The Pedagogy of Empowerment

The Pedagogy of Empowerment

Community Schools as a Social Movement in Egypt

Malak Zaalouk

The American University in Cairo Press
Cairo   New York

Copyright © 2004 by
The American University in Cairo Press
113 Sharia Kasr el Aini, Cairo, Egypt
420 Fifth Avenue, New York, NY 10018
www.aucpress.com

All royalties from this book go to UNICEF

First paperback edition 2006

Dar el Kutub No. 8077/06

Dar el Kutub Cataloging-in-Publication Data

Zaalouk, Malak
    The Pedagogy of Empowerment: Community Schools as a Social Movement in
    Egypt / edited by Malak Zaalouk.—Cairo: The American University in Cairo
    Press, 2006
            192p.   25cm.
            ISBN 977-416-026-6
            1. Community schools
            371.03

Designed by H Hughes/AUC Press Design Center
Printed in Egypt

To my parents, who anchored me with all the values I cherish.

To the people of Asyut, Sohag, and Qena who made the
Community Education movement in Egypt possible.

Contents

Acknowledgments   ix
Introduction   xi
List of Abbreviations   xv

1: Community Schools as a Social Movement   1
    The Problem Stated   1
    Worldwide Calls for Educational Reform   4
    Different Approaches to Educational Reform   5
    Social Movements Defined   6
    Education and Social Movements   9
    Education and the Global Political Economy   10
    Traditional Approaches to Education   12
    Toward a Modern Theory of Quality Education   14
    On Education, Individual Transformation, and Social Change   26
    Conclusion   29

2: Community Schools in Egypt   31
    Education in Egypt: The Historical Context   32
    The Community Education Model in Egypt: History and
    Underlying Objectives   34
    Core Components to the Initiative   36
    Major Inputs to the Community School
    Initiative in Upper Egypt   42
    Within the Classroom: Quality Education and Processes   74
    The School Day   83
    The Planning Cycle for Starting a School   88
    Phases of the Project   91
    Conclusion   99

3: Results of a Movement in Progress   100
    Outputs   102
    Outcomes   106
    Impact   115
    The Cost of Community Schools in Egypt   157
    Conclusion   160

4: The Way Forward: The Road to Sustainable Learning
    and Reform   162
    Community Schools and the Multi-Level Dialogue for Reform   163
    Critical Structures for Supporting Reform   173
    Lessons Drawn from the Dialogue   174
    The Political Economy of Educational Reform   175
    Conclusion   184
Notes   185
Index   195

Acknowledgments

MANY PEOPLE MADE THIS BOOK POSSIBLE; it is the outcome of the hard work of all those who joined the movement: all have, directly or indirectly, participated in every word and line. I would like to acknowledge UNICEF for enabling me to carry out this work, both practically and intellectually. I was fortunate enough to have had three representatives who greatly encouraged this work: Baquer Namazi, who saw the initiation of the community schools and was a great source of wisdom and support; Leila Bisharat who constantly pushed for documentation of the initiative; and last but not least, Shahida Azfar, who raised the initiative's visibility, both nationally and internationally, and who made its documentation possible.

To my colleagues at the UNICEF Cairo office, I am grateful for the wonderful team work and support received in implementation and for their reading of the manuscript during its early phases. I would also like to thank Professor Talal Asad of the Graduate Center of the City University of New York, and Professor Michael Connelly of the Ontario Institute of Studies in Education, who read the manuscript and recommended it for publication.

To the teams working on the ground in Asyut, Sohag, and Qena, I am forever indebted for their love, commitment, deep engagement, and hard work. I want to thank all the wonderful professionals at the Ministry of Education who made this work possible and who, along with colleagues at the National Council for Childhood and Motherhood, believed in the initiative. The officials at all levels in the governorates of Asyut, Sohag, and Qena have also been a source of great support. A big vote of thanks to the Canadian International Development Agency and colleagues therein for supporting this initiative since 1994. Many are both personal friends and friends of the initiative.

To all my dear friends who greatly supported me in times of hardship and who nagged me to put the experience in writing I want to express my deepest gratitude.

Finally to the children in the community schools and the graduates a hearty thanks for the emotional reward, inspiration, and pride they have given me.

Introduction

I N 1992 THE EDUCATION PROGRAM AT UNICEF (United Nations International Children's Emergency Fund) began its community education initiative through the community school model in four hamlets in the southern governorate of Asyut in Egypt. The initiative began with a signed agreement with the Ministry of Education (MOE) to jointly launch the experiment. The contract signed stipulated that the UNICEF education section would design, develop, and coordinate a community school model in deprived hamlets of rural Upper Egypt, while the MOE, the primary partner, would ensure that the initiative was sustainable, able to expand, and be adopted by the wider educational system. The objective was to achieve "quality education for all" by concentrating on the areas of greatest resistance, the least serviced and most remote areas of rural Upper Egypt, in sum the hard-to-reach.

The overall objective as stated in official documents was to demonstrate a replicable approach for increasing access of girls to primary education in remote rural areas where no schools exist, and develop innovative learning methodologies which can be applied to the formal education system. The initiative would, in accordance with MOE policies, ensure that each child had access to school, and empower local communities (especially girls and women) with access to schools, non-formal educational opportunities, participation in public decision making and allocation of communal resources. Finally, community schools would provide innovative pedagogies for quality education that would focus on active learning, acquisition of life skills, values-based learning (with an emphasis on practicing rights), and brain-based learning that would awaken all a child's intelligences including his or her spiritual and emotional ones.

Moreover the initial agreement between MOE and UNICEF accepted that while the initiative would begin as an experimental pilot, it would later grow as a model for mainstreaming into the educational system. Once the initiative had been evaluated it would expand, and the lessons learned from it transferred to the broader educational system. What began as an experiment has flourished into a fully fledged movement. It has been mainstreamed by the Government of Egypt (GOE) and strongly supported by the Canadian International Development Agency (CIDA), and replicated by the Social Fund for Development (SFD), non-governmental organizations (NGOs), and other international development organizations.

Informed by international wisdom, the community-schools movement emerged as an Egyptian model. It was, in the experimental phase, tailored to the rural regions of Upper Egypt, the governorates of Asyut, Sohag, and Qena in particular, and the model's design process was totally participatory. The growth of the model was an iterative[1] one which grew and gathered momentum through its many partners and alliances. It developed ultimately into a nation-wide community education movement.

As time went by it became clear that the community-school movement of Egypt aimed not at just introducing innovative learning methodologies but at individual and societal transformation. Quality education in such a movement, although a right in itself, was viewed as a means to attaining far-reaching personal and structural transformations in society, all of which should ultimately allow humanitarian values to prevail and the fullness of human nature to surface.

The process of transformation is a complex one, during which change occurs at many levels. There are many actors and parties to the movement, and as this book will demonstrate, the flow of change will move between the micro level with all the intricate details and processes of a dynamic classroom situation, to the macro level where policies, institutional structures, and legislation are developed and put in place to sustain the movement.

This book is divided into four chapters. The first chapter puts the initiative in a global and national perspective. It touches on issues of educational reform, social movements, and education as an entry point to social movements. It weaves these issues together to contextualize the community-school initiative in Egypt within a broader and deeper debate about what quality education is and what it means to be fully human. Educational movements such as the community schools movement are also made directly relevant to global issues such as poverty, growing income disparities, and the deteriorating conditions of the world of today.

The second chapter offers a meticulous, detailed description of the history of the community school initiative in Egypt, how communities were mobilized, how the initiative was mounted, the phases and strategies employed in and out of the classrooms, the training pedagogies used, and the initiative's core inputs and processes.

The third chapter looks closely at the outputs (immediate, quantifiable results), outcomes (short-term qualitative results), and impact (deeper, long term results) of the initiative. Although the many evaluations relied upon used a mix of quantitative and qualitative approaches, the methodologies used for examining the movement in progress, were very rigorous and relied heavily on qualitative assessment, as they described perceptions, attitudes, and transformations. This section ends with an overall cost analysis of the initiative, showing that investment in the movement is yielding far greater results than allowing a few more girls into school and ensuring their acquisition of reading, writing and arithmetic skills (the so-called three Rs).

The fourth and final chapter poses some strategic questions and, through a political economy of reform analysis, attempts to assess the community schools movement's sustainability. It also looks at the contribution of the community school initiative to national (and possibly international) educational reform.

My desire to write this book grew out of a strong need, as the initiator of this movement in Egypt, to recount the story of its genesis and development, and provide a source of hope to others for a better future. Through my own deep emotional involvement with the community schools for the last twelve years, I also feel compelled to give all those who have been involved with the movement their just due. Finally, I am also responding to all the pressures from friends and colleagues to document the movement's progress.

This work is deliberately aimed at a diverse audience. The practitioner and various development agencies worldwide wishing to emulate and be inspired by such an initiative may find within these pages a 'how to' handbook directly relevant to their work. Educators and academics may find the theoretical debates about learning and teaching methods insightful material as a basis for teaching and research. Anthropologists will undoubtedly discover how closely they in fact work with educators, while feminists will find practical ways of promoting the cause of female education. Finally, I hope that policy makers at all levels will discover some wisdom in what communities and people have learnt to do best.

Abbreviations

ASCD	Association for Supervision and Curriculum Development
CARE	Co-operative for Assistance and Relief Everywhere
CCIMD	Center for Curriculum and Instructional Materials Development
CIDA	Canadian International Development Agency
CRC	Convention on the Rights of the Child
ECCD	Early Childhood Care and Development
EEP	Education Enhancement Programme
EFA	Education for All
EIC	Education Innovation Committee
EMIS	Education Management Information Systems
FOE	Faculty of Education
GAEB	General Authority for Educational Buildings
GEM	Girls' Education Movement
IIEP	International Institute for Educational Planning
JICA	Japanese International Co-operation Agency
MENA	Middle East and North Africa
MOE	Ministry of Education
NCCM	National Council for Childhood and Motherhood
NCEEE	National Center for Examinations and Educational Evaluation
NGO	Non-Governmental Organization
OISE	Ontario Institute for Studies in Education
PAT	Professional Academy for Teachers
PPMU	Programme, Planning and Monitoring Unit
SFD	Social Fund for Development
UBE	Universal Basic Education
UN	United Nations
UNDP	United Nations Development Programme
UNESCO	United Nations Educational, Scientific and Cultural Organization
UNFPA	United Nations Population Fund
UNGEI	United Nations Girls' Education Initiative
UNICEF	United Nations International Children's Emergency Fund
USAID	United States Agency for International Development
WEEF	Women's Equality and Empowerment Framework
WSC	World Summit for Children
WSSD	World Summit for Social Development

1

Community Schools
as a Social Movement

"One of the greatest injustices and one contributing most to the destruction of civilization is the unjustified imposition of tasks and the use of the subjects for forced labour . . . an injustice even greater and destructive of civilization is the appropriation of people's property by buying their possessions as cheaply as possible and then reselling the merchandise to them at the highest possible prices."

Ibn Khaldun

The Problem Stated

T HIS WORK IS WRITTEN WITHIN A RIGHTS FRAMEWORK, taking a human- and child-rights approach to all modern forms of social movement encompassing educational reform. Looking through the articles of the Convention on the Rights of the Child, and important documents such as *A New Global Agenda for Children, The Global Movement for Children, Emerging Issues for Children in the Twenty-first Century, The Outcome Document: A World Fit for Children*, and the report, by Jacques Delors et al, of the International Commission on Education for the Twenty-first Century,[2] one reads beyond a moral directive to abide by global standards of conduct with regards to children, to the emergence of a new social consciousness. In addition to the four pillars of learning delineated by the Delors report,[3] "The Global Agenda for Children: Learning"[4] adds a fifth pillar, namely; "learning to transform oneself and one's society." In the world of today, one plagued by disparity and uneven development, all of the above represent a quest for change: a revival of a rights movement calling for equity and participation.

In 1998, Carol Bellamy, the head of UNICEF (United Nations International Children's Emergency Fund), declared that "the end of the UN [United Nations] reform is to bring about the total realization of child rights . . . the convention is the bedrock foundation of everything we do . . . [Which means among other critical issues the creation] of an enabling environment for learning including universal access to quality education . . . The strategic vision for the twenty-first century that we are developing has precious little to do with the calendar—and everything to do with the persistence of the dangers facing children and their families—dangers that grow out of poverty, which is deepening in many regions even as the global economy continues to swell; that stem from inequalities of wealth and access to basic services, both within and between nations; and from the steady erosion of many societies' capacity to maintain social safety nets for the poorest and most disadvantaged."[5]

The World Summit for Children which took place in 2002 drew the attention of the world and its leaders to a range of issues requiring immediate and urgent attention if progress and development were to be sustained. Although great achievements have been made, many challenges remain. These challenges can be summarized in the form of statistical indicators, which point the way to a crisis of unacceptable proportions:

- A total of 11 million children die each year, mostly from preventable causes, including poverty and hunger.
- An estimated total of 113 million children are out of school, 60 percent of whom are girls.
- Over 2.5 billion people live without access to sanitation facilities.
- Hundreds of thousands of women die every year from preventable causes.
- One out of every ten children lives with a moderate or severe disability.
- Over 200 million of the world's children are malnourished, contributing to over half of infant and child mortality rates. Meanwhile it is estimated that 20 percent of the world's population own and consume 82.7 percent of the world's wealth.
- Each year millions of children are the victims of violence, abuse, neglect, and exploitation, and are separated from their care givers. In the past decade alone some estimates place the impact of armed conflict on children to include two million killed, six million seriously injured or permanently disabled, 12 million left homeless, more than one million

orphaned or separated from their families, and 10 million psychologi-
cally traumatized.[6]

These were some of the challenges pinpointed during the United Nations
Special Session for Children held in 2002, when a renewed commitment was
made to the creation of a world fit for children. Most analyses have traced the
current global crises to a set of complex and intertwined factors, linked to and
reflected in systems of education, governance, and services worldwide, and to a
decline in morals and values, which in turn reflects a dwindling commitment
to social justice.

To meet the challenges of educating every child, it has been estimated that a
total of US$ 7 billion needs to be allocated each year for the next ten years. This
is far less than the amount spent every year in the USA on cosmetics and in
Europe on ice cream, not to mention the outrageous estimates of US$ 781 bil-
lion a year expended on defense worldwide.

The delegates to the World Summit for Social Development in 1995 agreed
that "almost each day brings ever-grosser manifestations of abuse, exploitation,
greed, violence, corruption, deprivation, conflict, exclusion, injustice, intoler-
ance, an obsession with materialistic self-gratification counter-pointed by the
indifference to the welfare of others, disregard for anything beyond the immediately present and an overall cheapening of human life. There is now a crisis in
the moral fabric of society, a crisis of values." [7]

The traditional model of world development that is focused on state power
and economic growth needs to change drastically, and the focus needs to shift
to human development.[8]

All the documents so far cited represent a cry for global reform. Most have
clearly declared education—and girls' education in particular—as the entry
point to that reform. The solution advocated by the international community
is to focus on early childhood care and development, democratize and univer-
salize high-quality education, and ensure the protection and participation of
youth and adolescents in all walks of life.[9] None of the above, surprisingly, is
new: the forefathers of educational theory, such as John Dewey, Robert Gagne,
Lev Vygotsky, Paulo Freire, and Maria Montessori were clear in their own
minds as to the relationship between educational reform, community development, and democracy. Although some educational analysts, in designing educational policy, tried to pit equity against excellence, utilitarianism against
humanitarianism, and finally, individuality against community, for John
Dewey, educators had an obligation to tailor their pedagogy to the needs of
both individual and society. According to Dewey, the role of school and educa-

tion was to raise democratic citizens; he regarded democracy as a way of life that extended far beyond the confines of formal institutions, to every part of a given community. Democracy in the broadest sense of the term, was conceived as a learning process, a mode of interaction among citizens.[10] From as early as the beginning of the twentieth century, Dewey made his position very clear with regard to the right of each individual to education, and the question of equity was expressed as the need to attend to the growth of *all* individuals.[11]

Worldwide Calls for Educational Reform

Increasingly, educators worldwide are calling for the kind of systemic reform that strives ultimately for the three E's: Equity, Efficiency,[12] and Excellence.[13] Today there is a pervasive discontent worldwide with existing structures and systems of education. As a result, reformers and proponents of change have established some 8500 educational alternative pathways, or methods of education.[14]

The desire for change is ever-growing as people show increasing dissatisfaction with their lives. Many trace this 'malaise' to a crisis of values and systems of education, which continue to serve a world torn by individuality, competition, and monetary pursuits. Education, a public good, is tailored to serve private goals and the exclusive interests of those in power, and to the enchancement of career development in its narrowest sense, and not to vocations or principles and causes.

More and more people are looking for alternative definitions of education. This signals a return to the fundamental purpose of education, that is, human development. *Learning is a process whereby individuals are able to enrich and enhance their relationship with the inner self, their families, communities, and the world at large.*

Voices of protest are increasingly being raised against the crises confronted by humanity at large. A good example of this protest movement is the group of educators who presented a vision statement in 1991 during the conference sponsored by the Global Alliance for Transforming Education.[15] This group issued some moving statements which represent the views of many of those concerned with education and its relationship to human development: "We believe that our dominant cultural values and practices, including the emphasis on competition over cooperation, consumption over sustainable resource use, and bureaucracy over authentic human interaction, have been destructive to the health of the ecosystem and to optimal human development as well."

The group proposed an alternative vision, one which reemphasizes the goals of the pioneers of educational theory and stresses the significant relationship between becoming human and being educated. "Education means caring enough to draw forth the greatness that is within each unique person. It is a life-affirming and democratic response to the challenges of the 1990s and beyond."[16]

Moreover it is becoming increasingly clear that the complexity of the current crises confronting humanity at large cannot be solved by individual leaders alone. The number of global problems is truly staggering: nuclear war, ecological decay, terrorism, homelessness, drug and alcohol abuse, poverty, malnutrition, illiteracy, corruption, armed conflict and occupation, to name a few. This only goes to show that, in global terms, the traditional methods of solving problems no longer hold. Courageous leaders need to realize that they must surrender the illusion of control in order to allow communities to seek solutions to problems through an infrastructure of trusting relationships and empowering institutions.

Different Approaches to Educational Reform

There are currently two approaches, broadly speaking, to educational reform: the 'project approach,' also known as the 'isolated pilot approach' or 'demonstration project approach,' and the 'movement approach' or what some analysts refer to as the 'structural approach,' which aims at developing a *reform support infrastructure*,[17] that is, where sufficient institutions have been put in place to create an enabling environment for reform.

The project approach to reform has striven mainly at improving material conditions within schools, such as creating more classrooms to improve enrollment rates, or providing more textbooks, in most cases for a limited amount of time, and within the restricted confines of formal schooling.[18] It has yielded very modest results on the global scene.

The movement approach, on the other hand, attempts to tackle the root causes that lead to lack of participation, inequity, and disparity, as well as inefficient education. Unfortunately most national and international actors have opted for the seemingly easier and more manageable project approach in the short run. It is no wonder, then, that most isolated, school-based project approaches fail to yield significant sustainable change.

For a reform to take root it needs to operate in a political economy of reform where conditions are being created to replicate that reform. These conditions are both ideological and structural. Hence leaders of reform need to work on the attitudes of policy makers and communities at all levels, in addition to creating structures and institutions that will survive those leaders and sustain the reform. As the demand for reform and quality education spreads and develops into a movement, structures are put into place to allow the movement to develop into a fully fledged and recognized source of pressure and interest, which sustains the momentum of innovation. Rational *constructivist* leaderships as agents of change facilitate this dialectical relationship between movement approaches and structural change. They do so by allowing communities to construct meaning in their lives and propose their own vision of how they want to be; a dialogue between communities and policy makers ensues.

Certain key preconditions need to be present for any given reform to develop into an ongoing process rather than a finite phase. This then begs the whole question of how one evaluates successful experiments.

This chapter will attempt to define social movements, since it is my belief that they provide the broader context for successful educational reform. It will also look at the conditions needed for far-reaching and sustainable change, as well as the significance of quality education, the ultimate goal of all reforms. This short theoretical framework to the current work is presented for the purpose of answering questions such as:

- Can the current community-school project in Egypt become a catalyst for a sustainable and deeply grounded social movement?
- Can this small experimental project contribute significantly to educational reform on a national scale?
- How does one measure a program's success and sustainability within a movement approach?

Social Movements Defined

Writing on social movements from as early as the late 1950s, Turner and Killian defined a social movement as "a collectivity acting with some continuity to promote or resist a change in the society or group of which it is a part."[19] The definition carries within it essential concepts such as change and continuity, while alluding to the significance of continuity for movements to result in structural change.

Although some movements may begin spontaneously, they eventually manifest elements of structural change. This occurs as a result of norms and values becoming a source of anchorage, identity, and mobilization for the group over an extended period of time. As the movement gains momentum, its set of norms become an encompassing way of life for its adherents. After the group ideology and the set of norms adopted have been imprinted in the group consciousness, the movement begins to set its policies, critical goals, and means or strategies of reaching those goals. This entails a certain amount of organization and a clear division of labor within the group, which often involves a certain degree of hierarchy. Whenever the movement attains its intermediate goals, it is propelled into a new phase, where newly defined goals allow its deep involvement in the society to continue while developing a new raison d'être.

Social movements usually spread through a process of diffusion. Ideas are passed on from one individual to another, and from one group to the next. Predicting the speed of change is contingent upon many factors and is therefore difficult. Elements or factors determining the speed of change in any given social situation are: the duration of interaction between those groups aiming at change and their external environment; the strength and power of those desiring change; and, finally, the cohesiveness of the groups desiring change on the ideological level, and the degree to which they are willing to stick together.[20]

In current-day definitions of social movements, much of the essence of the above is maintained, as definitions continue to include a personal ideational transformation component as well as a strong element of structural transformation. The parameters for partnerships, between different groups, state constituencies or parties, are wider, however, and the stated imperative for a democratic environment that will allow for participation and dialogue is greater. Meanwhile the creation of a demand for change, hence popular mobilization, is a significant prerequisite for a social movement's success.

In many parts of the Third World, notably in Latin America, as deepening crises prevailed within state-led models of capitalist development and, later, structural adjustment policies, with resulting widening disparities, social movements provided collective responses to survival challenges. This was in many instances done by engaging the formal arenas of political institutional power in an attempt to influence public policy.[21] States can and do become part of this configuration, as states are not homogenous entities, and they do enjoy relative autonomy.[22] There are different parts of the state apparatus that can be independent from the ruling power.

In essence, these forms of contemporary social movements embody a search for forms of democracy that bring about the empowerment of people and give them a greater control over their lives at work and at home. These movements represent the will of any given community to acquire the powers of decision-making, which is in turn reflected in grassroots mobilization and the development of community-based modes of democracy.·

Participatory grassroots democracies are both a means to and an end of the type of progressive movements needed today to counteract poverty and underdevelopment in the Third World, the latter characterized by enormous bureaucracies, centralized governments, and transnational economic and political entities that monopolize power, leading to great disparities of political, social, and economic participation.[23]

The disparities between the underdeveloped Third World and the over developed First World and its allies, as described by the proponents of dependency theory,[24] have stimulated a global interest in finding models of development that are directly relevant to the majority of the world's population. The structural adjustment model, enforced by the International Monetary Fund (IMF) on those economies of the Third World that were unable to service their debt, imposed policies that restructured economies away from government regulation and a dominant public sector toward privatization and free markets. Although this model created some pockets of growth, it has not proven to be an equitable method of reaching out to the majority. The world of today truly needs new forms of popular power that operate directly from the grassroots up.

Popular participation at the community level is the only viable form that will allow for the kinds of governing structures that can overcome social, political, and economic inequalities. At the heart of this process of structural transition and transformation lies a much needed change in power relationships that would ultimately lead to the empowerment of the vast majority of people. Hence, once again, it is the concern with structures and relations rather than material conditions per se, that is at the heart of reform within a movement approach.

Theoretical Paradigms of Social Movement

Within the context of post-industrial societies, social movements are dominated by two theoretical paradigms: the new social movement (NSM) approach, and the resource mobilization (RM) approach. The NSM stresses the cultural nature of social movements. The RM, on the other hand, stresses the political nature of movements, and tends to interpret them as conflicts over the allocation of resources.[25] This approach does not however view the subjective perception of inequalities as a sufficient condition for a movement to take off. There must be, along with that, an availability of resources and changes in the opportunity for collective action.[26]

Looking at the NSM approach, Touraine argues that the transition from one societal type to another requires an external agent of change. The best candidate in his view is the state. The state becomes the agent of structural transformations at what proponents of this theory call the diachronic (or historical and cultural) level. Along with structural and political levels of transformation, both Habermas and Touraine argue, there is a further level; the synchronic, that is, one made without reference to history, which deals with the generation of conflicting norms, social institutions, and cultural patterns. This is the domain where people and communities are most active. Others, such as Laclau and Mouffe, do not accept the separation of the social and the political, but view politics as a wider domain and assert the primacy of political articulation. For both the latter theorists, the political and social domains are mingled into one, and they believe that social movements emerge when the identity of a given group or subject is denied. This form of negation or denial may occur when acquired rights are called into question, for example, or when certain social relations are transformed into ones of subordination.[27]

Movements have a wide array of goals, such as the eradication of discrimination and oppression, the rejection of traditional roles, the reappropriation of physical space, the re-definition of the relationship with nature, and the creation of new identities. Movements advocate values of equality and participation, democracy, and individual autonomy. Many thus view that the field of conflict and transformation is no longer an exclusively political one, but is also a cultural one that manifests itself in civil society. Hence the best approach to social movements is a comprehensive one that takes account of both cultural and political domains.

There are, however, certain conditions for the success of social movements: organization, leadership, political opportunity, and the nature of the political institutions in place. We will look at each of those components in turn, to show how management structures and styles are part and parcel of a movement's identity and components of its success.

Education and Social Movements

Quality educational programs, with the appropriate management and leadership styles, can evolve into social movements that lead to transformations on both the personal and structural levels. It is unfortunate that, for the most part, formal established schooling has historically sought to promote the existing order. As a result, both intended and unintended, formal schooling has caused fragmented educational experiences that place a great emphasis on compliance with and adherence to an existing order, and on abstract academic content, at the direct expense of a learning experience that connects to the daily lives of children and allows them to serve their wider community and promote change where necessary.

Movement education is instrumental, therefore, in the articulation of problems and in assisting in the formulation of solutions. It is also instrumental in bringing education to people who are not reached by the formal educational establishment. It is furthermore able to provide education at lower costs, and to direct educational efforts toward goals that are more practical or relevant to learners' needs in the society of which they are a part.[28]

Meanwhile, movement education helps create fertile ground for movements leading to reform. Movements have manifested a proven ability to increase the capacity for collective action by fostering solidarity and community, to increase opportunity and choice, and finally to strengthen people's organizational and problem-solving abilities. Moreover such movements enhance the ability of societies to reach the ultimate objective, namely that of democratizing education.

The role of education within social movements is to assist individuals in articulating needs; in mobilizing resources to meet those needs; and in the organization of participatory activities that enable communities and societies to reach their ultimate goals.[29] Thus movement education seeks to emphasize the fact that school is supposed to be a place where those wanting to learn can find help. All too often school has developed into a place where those not wishing to attend are forced to remain, and those wishing to go are unable to attend for a variety of reasons.[30] If a society is able to tolerate the continuous relationship between reformist social movements and educational reform, people will be able to realize themselves through structures as they evolve in their path to growth.[31] In sum, only quality learning offers a genuine opportunity for change on both the individual and structural levels.

Education and the Global Political Economy

The quest and need for quality education as it is defined today represents a paradigm shift of not insignificant proportions. It has been triggered by new scientific knowledge and a greater appreciation of the need for values in our increasingly barren lives.

The world of today is characterized not only by very high levels of manifest economic and social disparities, as earlier mentioned, but also by accelerated, compressed, and rapid change. It is a world where certainty has given way to scientific uncertainty, acute relativism and diversity, national insecurity, and great technological sophistication and innovation accompanied by a marked compression of time and space.[32] It is a world of uncontrollable complexity and change, one which offers a limitless capacity for knowledge storage and retrieval, sophisticated information and data analyses, instantaneous global communication, and artificial intelligence and simulation. There needs to be a matching human resource component for a truly knowledge-based society, one based on research, reflection, knowledge generation, and scientific methods of inquiry and analysis.[33]

It is clear from all the above that education is increasingly becoming the center of the knowledge-based society, with the school as the leading institution. There is necessarily a need for more knowledge of an advanced type and of an elevated quality. An educated person will be someone who has learned how to learn throughout his or her lifetime. The school, a pivotal institution, will be expected to perform in ways that support these new changes. The performance of the schools and their basic values will become of increasing concern to society at large and will no longer be left solely in the hands of professional 'educators' or economists concerned merely with market requirements.

During an era of grave uncertainty, both in the moral and scientific domain, educational sectors will be confronted with the challenge of reasserting old cultural certainties or creating new ones. Values have been much in demand. In the face of globalization and the ensuing malaise of widespread poverty, illiteracy, and high mortality rates, schools have been called upon to carry the responsibility of national reconstruction. They have, in addition, been sought for the implementation of the new paradigm shift, namely learning for understanding, rethinking, restructuring, redefining the self and the questioning of existing relations. School is increasingly viewed as a creator of enabling environments and relationships for learning. It can no longer play a limiting and disciplinary role: it is there to enhance moral imperatives and cultural values, which include the democratization of learning, the empowerment of the self and whole communities, as well as the alleviation of increasing global poverty and inequity.

These are not the only justifications for a paradigm shift in education. An added impetus to the need for change is new knowledge on brain-based learning. Educators have stayed with folk psychology for too long. As some have put it most cogently:

> Our society is well into the information age, and education has no choice but to follow suit. The challenge is to participate intelligently in the change. To meet the challenge, educators must have a state-of-the-art understanding of how the brain functions and people learn. Education needs to be extremely well grounded in what is possible for humans to participate more fully in what they and society ultimately become. Thus we begin with some emerging understandings about the brain and education.[34]

Brain research is not sufficiently used by educators. The most striking findings from this body of research to date is the fact that the human brain has immense potential yet untapped, and, more importantly, that the brain is an interconnected whole. Our emotions, physical well-being, social interactions, and the time and space in which they are activated are all interconnected, affecting each other mutually and representing different gateways to our cognition, perception, and affect (emotions and moods).[35] Previous theories viewed the human brain as a container that functioned separately from emotions and experience. The results of this new body of research have huge implications for the way we learn. An infant is born with enormous potential and more brain cells and synaptic connections than he or she will ever utilize. The connections and related learning processes occur through the interconnected and multiple social, emotional, and sensory experiences that the child is engaged in. All these experiences form the basis of learning and cognition, not just the programmed information presented in school textbooks. The brain does not distinguish between what is learned at home or at school, nor does it function in a fragmented way: how we feel determines what we learn and many more such complexities to be tested and discovered.[36]

Traditional Approaches to Education

While neuroscience is making great strides forward, educational theory continues to lag behind, functioning on the basis of old assumptions that view the mind as a container, ready and willing to absorb information that can be retrieved upon test or request.

Most educational approaches are still based on behaviorist theories, which assume that learning occurs sequentially, in one stage following the next; thus curriculum development simply entails the ordering of a hierarchy of goals that are in turn imparted to students through direct instruction. The teachers seek to direct pupils and correct their errors, which are a result of the latter's inattention and incomplete learning.[37] Teachers are the sole source of knowledge transmission, and pupils are viewed to be of varying degrees of intelligence. Intelligence is viewed as an individual trait that sets a limit on the maximum rate at which cumulative learning can take place.[38] This approach to education is obviously a holdover from the industrial era when only a few people, that is, the heads, were required to plan and innovate, while the masses, that is, the hands, were expected to execute boring and repetitive tasks. School was therefore the perfect selection mechanism for that type of job market and hierarchical mode of individuated management.[39]

As a result of the above approach to education, a number of assumptions continue to survive, rendering many aspects of today's schooling system irrelevant to the world we live in. Torres cogently summarizes the current assumptions behind much of modern-day schooling:

1. *Learning takes place mostly in school.* This assumption completely ignores recent scientific research on the way learning takes place; it particularly ignores non-school-based learning experiences, which lie at the heart of our brain map and its construction (cells, neurons synaptic connections and neuronal networks).

2. *Learning requires teaching.* This assumption completely ignores learning that takes place on one's own (self-learning) and throughout one's life (life-long learning).

3. *Teaching results in learning.* This assumption ignores the fact that a great deal of teaching does not result in learning. Moreover it continues to negate diversity in learners and to label those that do not learn as having learning difficulties when a single teaching approach is applied.

4. *Learning relates (only) to students.* This assumption totally negates the notion of a "community of learners," in which school teachers, principals, and the surrounding community are not passive actors but engaged in finding the best and most suitable teaching practices; it presumes that teachers and head teachers do not learn but instead implement and 'administer' lists of prescriptions inherited over the years. It furthermore assumes that educational research does not exist, and if it does it is futile academic fantasy.

5. *Learning relates (mainly) to children.* No attention is paid to later years of learning or to the fact that a child has in fact learned a great deal before even entering school.

6. *Teaching and learning revolve essentially around an adult-child relationship.* No recognition is accorded to the importance of peer education, despite all relevant research to date.

7. *Learning depends on listening (to the teacher) and reading (books).* All evidence on the different intelligences and diversified approaches to learning are totally ignored.

8. *Teaching and learning are mutually exclusive.* Activities involving students teaching others or teachers learning are not acknowledged.

9. *Learning is restricted to content (the written instructional subject-related material).* Contrary to the needs of learners discovered through observation and research, this approach takes content to mean facts and con-

cepts. It ignores values, skills, competencies, procedures, processes, beliefs, emotions, spirituality, social interaction, and physical needs.

10. *Learning is measurable with tests and is reflected in scores.* The acquisition of life skills and other competencies, such as critical thinking, creativity, problem-solving skills, self-esteem, and so on are not accounted for. Moreover, methods of identifying and assessing qualitative developments in learning are not sufficiently developed.

11. *Educational improvement is limited to teacher training and learning.* Methods of improving the learning process are oversimplified and do not account for other influences on the learning process, such as management systems and the general school environment.

12. *A given set of inputs will predictably result in learning as an output.* Again, this takes an oversimplified view of the learning process and educational improvement generally. It derives from an economic bias in the approach to educational reform. Such an approach often stresses the need for technological expansion (more computers in the classes) as a requisite for educational improvement. It steers away from experimentation and abides by general recipes for educational enhancement (textbooks, technology, teacher salary, teacher training, and so on).[40]

Toward a Modern Theory of Quality Education

Educational reformists have pointed out that the origin of the meaning of learning is to 'draw out' from the learner, to educe, implying in turn that education is based on, indeed centered on, the learners' interests. It builds on the learners' real experiences while respecting him or her as a valuable person, worthy of trust, confidence, and esteem. It believes in the capacity of the learner to learn and teach him or herself, and to find meaningful answers to her own questions.

It is the sheer evidence of modern research that has provided the basis for a huge array of literature on learner-centered, activity-based learning. This research not only takes into account the needs of the modern era, but is based on experiments and observations that indicate how the best learning results are obtained and how learner well-being is most effectively realized. In sum, new theories of constructivism, socio-cognition,[41] and multiple intelligences,[42] take it as their ultimate goal to ensure that children are taught and allowed to learn in ways that make sense to them and that are pleasurable. Moreover these approaches take into account the learners' individual stage of physical and mental development, as well as their preferred learning style.

The initial urge for educational reform in the developed world was triggered by an increasing awareness of and respect for the research on learning which accounted for the findings of neuro-scientific endeavor, and a realization that schools, as the deliverers of essential information, are slowly being made irrelevant. Schools have long served to prepare students for bureaucratically organized and controlled environments.

With regard to neuro-scientific research, findings seem to indicate that every brain is uniquely organized.[43] Moreover, the human brain is by no means formed completely at birth. It is experience, mostly during childhood, that 'sculpts' the brain. The human brain continues to shape itself through life. At birth the human brain contains many more neurons than it will ever need or use. Through experience and a process best known as pruning, those neurons that are used the most remain and are strengthened, while those neuronal connections less utilized are in fact lost. It is the way synaptic connections and neurons are made to thrive and relate that therefore creates a brain structure unique to each individual. Hence experiences will impact on brain structure in immediate and unique ways.[44] This lends credence to educational theories and practices that respect diversity and difference in learners.

As for the second point, schools were increasingly observed to fail to produce self-motivated individuals who can live with the complexities and ambiguities of today's world. The new organizations of today need people who are creative and adaptable. More specifically, today's world requires individuals who possess:

- An inner appreciation of interconnectedness.
- A strong identity and sense of being.
- A sufficiently large vision and imagination to see how specifics relate to each other.
- The capacity to 'go with the flow' and to deal with paradox and uncertainty.
- A capacity to build community and live in relationship with others.[45]

Learning is by no means an exclusively school-based activity, even though the role played by formal schooling continues to be pivotal. Learning is present in every atom of this universe. It is an infinite, universal, and continual activity, and a process by which the lifelong human capacity to enjoy and share the process of learning is enhanced.

In agreement with all the above, a group of reformists, calling themselves holistic educationalists[46] have outlined ten key principles to guide the way out of the current crises in education today:

1. The fundamental purpose of education is human development. Learning is about enriching and deepening one's relationship with oneself, the family, the community, and the globe.
2. Students as learners should be honored as individuals who are inherently creative, unique in their needs, and have an unlimited capacity to learn.
3. Experience is central to learning, which is a multi-sensory engagement with the world.
4. Learning is a holistic activity: one attends not just to the intellectual, but also to the physical, social, moral, aesthetic, creative, and spiritual needs of the learner.
5. The role of the educator is to facilitate learning and, in turn, become a learner.
6. True learning is conditional on freedom. An atmosphere of freedom fosters freedom of inquiry, exploration, discovery, and expression.
7. Education is for participatory democracy. This means a return to Socrates's ideas of critical thinking and the development of shared human values.
8. Education aims at producing model citizens, that is, people who are responsible for and engaged with the well-being of their families, communities, and the world at large, and who accept difference and cultural diversity.
9. Education aims at promoting an awareness of ecological concerns. Education should ensure that the outcomes of the learning process result in individuals who are responsible custodians of the planet earth and understand the interdependence of its parts.
10. Ultimately education aims at cultivating morality and spirituality; at developing a deep connection to the self and others, and a sense of meaning and purpose in daily life.

I would personally like to add another principle, which is that education and learning, seen in the context of development, morality, and spirituality, are a movement toward greater social justice. It is important to single out the deprived for concern and attention. After all, as Aristotle once said, "the greatest inequality is to treat unequal things equally."

The Methods and Processes of Quality Learning
The methods and processes of quality learning are indeed intertwined and interdependent. Moreover the holistic nature of a quality-package approach

looks at the inputs as well as the processes and outcomes of quality learning. With regards to the inputs, the learners and their families, their experiences, physical condition, health, and nutritional status are all important dimensions of a quality package. Parental support and involvement in the learning process are other vital inputs. Classroom environments in terms of care, a sense of community, and gender sensitivity and equity are significant contributors to a quality package. Concern with learning content looks at the relevance of that content, both to the lives of learners and to wider goals of human development. Hence, the extent to which the content of learning assists learners in developing to their full potential and operating in a competitive and increasingly complex world of science, technology, and communication, is an important consideration in the complex package of quality education.

With this new approach in mind, the nature of many aspects of the learning process in schools are required to change, foremost among which are:

- Learner participation, self-efficacy, and empowerment.
- Community participation.
- Objectives of learning and instruction.
- Teacher use of time.
- Sources for curriculum and instruction.
- Teacher approach to assessment.
- Teacher approach to discipline.
- School environment, management, and constructivist leadership.

Taking each one of these subjects in turn:

Learner Participation, Self-efficacy, and Empowerment

This concept is at the heart of child-centered learning. It refers to the ability of teachers to spark genuine interest in their students and to actually follow the path pointed out to them by children. The empowerment of students is a conscious process wherein teachers reflectively make the trajectory from power over others to developing the self-efficacy of their pupils. Through that process, students are able to take charge of their learning and make things happen. Children have, through that process developed higher self-esteem and are therefore clearly motivated; they develop the characteristics of self-efficacy (the opposite of dependency), a much-desired trait needed for survival in the technologically rich future. Students believe in themselves and their abilities, and teachers enhance this by containing their own power and by steering away from undermining and curtailing children's drive.[47]

Community Participation

This notion complements the above. It reiterates the fact that the learning process, far from being the transmission of knowledge from experts, is the act of knowledge acquisition by the learners themselves. Knowledge is acquired through active exploration. The "community of learners" approach is one in which both experienced and novice learners enter into a partnership and participate in a learning endeavor that ultimately leads to transformation. The old transmission model belonged to the factory era wherein managers and supervisors ensured that standardized outputs came out of a centrally directed mode of organization. In a community-of-learners model, all participants are active. No single person or entity bears all the responsibility of learning. All participants are active, no one is passive, and children take an active role in managing their own learning. Adults provide guidance while also learning in the process. Although the responsibility may be unequal at times, with adults guiding the process, children are nevertheless constantly encouraged to participate in structuring the inquiry and managing their own learning. This strategy, although apparently chaotic on the surface, is a very well thought out pedagogical technique that allows both teachers and students to learn together.[48]

At a wider level, another dimension of the notion of community participation is the fact that learning is such a complex process that it necessarily requires a wide range of partnerships. If education is viewed as a societal responsibility in which learning, a process that happens in and out of schools, occurs, then many partners need be engaged. The participation of whole communities, parents and families, governmental and non-governmental organizations, other institutions, and the private sector therefore becomes imperative.[49]

Objectives of Learning and Instruction

Literacy and numeracy are no longer sufficient objectives of learning or schooling. Other life skills are also important aims of learning. With regard to learning objectives, considerable emphasis is currently placed on collaboration and teamwork. Management experts worldwide have noted that behind the Japanese technological, economic, and educational success story has been the ability to work in groups and develop group loyalty. The ability to work in groups is now being recognized as an educational objective, as important as literacy and numeracy.[50]

Also important to group formation and on a par with literacy and numeracy are communication skills that are not necessarily reducible to reading and writing, such as planning, presentation, critical and logical thinking, and nonverbal communication.[51]

In a knowledge-based economy, another clear objective is not just clear access to and the use of knowledge, but the processing of that knowledge, and making sense of and attaching deep meaning to it. Hence creativity and knowledge-processing skills are of paramount importance. The ability to interact with and create knowledge is an ultimate value of the modern educational era and one that becomes of necessity translated into school objectives.[52]

Emotional literacy becomes, in the context of current thinking, another critical objective of educational institutions. Identifying our emotions, caring, and neutralizing impediments to learning are imperative skills if any learning is to take place. Much research indicates that emotions are the gateway to learning. Emotional-literacy programs, in a great number of cases, arose as a means of alleviating violence in schools, through the introduction of conflict resolution skills. It was discovered, however, that heading off violence could not be separated from the larger spectrum of desired emotional competencies, which include: emotional self-awareness, managing emotions, harnessing emotions productively, empathy and reading emotions, handling relationships, and developing morality. These new challenges and mandates for quality schooling emerge as the family, during the post-modern era, is no longer able to fulfill its socializing and nurturing role. This challenging role of the school however requires that teachers go beyond their mission, and communities become ever more involved with schools.[53]

In keeping with the above, schools and educators are now being called upon to promote a harmonious and holistic form of human development through value-based education. This program of education aims at providing students with a whole philosophy of life. Through values such as cooperation, freedom, happiness, honesty, humility, love, peace, respect, responsibility, simplicity, tolerance (accepting others) and unity, students are able to develop the spiritual and emotional tools and skills that will allow them to make good choices in life. The selected values should fit what best suits every society.[54]

Educators have recently come to realize that students, despite some governments' desire to secularize schooling, are in great need of a spiritual life and a deeper sense of connection to their inner souls, to others, the universe, and a higher power. It has been observed that students who feel deeply connected in one way or another are less marred by stress and are better able to function in the learning environment and in life, generally.[55]

Some believe that religious and morality-based education might be needed to develop certain types of thinking skills and strategies for theological thinking. More and more educationalists are coming around to the fact that modern, secular styles of education leave children with a void and a hunger for spirituality, the absence of which has a direct effect on their cognitive abilities. The cognitive process in such programs is divided into:

- Problem solving/finding (focusing, information gathering, analyzing, generating).
- Decision making (organizing, analyzing, integrating, evaluating).
- Critical thinking (information-gathering, analyzing, integrating, evaluating).
- Creative thinking (focusing, information-gathering, generating, integrating, evaluating).[56]

Other critical objectives of the learning process are life skills and thinking skills. At the heart of this concept-based approach is the view that education needs to be made relevant to students' lived experiences. Learning should empower young individuals to live better lives by equipping them with the skills to know *how* to know, to do, and to work together, and finally, how to be. There is no set list of skills, and different programs will categorize them in different ways, according to the community they are tailored for. The basic learning competencies of the UNESCO (United Nations Educational, Scientific and Cultural Organization) program, for example, divides life skills into:

- Awareness of environment (both physical and social).
- Self-preserving skills (including health, nutrition and hygiene).
- Social skills (such as gender roles, participation and caring for others).
- Study skills (research and learning how to learn) and manipulative skills (using household gadgets and tools).[57]

The UNICEF Education Cluster has a similar but slightly different figuring. Life skills are divided into:

- Inter-personal skills (including empathy building, active listening, assertion and negotiation).
- Skills for building self-awareness (self-assertion, positive-thinking skills, values and acting on rights).
- Critical and creative thinking skills (analytical skills, creative skills, information gathering, evaluation skills and skills for generating ideas and alternatives).
- Decision-making skills (critical thinking, problem-solving skills, skills for assessing risk, skills for assessing consequences, goal-setting skills).

- Coping and stress-management skills (self-control skills, coping with pressure, time management, dealing with anxiety, dealing with difficult situations, seeking help).[58]

Thus learning must no longer be limited to reading, writing and arithmetic, but to the attainment of life skills. The UNESCO and UNICEF lists are complementary and equally important.

Teacher Use of Time

Planning and preparation remain the fundamental components in the facilitation of an effective and progressive learning experience for all pupils. Lesson planning is a key teacher skill, which should reflect a theoretical approach to teaching and clear knowledge of the subject matter. More importantly, it reflects the capacity to manage a classroom and create the kind of environment that leads to learning and the attainment of learning objectives. Planning should entail the best use of the teachers' time. It involves the specification of relevant learning objectives, the selection of learning materials, the organization of learning activities, the specification of evaluation and assessment procedures, and the preparation of materials, resources, and props.

Planning is usually the result of considerable thinking and reflection. It takes into account the diversity in the classroom and all the different needs of each student. Multi-ability teaching requires meticulous planning and preparation. Moreover planning is an ongoing and complex matter that even allows teachers to prepare for the unexpected.

Another component of good planning is classroom management and the establishment of routines. Effective classroom management refers to the arrangements made by the teacher to maintain and establish an environment in which learning can occur with students actively engaged in that learning. Rules and routines are planned in order to enhance discipline and ensure a smooth flow of learning.

Another big chunk of teachers' time is employed in class monitoring and assessing the progress made by students. Recording and discussing with peers and mentors is also a very significant part of teachers' time employed for growth and enrichment.[59]

Sources for Curriculum and Instruction

The strongest source of curriculum and instruction, despite learner diversity, is experience. More specifically, student's experiences are the essence of any course of study.[60] A curriculm, despite all formal and traditional definitions of the word, is much more than what we see in curriculum guides, textbooks, and teachers' guides, which tend to define a curriculum as the sum or aggregate of courses given. Built within what children learn, is the intended curriculum, the taught curriculum, the learned curriculum, and the hidden, or implicit, undeclared as opposed to declared and planned, curriculum, all of which contain critical layers of skills acquisition. Hence other sources of curriculum are national, communal, and school experiences and situations. A key source of curriculum in all this is, of course, the teacher.

Because a curriculum is essentially also about the relationship between pupils and teachers, and pupils with other pupils, a significant source of that curriculum is the classroom situation. Classroom situations are about experiencing relationships; thus it is those relationships that are at the heart of the course of learning, often more so than the subject matter in the books.

Children normally do not learn in boxes, thus the strict division of curriculum into subject matter does not lead to effective learning. Thinking-based curricula, which encourage and allow children to think, if handled in a multi-disciplinary and integrated fashion, yield the best results. Bearing this in mind, the sources for a relevant updated curriculum in a fast-moving age will rely far less on standardized textbooks than on carefully prepared materials by teachers and community members. Examples of these may be newspapers, reading corners, and web sites.[61]

Teacher Approach to Assessment

Learning and the assessment of what is learned tend to be much more effective when learning outcomes and performance standards are established first. The establishment of clear learning outcomes provides the context for practical assessment. Meanwhile, it has become increasingly clear that using one assessment task or testing occasion to generalize about an individual student, classroom, or school cannot lead to authentic and useful knowledge. Authentic assessment needs to be carried out using several methods, tasks, or occasions over time before judgments can be made.

A number of educators have advised teachers to turn to portfolios as a means of authentic assessment, as they appear to include multiple measures taken over time. Moreover, portfolios measure student performance within a context of several other issues related to learning, including affect and other cognitive skills. Well-designed portfolios allow for the inclusion of samples of students' completed work and work in progress. Meanwhile well-conceived portfolios can help to enhance students' self-evaluation and reflection. Portfolios are flexible enough assessment-conduits to measure against learning outcomes of all forms of curricula, and also to indicate the processes by which the outcomes were achieved. They can capture group and individual work as well as independent and guided/supported work.

Most importantly, portfolios are ideal channels for parental involvement. Conferencing with parents on the skills, knowledge, and attitudes acquired by their children are very significant components of authentic assessment. Portfolios and other forms of classroom-based assessments, other than standardized tests, are ideal methods of multi-ability learning and of unleashing the different talents and intelligences that children hold within them.[62]

Teacher Approach to Discipline

The questions of discipline and control are treated quite innovatively in the "community-of-learners" approach. In such communities, the classroom and school are viewed as an extended family. They are a community in every sense of the word, whereby goals and common cultures are shared. Relationships are personal, and learning is cooperative. Moreover relationships are long-term and not transient. Not only are relationships personalized, but so is instruction. There is a sense of personal accountability and citizenship. A social contract is formulated and agreed upon. Students become citizens in that context and abide by an ethical code they have formulated, which includes rules about students being prepared for classes each day, paying attention in class, behaving and being at their personal best, and respecting other people and their property.

Peer and cooperative teams help create such an environment. Students are taught to be peacemakers. Students in this new learning environment learn to resolve their own conflicts, and moreover mediate their classmates' conflicts. Hence classroom and school discipline is based on teaching students the skills and competencies required for resolving their interpersonal conflicts constructively. The focus is inwardly rather than outwardly oriented. The disciplinary system relies on students regulating their own actions and helping their peers to do the same.[63]

School Environment, Management, and Constructivist Leadership

All the above-mentioned innovations in education, the community, school, and classroom cannot take place unless a critical revision of management, organization, and leadership takes place. The worldview on management and organization needs to shift radically if any real headway in learning is to take place. Organizations must be viewed through the lens of living rather than mechanical systems. The latter view has pervaded our thinking for long, hence the result-based management that has been in vogue as of late. Unlike machines, living systems are not predictable and allow for chaos within organization. Exploration and experimentation in fact create new opportunities. Most of life is to be unraveled and discovered, and is a source of surprise and wonder. Life is in constant motion, hence imposing a solution generated by one system on another, or transferring a program from one place to another is unrealistic and a waste of time. The underlying assumption here is the discovery by some social scientists that organizations are living systems, and therefore intelligent, creative, adaptive, self-organizing, and value-seeking organisms. The key elements of this logic, as spelt out by Wheatley and Kellner-Rogers is:

- Everything is in a constant process of discovery and creation.
- Life is by nature organized and uses messes to get to well-ordered solutions.
- *Life is intent on finding what works, not what's 'right.'*
- Life creates more possibilities as it engages with opportunities.
- Life is attracted to order.
- Life organizes around identity [everything in life is ultimately identifiable].
- *Everything participates in the creation and evolution of its neighbors.*[64] (Author's emphasis and clarification)

The two critical components of this new way of perceiving organizations in my view are, first, the notion that a reform movement's key to success is for the main participants to find out what works for them through action, experimentation, and discovery. This view is based on the assumption that success does not come about through blueprints and highly sophisticated plans that are perceived as a priori correct. Meaning is constructed on the way and fears of error and missed opportunities are cast aside. Exploration and experimentation can only make way for new opportunities and venues that are different and that work. They are not necessarily better or worse paths, but they are what work for now. The second critical component is the idea that we live in a relational world and that symbiosis is strength. Not only do living systems contain their own solutions within them, but the solution also always works to bring the parts of a system together so that it can learn more about itself from itself. In organizations, one works with webs of relations. It matters not where the solution or change begins: it will work its way to the rest of the system in the most remarkable of ways, since healthy relations within the system are a source of great energy. What matters is for a system to be provoked or stimulated rather than ordered.

The real transformations in life occur when the nature of relationships has been revisited and the members of any given system share new meanings. Hence systems work best through partnerships as opposed to hierarchical structures: in partnerships people create meanings and set regulations together instead of having others impose them. Change truly comes about when old meanings are questioned and no longer work. Moreover genuine transformation occurs when images of the self and other are changed, making way for new forms of relationships.

In school management, significant changes will occur when:

1. Cognition takes place of what is meaningful to a community of learners. No one is left out, and all share in designing the school's mission statement. More important is the need for all the stakeholders or participants in a movement, in and out of the school, to understand the fundamental intellectual and theoretical underpinnings of their choices.

2. Relationships are such that the hierarchies and divisions that separated teachers from principals, and educators from communities are greatly diminished. Members of the community of learners rediscover each other as colleagues who can work together toward what they have identified as meaningful to them.

3. The entire system is engaged in living networks that allow them to constantly conduct practical research. All the actors are able to reflect on and practice the results of their findings as they learn to make the school and community better environments for learning.

4. Change can occur at any one point of entry. There is no need to achieve a critical mass or develop programs for the entire organization. One can work locally, finding what creates energy in one area of the system, which will in turn spread to its other parts.[65]

5. Participants in this new community of learners are constructivist leaders. By sharing their authority, these leaders engage people in a process that is empowering and conducive to learning. The new, as opposed to the conventional, type of leader is one who assists others in attaining a shared goal. The leader does not influence others, but, rather, helps release the creative talents of those with whom he works and recombines those to reach higher forms of experience and learning. Knowledge is generated, not through transmission, but as a result of the respectful relationships created between people. Those relationships form an ecological social system where there is interdependence, respect, mutual trust, and often,

love. The sustainability of such systems relies on the existence of the joint construction of knowledge and meaning around common causes. Those leaders, whose purpose is control and conformity to regulations, as opposed to collective endeavor and meaning, will risk the balkanization of communities and ecological systems. Leadership is the act of facilitating the work of others and creating an enabling environment for meaningful exchanges, growth, and learning in an environment of acceptance and trust. Its tools are genuine dialogues—listening with respect as collective decisions are formulated and consensus is built.

Critical to this notion of leadership is the concept of 'acts of leadership,' which points to the existence of many leaders. The traditional lines of authority are broken and power relationships are equalized through the replacement of hierarchies with collaborative networks. The acts of leadership are many: students are leaders; teachers are leaders; parents are leaders; community members are leaders; women are leaders; men are leaders: administrators are leaders.[66]
In this comprehensive ecological system I would like to single out teachers as special leaders and agents for change. Teachers are privileged in the sense that they play a central, though not exclusive role, in revitalizing political culture, ethics, civil virtue, and intellectual intelligence. Teachers need to view themselves as public intellectuals. They actually combine theory and practice within a political project that strives for liberation, development, equity, rights, and justice. Teachers must therefore, as facilitators of empowerment, provide leadership models that can bring about school and societal reform.[67] They are significant producers of the public good, namely education, humanness, and morality.

On Education, Individual Transformation, and Social Change

In defining quality education we have already alluded to the complex and multi-dimensional nature of the inputs and processes constituting an integrated package approach. Included in the dimensions are the quality of the material resources available for learning, the quality of learning practices and processes, and, finally, the quality of the results and outcomes of learning.

The results of learning are measured according to the desired objectives developed by an educational system within a given society—its state-mandated or nationwide standards on the one hand, and the extent to which the knowledge, skills, and values acquired are relevant to a community's more immediate and local human and environmental needs, on the other. Consensus is not always guaranteed on all of the above fronts, particularly on whether or not it is possible to balance state curricula and testing standards with educational values rooted in local communities and practices.

What is clear, however, from all systems striving for educational reform, Egypt being a case in point, is that the ultimate objective of learning is to produce young, democratic citizens empowered with critical thinking, equipped with the necessary tools for life-long learning, and able to develop creative thinking and talent to their full potential.

Before bringing this section on the quality of education to a close, it is important to conclude by stating that quality education is not just about learning for the sake of understanding, rethinking, reconstructing, and creating knowledge, but most importantly it is about learning to question existing power relations. Power relations do not exist in a vacuum. These relationships are situated within a social context that allows that power to be exerted. Power relations are actually structural and do not operate on individual will. It is because our societies are by and large patriarchal that husbands can order wives around with great ease and high impact.[68] Liberating transformative education occurs when those engaged in a learning dialogue revisit the nature of existing relationships and create new norms and social meanings. It is when members of a community enter into consensual relations within a shared value system of their own. It is furthermore when members of the same community are able to comprehend that different alignments are possible and that existing power relations are not immutable.

As Freire cogently puts it:

> . . . [T]ransformation is not just a question of methods and techniques . . . the question is a different relationship to knowledge and to society . . . liberatory education is fundamentally a situation where the teacher and the students *both* have to be learners, *both* have to be cognitive subjects in spite of being different . . . *both* have to be critical agents in the act of knowing.[69]

Education has a very significant role to play in transformation. It is through a specific form of education that the cognitive mapping and consciousness of individuals is changed. Individual transformation is important in the trajectory to societal transformation. The kind of personal transformation pertinent here to social change within movements is the kind that invites students to think critically, to challenge, and to question. It is the kind of education that allows for an unveiling and critical reading of the reality surrounding us.[70]

One must not imagine however that education alone can bring about change. Radical education, whether adult or not, formal or nonformal, must be sustained and nourished by potent social movements.[71] It is important for radical educators to create alliances with other political actors seeking change. Alliances may be created with numerous movements thus constituting what Gramsci called a *historical bloc*. Although Gramsci used the concept nationally to refer to the ways in which a rising hegemonic class could revolutionize past structures of dominance by combining the leadership of a bloc of social forces in civil society with its own leadership in the political and economic spheres, it is possible to extrapolate the concept globally.[72] A coalition of movements seeking to reverse situations of multiple oppression are the best guarantee for education to make a difference. In the globalized world of today, international movements of those who dream of a just society are very potent civic allies for the achievement of a world paradigm shift in power relations and governance. New social movements with a strong national and international character, networking with the various coalitions seeking change, are more likely than national institutions to make a headway nowadays. Examples such as women's and environmental movements are cases in point.[73] Other significant movements have been the debt relief movement spearheaded by the Jubilee 2000 campaign, which has been hugely successful for a number of African and Latin American countries. Other examples are the de-mining campaigns and the civic groups that caused nuclear states to at least recalculate the costs and benefits of continuing nuclear testing.

In light of all of the above, a very significant and critical movement needs to be singled out for special attention: the human rights movement with child rights at its core. The latter movement is indeed experiencing a comeback and an unprecedented revival, rendering the dream of the impossible actually viable. A number of countries have formed national coalitions that network with and have been supported by international coalitions and agencies working for the same cause and vision. This movement is immensely pertinent and instrumental in strengthening educational reform and paving the way for important structural and individual transformations.[74]

Moreover the necessary personal transformation needed for social change within a rights-equitable perspective is that which helps individuals become persons—with all the ethical, moral, ideological, and value underpinnings that entails.[75] It is mostly about triggering the inherent capacity of individuals to think critically and imaginatively; to dream the possible and to have the courage to engage in making it happen. After all, transformation needs to be accomplished by those who are capable of dreaming about reinventing society and human relationships to bring about democracy, social justice, and dignity of all human beings. It is also the realization by individuals that human beings, to borrow from Murphy, are possibilities *in process*. Change, as opposed to inertia, is an inherent part of our being. The process discussed is one where we become increasingly empowered to be, and in turn change our surroundings.[76]

Finally, learning to be persons has everything to do with learning to trust ourselves and others. Personal transformation and growth are valid only if they translate to social capital, capital that teaches us to live in community and within an atmosphere of *trust*.[77] The basic idea of the concept of social capital is that networks have value. Social capital is one of the most important assets that a community can have. Societies can be rich to the extent that its people take part in community organizations and are able to trust one another and engage in reciprocal relationships.

Movements clearly involve both personal and structural transformation, and the two processes are intertwined. It is useful, however, to isolate individual trajectories and show how they relate to structural change, as this helps to demystify the process of change. It is also useful to acquire such an approach in order to enable one to understand why some changes take on and build roots in one area and others do not.[78]

Conclusion

We have observed that most recent learning paradigms are driven by a core assumption about what it means to be fully human, so that education is regarded as a means to personal development, ethical decision-making, and active participation in civic life.

This section has placed the quest for a new learning paradigm within the context of social movements. It explains the nature of social movements and shows how educational reform and participatory social movements are mutually reinforcing. Learning is a process whereby individuals are able to enrich and enhance their relationship with the inner self, their families, communities, and the world at large. It shows how moving toward this new definition of learning can contribute to a redefinition of social and power relations, leading to transformations at both the individual and structural levels. Education is regarded as the gateway to a deep structural transformation that spans both the cultural and political aspects of a movement.

Taking a movement approach to educational reform, this section has shown the relevance of educational change to the global crises we live in. It has pointed to the need for the globalization of social movements to reestablish a balance in our global ecosystem, and has argued that an already powerful candidate for such an alliance is the child rights movement.

2
Community Schools
in Egypt

"We want more schools, it is more important than anything else, it is more important than having electricity. The lamps will light the roads, but the schools will light our minds."

> *Nagwa* (member of the Education Committee in the hamlet of Abu Risha, Asyut).

HAVING CLARIFIED CONCEPTS, THE GENERAL STATE of the art in social movements, and approaches to quality education in chapter one, this section will look closely at the community-school model, as it took root in Egypt. The model has been informed by all the approaches and concepts discussed in chapter one, and is still in the process of evolving. Narrating the history of the community-school experiment in Egypt can serve as a reflection on the past and a search for meaning in the present, and, possibly, help catalyze a future.

This chapter will look at the global and national educational context within which the community-school model emerged, before moving on to closely examine the community-school project in practice in Egypt. Emphasis will be placed on the model's underlying philosophy, as well as the pedagogy it employed, as portrayed prominently in its classroom management style and training methodology. Hence processes in the classroom and training, as key aspects of the model, will be addressed in some detail. Similarly the whole issue of community mobilization will be looked into in some depth, as it is one of the key components of a social movement approach to educational reform.

Education in Egypt: The Historical Context

The community-school education model in Egypt was established during the period following the Jomtien Education for All (EFA) world conference. The conference, which was held in Thailand in March of 1990, was convened with the purpose of mobilizing the global community to ensure a sound basic education (with emphasis on primary education) for all children. Major partners during this historic meeting were: UNICEF, the United Nations Development Programme (UNDP), the United Nations Educational, Scientific and Cultural Organization (UNESCO), the United Nations Population Fund (UNFPA), and the World Bank.

The EFA world conference emphasized the significance of basic education to human development. It triggered regional and national commitments to life-long learning and the kind of learning that would be relevant to the needs of the young child, the older child, the adolescent, and the adult. Special emphasis was placed on girls and those sectors of the world's population that were hard to reach, whether it was because they were underprivileged, impoverished, illiterate, or living in physically remote areas. The latter two groups became a priority for UNICEF.

During that same decade many other forums promoted equal and quality education for all. Examples were the 1990 World Summit for Children (WSC), and the 1995 World Summit for Social Development (WSSD). From the mid-1990s, UNICEF has moved a step further and adopted a rights-based perspective to education, as mentioned earlier in the general introduction. This approach not only strives to ensure education for all, but to promote the kind of quality of education that would allow children to develop to their full potential.[79]

Egypt has been a prominent partner in all the above forums, and a country which has in fact taken a leadership role in the World Summit for Children. It is also one of nine Third World countries, the so-called E9, of which it is one of the most populated, selected for the EFA's special focus. Hence the decade beginning with 1990 was one where education featured as the main entry point to the country's development, and which was declared by the highest political power in the land as the decade for educational reform.

Egypt has a long tradition as a seat of learning and scholarly endeavor. In the fifteenth century, Cairo alone had 155 schools. These, along with the many libraries then in existence were well-established centers of learning, in contrast to Europe, from where many Europeans were just beginning to set off on their first long voyages of discovery.

Today's modern systems of education date back to the early nineteenth century and the rule of Egypt's modernizing leader, Muhammad 'Ali. A council of 'public instruction' was formed in 1836. Muhammad 'Ali's descendants maintained his dedication to education as a catalyst for modernization. Ismail Pasha (r. 1863–79) put education at the center of the state policies. The Ministry of Education (MOE) was established in 1886. 'Ali Mubarak, the then Minister of Education, introduced the first education plan. Its objectives were to enroll the largest possible number of students in quality schools.

Girls' education was very much a part of the modernization drives that took place after the mid-nineteenth century. In 1936 the 'Council of Public Instruction' recommended the foundation of girls' schools. The first modern Egyptian school for girls was established in 1873, during the reign of Ismail Pasha. Even earlier, during the reign of Muhammad 'Ali, some nursing and technical opportunities had been open to girls.[80]

After a brief interruption due to the British occupation, early in the twentieth century, the incremental increase of student enrollment continued. In 1913 the number of students in Egypt's schools was four hundred thousand. During that time, talk of reform and the need to improve both the quality of schools and enrollment in them were topics of the day. The concern for the democratization of education was also expressed. More importantly investment in education, as reflected in student cost, was not too different from the then industrialized world. During that very early stage of the educational system's development, expenditures and per capita student costs compared very favorably with many parts of the world. As an example, an elementary student cost US$ 1.89 in Egyptian government schools, while the same type of student cost US$ 1.22 in British schools.

Between the first and second world wars, the number of schools in Egypt increased many times over. In 1914, there were 142 schools in Egypt; by 1930 there were 2003 schools, or fourteen times as many. Education was made compulsory in 1923. The 1952 revolution deepened the state commitment to free and compulsory education, and free education was extended to the university level. During the 1950s, the government pursued a policy of building a school every three days. This policy continued, interrupted only by the needs of defense expenditure. In the 1970s, the open-door economic policy allowed for substantive labor migration to the oil producing countries. Prominent among those who sought employment opportunities in those difficult times were school teachers. The mass exodus of teachers led to the development of educational systems in neighboring Arab countries, and the weakening of the Egyptian educational system. In the1980s, due to a large fiscal deficit, the share of social expenditure in Gross Domestic Product (GDP) decreased. The percentage share of expenditure on pre-university education regressed from 2.2 percent to 2.0 percent of GDP between 1980–81 and 1989–90.

In addition to the overall shortage of financial allocation to the education sector, there seems to have been a misallocation of resources in favor of salaries and other running costs coupled with a neglect of long-term investment expenditure. Moreover a clear bias in favor of secondary and higher education was readily apparent. These features did not serve as a solid background or heritage for the decade to come.[81] It is very important to emphasize clearly that the 1980s left behind a dilapidated educational structure. A serious brain drain, coupled with a weakened infrastructure, with school buildings in great shortage and poor condition, was certainly not helped by overall levels of investment. A very serious overhaul of the system was absolutely necessary.

The 1990s have, as mentioned earlier, both in Egypt and as part of a world movement, witnessed a very special concern with education. Early in the decade some challenges required immediate attention. One critical challenge in Egypt was to get all children into school—in 1993, the number of girls out of school was reported to be in the order of six hundred thousand. These were located mostly in the southern part of the country where enrollment rates for girls were on average 71 percent.[82] A great number of the sparsely populated areas in the south had in fact no schooling services, as discovered through field visits undertaken by UNICEF teams.

Meanwhile the quality of education was a source of great national concern. In 1991 the President is quoted to have described the educational system as one in crisis in which large investments were being made for very poor returns.[83] Indeed a sample household survey administering achievement testing during 1993–94 validated the above concern and showed that school learning in arithmetic and language left much to be desired.[84]

The Community Education Model in Egypt: History and Underlying Objectives

In an attempt to respond to the situation during the late 1980s and early 1990s described above, the community-school initiative began in Upper Egypt in 1992 (as one of many initiatives forming part of the reform movement). A signed agreement (memorandum of understanding) between the MOE and UNICEF was the fruit of many weeks spent in negotiation to work out the details of the proposed project. The genesis of a strong partnership was created. This partnership, at a very initial stage of the foundation of the community schools, was extremely critical to the initiative's strength and success. Cementing the partnership at all levels of the MOE was no mean task. The ministry, like every state institution, harbored progressive elements alongside a majority of extreme conservatives. The latter questioned the founding principles of the initiative; that is, the role of teacher-as-facilitator, and community ownership and involvement. The dialogue proved very trying and discouraging at times.

The historical configuration at the time and the prominent figures leading the partnership between the MOE and UNICEF resulted in a successful agreement. The visionary role played by the then Minister of Education, Dr. Hussein Kamel Bahaa El Din, tilted the balance in favor of the ministry's more progressive elements. Under his leadership an agreement was signed on April 29, 1992, between the MOE and UNICEF.

The agreement established an alliance with ground rules, with the purpose of launching a joint venture for quality innovative education through genuine community participation. The overarching objective of the initiative was to provide *quality* education for all. The initiative needed to be both sustainable and capable of inspiring wider expansion.

The model took the following main objectives as its starting point:

- Ensuring that all children of school going age, particularly girls, are in school.
- Encouraging self-help, participation, and non-governmental resources for the provision of school buildings and maintenance.
- Introducing effective and innovative models of schooling and management.
- Emphasizing the development of critical thinking, creativity, and problem solving capabilities.
- Reinforcing democratic behavior.
- Rendering learning materials relevant and suited to children's preferences and needs.
- Enabling children to acquire the skills required for life-long learning.
- Complying with the core principles of child rights.

Roles and Responsibilities of the Major Participants

The above-mentioned agreement delineated roles and responsibilities clearly in the following manner:

The MOE would support the initiative by paying the salaries of the facilitators/teachers who would be selected jointly by the communities in question, Non-Governmental Organizations (NGOs), local MOE officials, and the

UNICEF team. The ministry would also provide school books and guides. It would give guidance and assistance on curriculum matters and participate in the training of facilitators. Finally, the ministry would provide the children in those schools with a small school meal.

UNICEF would design a model for community quality-education for those deprived areas of Upper Egypt. It would design and be responsible for the training of all those involved in the initiative. It would act as the catalyst to the initiative and oversee its management through its partnership with NGOs in the south. Finally, it would design and provide classrooms with furniture, equipment, stationery, and learning materials.

Communities supported by NGOs would provide adequate space for the schools, and they would manage the school through an education committee, one of which would be created in every hamlet. Local leaders and donors would make up the committees' members, and the community's different social categories, including women, men, and youth from all socio-economic levels would be represented. Normally, these communities tend to be fairly homogeneous. The committee was to function like a board of trustees and take all the daily decisions for the school's administration. It was also to ensure that the school was well connected with the local community and that it met its needs.

Furthermore, the committees would nominate potential teachers/facilitators in the various hamlets when they were needed. Teachers/facilitators would be selected from the local communities of the hamlets in Upper Egypt. They would have to be graduates from intermediate education. The selection process for teachers/facilitators would have to be a very rigorous one. In practice, it was done through a committee of the managers in the initiative, professors from the faculties of education, MOE local officials, and members of NGOs. Normally, word-of-mouth announcements of vacancies were made in the various hamlets. The candidates were then interviewed and assessed through oral and written methods to ensure that they were interested in the job as a mission, had the necessary basic competencies, and possessed a positive attitude toward children, which would enable them to teach within a rights perspective. Finally, the local community could set up income-generating and income-saving projects to sustain the school.

Core Components to the Initiative

The community-school model in Egypt is characterized by a number of key components without which it would be hard to develop similar initiatives. The following are some of the critical pillars of the project:

Community Participation

The involvement of communities through the education committee is critical to the empowerment of communities in the ownership and management of their schools. It is only through committees such as these that the real heart of the model can reveal itself in treating the child holistically and bringing about a much-desired transformation.

Moreover the school greatly emphasizes the importance of agricultural work and encourages pupils to feel proud of the communities to which they belong. A sense of community is established in and out of school and students are encouraged to participate in solving the problems of their own communities. This is where citizenship begins.

Convergence of Development Activities around the School

The model presents a convergence of activities and initiatives around the school to reflect an integrated holistic approach. A life-cycle approach is adopted for education. Families in the community receive parenting education and training to look after their young pre-school children; they are equipped with methods to stimulate the young child, develop his or her health, and provide him or her with care and safety. The Early Childhood Care and Development (ECCD) initiative around the schools has not only resulted in better parenting, but has created community-based daycare centers. The older adolescents in the communities were provided with non-formal education in the community-school sites after school hours. The integrated approach also involved health, hygiene, and nutritional and environmental education. The provision of water and sanitation will complete the cycle of integrated development, as well as the increased integration of disabled children. Finally, the possibility for income-generating activities is being developed.

Partnerships

The partnerships that have been most critical to the success of the community-school initiatives have been those between communities, NGOs, universities, and the MOE. These have constituted critical partnerships from the model's inception. Other partners have joined the movement through the years, such as donors and specialized institutions, such as the National Center for Examinations and Educational Evaluation (NCEEE) and the Center for Curriculum and Instructional Materials Development (CCIMD).

Adequate Facilities

Although the facilities provided by the communities are fairly modest, they are in most cases sufficient for conducting the desired activities during learning time. There are, however, clearly developed specifications regarding school space, child and staff safety, as well as specific criteria for selecting a site. The criteria specify the required proximity of the community to the nearest school (usually a minimum of two kilometers), the size of the community's population (no less than 1,500–2000 inhabitants), the number of out-of-school children (no less than fifty per hamlet), and the willingness of the community to participate (the community should agree and be eager to participate in the provision and management of the school). This of course entails systematic surveys and fact-finding early on. Meanwhile the modest buildings built and/or donated by the community also require minimum standards of safety and functionality. Ventilation and lighting are looked into. Each child is allocated a minimum of 1.5 square meters and some common space for the kinds of activities required by the school day. A classroom should accommodate a maximum of thirty-five students and an average of twenty-five. Some sites will have more than one school if the need arises and hence clusters of schools (called 'school clusters') are established. In some cases these will consist of up to five or six schools in one site. The spaces have proved functional despite the often negative comments made by some officials with respect to the poor building material and inadequate facilities of the buildings.

Free Education

What is even more critical than the mere physical existence of the school is the fact that education is truly free. The schools are provided with stationery, equipment, and learning materials for each child, thus truly abolishing all costs for poorer families. Facilitators and children are, however, made conscious of their consumption, are initiated to recycling in all their training, and are strongly encouraged to utilize recycled material and junk to create learning aids.

Meanwhile, children are not forced into school uniforms or any other obligations that might incur hidden costs. Transport is obviously another potential hidden-cost item, which is not needed. Most importantly, private tutoring is unheard of. The poor families are willing and prepared to make one-time investments in the provision of school space. They are, however, not prepared to carry the burden of regular running and/or hidden costs.

Flexible Schooling Hours

School time is flexible and often seasonal to accommodate the need for children to help their families in the field and at home. The possibility of organizing school demands around family needs is extremely important, particularly for girls.

Some school committees choose to start the school day very early in the morning to allow children to help their families after school; other committees choose to begin slightly later, to allow children to carry out family chores before school. In addition to their weekly holiday on Fridays, both teachers and students are allowed an added day off on village/hamlet market days.

During the year, specific agricultural seasons are taken into consideration, when children help families and communities at harvest. This is all a matter of consensual organization between the school and the family whereby learning is given priority but family and community life are not disrupted.

Multi-ability/Multi-grade Teaching

The formal pre-university system of education in Egypt is divided into three cycles. The primary cycle, which consists of five grades and which, in 2003, was extended to six. Children are admitted to the first grade between the ages of six and nine. Government examinations are administered during the third and final grades. The next cycle is the preparatory cycle and consists of three grades. At the end of this cycle a formal government examination is administered. Depending on their performance in these examinations students will be admitted to either technical or regular secondary schools, the former accepting the weaker children while the latter are reserved for the higher-performing students. The secondary cycle consists of three grades, after which students are examined and compete for university places and other academic institutions according to their grade levels.

Multi-ability grouping styles in the classroom describe any teaching style whereby children in a single classroom are divided according to ability, and managed by single teachers. In larger, mainstream schools, each class usually corresponds to a grade, or specific age group, and within that class, children are grouped according to their abilities.

In rural areas, however, particularly in villages with small populations, the total number of children attending school may come to no more than forty of fifty, in which case dividing the children into different classrooms by grade/age group can constitute a waste of resources. Hence in the community schools, which include the primary cycle, children are admitted between the ages of six and twelve. As the children enroll in the school for the first time they are basically all at the same level of reading and writing as they will have never been to school before. Their ages, however, range between six and twelve years. The older children will naturally progress at a faster rate. Pupils are therefore organized in grades according to their abilities and pace of learning, but within the same classroom, and activities and learning are therefore tailored in accordance to the children's pace. This is the multi-grade system of classroom management.

Through a system of self-management, authentic evaluation, and peer-driven and conscious learning, some children will manage to complete the primary cycle in three years. This is done through an acceleration program that functions best within a multi-grade system. Facilitators have been carefully trained on the art and techniques of managing multi-grade classrooms.

All the schools are run through multi-ability grouping styles and 40 percent of them are run through multi-grade management. The classes naturally develop into multi-grade classes, based on the needs in the hamlet and the age group that is out of school in each community. Preference for admission is usually given to older children since the communities view them as the most vulnerable, after the girls, and the most likely to have missed the chance of a formal education. It is therefore not unlikely that, in many of the hamlets, the age levels of the children will not vary too much.

Formal Recognition

The schools are not non-formal alternatives. Pupils of those schools are entitled to a formal, recognized primary-school certificate at the end of the cycle. They also take the formal and regular government examinations in the third and fifth grades. At present, the primary cycle is five years long, soon to become six years. Through an accredited acceleration program, pupils in those schools may complete the cycle in a shorter period of time. The graduates from the community schools are then admitted into regular government preparatory schools.

Selection of Facilitators

A rigorous system of selecting facilitators is carefully put in place. Key experiences, competencies, personality traits, and preferences are carefully looked into before a facilitator/teacher is selected. It is not just a question of adequate academic credentials or degrees. The young women selected for the business of facilitation are required to perform in ways that are innovative, sensitive, and child friendly, if any learning is to take place. The facilitators are rigorously trained and, along with the core group of facilitators who teach in class, a group of reserve facilitators are also selected and trained. They fill in when core facilitators drop out or are absent. Moreover some are meant to be constantly rotating in order to lend a helping hand to the weaker classes. They contribute positively to the growing human capital emerging from the initiative. They also reinforce team teaching and learning.

Classroom Furniture

To allow for activity-based, peer and group innovative learning, the furniture in these classes must be of a special type. The furniture is detachable and flexible. It lends itself to many creative configurations. It thus allows children to move freely and actively as they take responsibility for their learning. It also allows them to work in groups. The furniture is mostly made of trapezoid tables and chairs that can be shaped into U-shapes, circles, rows, and small working groups.

Pedagogy

The pedagogy is also very innovative and relies mostly on the creativity of facilitators and children. Together they develop learning materials that may be used for multi-grade learning, active learning, and the acquisition of life skills and values. The materials developed are attractive and child-friendly. They are mostly shaped by brain-based learning and the kind of learning that awakens all the intelligences (see page 14). Moreover peer and cooperative learning is widely practiced. Much more will be said on classroom management, learning processes, and quality.

Supervision of the Community-School Initiative

A strong team of well-selected and trained supervisors must operate within flexible management structures. A tight and supportive system of supervision ensures the quality of schooling and learning. Two supervisory teams are responsible for the management and monitoring of the initiative: a field supervisory team and a technical supervisory team. Both teams supervise and direct the schooling process and carry out on-the-job training. The teams are also responsible for on-going evaluation and for fostering the links between school and community. Members of these teams are constructivist leaders. They are graduates of universities and have some teaching/educational management experience. Together with the local communities they are responsible for much of the initiative's progress and development. Both teams work through the local NGOs in each governorate. This is the ultimate insurance of continued capacity-building and quality control. Each supervisor is responsible for 8–10 schools or classes. They routinely visit the schools in order to problem-solve, evaluate, and train.

Management of the Community-School Initiative

Egypt is divided into twenty-seven governorates (provinces). Each of these governorates is divided into districts and villages in the rural areas, and cities and towns in the urban areas. The management of the initiative is carried out by local NGOs at the governorate level. For each governorate there is a project manager and deputy or assistant project managers, in addition to the supervisory staff. The management tends to be flat and highly participatory, as opposed to rigid and hierarchical. The teams have been trained on team building and teamwork, where tasks performed in complementary ways are the determining factor in their evaluation. Although accountabilities are made clear, since specific individuals are in charge of specific tasks and the terms of reference are clearly defined, there are, however, team evaluation systems where it is the performance of the team as a whole that is measured.

Often the competition appears not between individuals, but is quite pronounced between the teams in the various districts. The initiative is based in three governorates and in six districts within those governorates. The three governorates are Asyut, Sohag, and Qena. Each has its own NGO. In Asyut the districts reached are Manfalut and Abu Tig. In Sohag the districts are Dar al Salam, Geihena, and Saqulta. In Qena the District is Farshut. All the six districts were selected according to a poverty index, and in partnership with the local authorities at the governorate level.

Training

This is one of the most powerful and dynamic pillars of the model. Training is mostly tailored to suit the needs and demands of a particular school and community. It therefore deserves a separate in-depth section of its own (see pages 55–70). It is totally participatory and based on a vision of transformation.

Major Inputs to the Community-School Initiative in Upper Egypt

The most significant inputs to the model are what I refer to as its human and social capital. It is not fancy buildings, glossy books, or advanced technology that determine the initiative's success in practice, it is the people. The most important inputs to the community-school initiative may be singled out as follows:

1. The rich and latent social capital that has been revived through community mobilization.
2. The human capital that has carefully been nurtured through training.
3. The leadership style that has been constructivist, decentralized, and, finally, totally localized.

Taking each one of these inputs in turn:

Social Capital and the Mobilization of Communities in Upper Egypt

To understand a people is to understand their history. There is no revelation as deep as that of social history, which delves into the collective consciousness of a given people at a given point in time, their image of self and other, and hence their lived reality. Social action is very often the result of perceived and inherited collective consciousness, performed within a structural reality. Within that reality, legends, myths, and facts are intertwined to give rise to a social-historical conjuncture that creates the specificity of each people and community, and constitutes a basis for future action.

Education in Upper Egypt

Egypt is a country that has for centuries revered science and education and in fact established one of the first universities in the world. Rural areas in Egypt are notable for their community education. *Kuttab* or Qur'anic schools have been fairly widespread in the Egyptian countryside as the first form of primary education, often held within a multi-grade type setting and completely reliant on community participation in setting up and running the schools.

Upper Egypt has been particularly famous for its self-reliant development patterns. Since ancient Egyptian times the country has been divided into two main constituencies: Upper and Lower Egypt. Upper Egypt attracted vast numbers of Arab tribes, even before the advent of Islam. It was in fact the Arabs who first called Upper Egypt *al-Sa'id,* meaning the elevated land. The whole of the Eastern Desert between the River Nile and the Red Sea was, from Pharaonic times, called the Arab country. During the early phases of the Islamic expansion, Upper Egypt and Nubia in particular continued to attract hordes of Arab tribes, the majority of whom were of Yemeni stock. The tribes flocked to this region for a number of reasons; some of these were economic, as Upper Egypt offered great trading opportunities and also had precious metals. The climate was also akin to that of the Arabian Peninsula and some parts of the Yemen, which allowed the tribes to settle comfortably into the kind of agricultural activity they knew best. Politically, the tribes were greatly attracted to the southern part of Egypt for they found secure asylum there. This is particularly true of those tribes that opposed ruling regimes during various, dramatic eras of history in the surrounding Arab lands. Some opposed the Ummayads, others the Abbasids, while many supported the Fatimids, who in fact eased their entry into Egypt.

The Arab tribes found great allies in the Egyptian Copts residing in the Sa'id. The Copts welcomed the arrival of the Arab tribes and soon became

Arabized themselves. The reason for this warm welcome was their adversity to Ptolemaic and Roman rule, which had greatly ill-treated them and shown a deep disrespect for their religious practices and beliefs. The Arabs showed tolerance and respect, which allowed for assimilation, coexistence, and alliance.

Arab rulers also encouraged the Arab tribes to migrate to the Sa'id, especially when they stirred domestic trouble through their opposition to rulers or their own internal strife and feuding. Those Arabs that did migrate to the south of Egypt were not just military men. Among them were very large numbers of *ulema* in the religious sense, as well as men of science—chemists, biologists, alchemists, medical men, logicians, and philosophers—and men and women of letters—poets, writers, specialists in grammar, linguists, artists, musicians, geographers, and historians.[85]

Politically and culturally, Upper Egypt developed more or less autonomously and became the cradle for many a revolutionary or opposition movement. In fact Upper Egypt became notorious for its separatist movements, creating, according to certain historical accounts, an independent republic during the early Mamluk era. Between 1301 and 1517, the Sa'id witnessed several upheavals and revolts championed by the settled Arab tribes against the Mamluks.[86]

The whole southern region became the cradle of tribal settlements, and by the eighteenth century Upper Egypt was completely ruled by the famous Hawara tribe. Governance had become decentralized as the Hawara spread their sovereignty over ten provinces and parts of the remaining twenty-one provinces in Upper Egypt.[87]

The southern provinces enjoyed a rule where the sense of community was very pronounced. Unlike the northern provinces, land was commonly owned and there was no allusion in historical documents to individual or private property. A strong sense of equity and justice was evidenced, particularly during the rule of Sheikh Hammam, a legendary leader of the Hawara tribe who earned the enduring love and respect of the southern inhabitants of the Sa'id. Exploitation by the central government was avoided, and care for the poor and marginalized was eminent. A very high level of organization and self-rule emerged, out of which evolved independent armies which were instrumental in fighting against Napoleon's campaign, as well as in protecting the peasants from pillagers. Meanwhile political dissidents from the specifically Egyptian central rule came to the Hawara for protection.

The southern tribal polity also developed a culture of tolerance wherein the Copts were invited to take important financial positions within their rule. Meanwhile a reverence for all forms of education, science, and knowledge was clearly manifest. Great philosophers and men of learning were invited to stay in Hawara territory and enjoyed tremendous respect, status, and privileges.

In fact during the latter part of the nineteenth and early part of the twentieth centuries, the Sa'id continued to be a stronghold for the learned elite. Many great literary and philosophical figures had their origins in the south, examples of whom include Rifaa al-Tahtawi, al-Aqqad, Hoda Shaarawi, and Taha Hussein.

Writing about Girga, the original capital of the Sa'id, 'Ali Mubarak states clearly that the town was famous for its scientists and men of knowledge from ancient times; it was the home of thousands of writers, teachers, theologians, muftis, and judges. Towns, cities, and villages in other parts of the country were, on the other hand, described as being famous for commerce or industry, or singled out for the piousness of their inhabitants.[88]

When 'Ali Mubarak, in his famous description of countries and places,[89] describes Tahta, a town in Sohag, he does so in ten pages of minute handwriting. After a brief description of the geographical location and services therein, he describes the inhabitants, who were, according to him, mostly people with knowledge in the arts, theology, and science. He mentions the prominent Sheikh Hassan al-Attar who traveled to France during the era of Muhammad 'Ali and managed to translate whole libraries of books from Europe. Attar was also instrumental in setting up the Alson school of languages and translation. No less than one thousand names of people of knowledge are mentioned in the pages. Mention is clearly made in those pages of a well-reputed theologian, 'Ali al-'Abidin, a leader of the Hawara tribe, whose ancestry could be traced back to Islamic nobility. Mention is made of his great wealth, generosity, hospitality, and leadership.[90]

The cult of leadership was important to the Hawara and Sa'idi existence. During the reign of the much-adored Sheikh Hammam, communities had been mobilized to carry out many public works in a self-reliant fashion. The man was so loved and admired that many folk songs about him have survived to the present day.[91]

The various historical accounts of the Sa'id capture some of the most vital values and characteristics of community education worldwide,[92] the most prominent features being radical thinking, equity, self-reliance, democratic leadership, tolerance, democracy, participation, and decentralization.

How Communities Were Mobilized in Upper Egypt

This section will attempt to answer the question of how the communities were mobilized, within this historical background so described, and with particular emphasis on the four schools from which the very first cohort of students graduated, while at times drawing examples from schools that were established later. This section does not have a single author, as all participants in the program were engaged in research and writing as the program expanded and grew. Students, facilitators, and project support staff wrote much of the data employed. Often, the support staff, using discussions with community members, recorded the data. Meanwhile as the project expands, the amount of records increases. Regular school and community records are kept by project staff and school committees, all of which render research and evaluation not only possible but a natural project activity. Research and development were very much part of the project's initial conception, and are carried out by home-grown experts from within the project.

Present-day communities approached for the creation of community schools were mainly small hamlets which had originally been tribal settlements. Dates of settlement varied quite a bit, ranging from the mid-nineteenth to the mid-twentieth centuries, hence spanning a hundred years. A great many of those communities had just been introduced to electricity during the 1990s, while clean drinking water was by no means widely available. Almost all those communities had no health services. Each catchment area had roughly a hundred or so families, all related, with an average of seven members per household. The main economic activity of these communities was agriculture. A few of the communities were involved in fishing when they were close to a stream. The members of all these communities were poor and by and large agricultural laborers. In some situations members of these communities owned small plots of land. Inhabitants of these areas all suffered from underdevelopment. Children were a particularly pathetic sight, with signs of malnutrition appearing on their fragile bodies and pale faces. Children tended animals and carried out other family chores, while women and girls, particularly, were not given adequate opportunities for development. They were married off very early and hardly had a chance to go to school. Many were kept occupied with field and household chores. The idea of educating them was not precluded provided that they did not forsake all their household chores.

The first communities and teams I approached were not immediately convinced. There was resistance at times to the initiative, because of poverty and the burden of contributions, and some of the younger men feared women's education. Reticence was most apparent, however, when community members did not trust the seriousness of the project and suspected that they might receive a second-class education. A very common reaction was a general disbelief that anyone might be interested in them. They had been marginalized and over-looked for so long that they found it hard to believe that a real and effective school would be set up for them, and which would be officially recognized by the authorities. Those communities were not averse to contributions for 'holy' causes, such as mosques and schools; they were, however, not sure that the contributions would be put to good use. They needed some reassurance. Personal rapport, trust, and leadership were key elements of the initial negotiations. Several months were spent building such rapport. The community members were extremely flattered at our many visits. A common remark was, "how very privileged we are that you have come all the way from Cairo to visit us and look after our interests!" It is interesting to note that despite the very common belief that women were unimportant, it is they who, on two occasions, made the final decision to accept the project in the first four hamlets (*ezbas*) and in fact identified the school site. They appeared more trusting and willing to take the risk.

After traveling around some thirty hamlets in Asyut, bridges were built with some fifteen communities as potential sites. The focus was then narrowed to four sites that appeared to be the most ready to initiate the experience; al-Kom, al-Akarma, Abu Risha, and al-Gamayla.

Each site required a different strategic approach for mobilization. The al-Kom community was relatively well off and had built its own mosque at the edge of the hamlet. The natural leaders were relatively cohesive and generally in agreement with one another. With them religious arguments were the most potent, especially as one of their leading figures, Sheikh Bakr, was responsible for religious education in the mosque. He had himself acquired secondary schooling, had great respect for education, and wished he had had an opportunity to obtain a higher education. To make up for that he was perfectly happy to teach school children religion if the project was realized. He was of course encouraged to do so. Soon enough Sheikh Bakr and the rest of the community offered the project a compartment in the first floor of the mosque.

Al-Akarma was a much poorer community, and the leading figures in the hamlet were eight brothers who had joint ownership of some estates, mostly poor peasant houses. Negotiations with that group were rather lengthy and tedious. Many arguments were presented by the project team including the fact that a school could act as a leverage for more services. It would empower the community to request better services, such as drinking water and electricity for the school once it was established. With some hesitation an old guesthouse inherited by all eight brothers was offered. The place was being used as a warehouse or storage space and was owned by all the brothers. Although the space was adequate, many repairs and cleaning were necessary, hence the need for additional funds. The brothers were clearly not prepared to bear the brunt of the expense alone. The method used in that situation was that the project leader and author, a woman, volunteered some personal financial contribution to the community and suggested that a contribution list be passed around the whole community through a contribution committee.

There was a sense of embarrassment that a woman had initiated the contributions, all of which encouraged all the men to come forth and make generous contributions. This technique was later discovered to be a very useful one and one which on many occasions, not only embarrassed the men of a community, but flattered them greatly. The fact that an outsider felt enough of a commitment to a school in their hamlet to contribute to it encouraged them greatly and endeared to them the idea of establishing a school in their community.

The third community school was set up in Abu Risha where the most active and leading family was contacted. After some rapport and trust was built, the team was introduced to the women in the family, who were made up of older and younger women, two of whom were newly wed brides. The women rallied around the project and the newly wed brides, who were sisters, convinced their husbands, themselves brothers, to donate their bedrooms to the school and reside with their mother-in-law and aunt in the extended family home.

The fourth site, al-Gamayla, was the last one mobilized of the four. The leaders of that community had been instigated to donate space and join the project through competition and emulation. They were the relatives of the nearby families in al-Akarma and felt insulted that the latter community, despite its poverty, had managed to set up the project. Their tribal pride conduced them to succumb to our solicitation.

Despite the diversity of techniques and the varying contexts within which mobilization occurred, a few common elements can be gleaned from all four experiences, based on the accounts of the community members themselves as to why they had joined the project. Two very clear sources of motivation in each of the sites were the great desire to be engaged in good deeds and also the great value attached to education and, surprisingly, particularly that of those who risked the greatest deprivation of all: girls.

A sample of about twenty community members and parents of the children in community schools, in addition to about seven members of the education committees in all four initial schools, were interviewed by the field support team in 1996 and 1997. The interviews covered issues such as:

- Why the community decided to participate in the project and provide school space.
- Why some community members opted to be members of the education committee.

- What was the nature of the community members' relationship to the school?
- What were their aspirations regarding the role of the school in their community?
- How did they regard the school and its quality?
- Did they want their children to continue their education in the school?

In al-Kom, some of the community responses indicated that they had been encouraged to begin the school because of the many visits of the project team from Cairo. In a respondent's own words, "The school has honored us and is a source of great pride; the fact that people came all the way from Cairo to set up a beneficial project for us is enough evidence of its importance." Other community members expressed their great gratitude for the school and what it had done for their children. One father stated, "My daughter goes to the community school and she has learned so much; she can in fact read better than her two brothers who go to regular schools." Another parent declared, "My daughter would have never managed to get an education as she was getting older than the regular school age limit for enrollment. Besides she has enrolled in a school, which seems to treat the children very well; the facilitators are just like sisters to those children. They are getting an excellent education." Another mother declared that the school did not have a single fault. Comparing her children's education she said, "My son, who is in the third preparatory grade in a regular school is not able to read or write as well as my daughter, who is now graduating from the community school fifth primary grade and can read and write fluently." The quality of education and learning in those community schools was highly commended on many occasions by several community members.

In addition to accepting older girls, the community was very grateful for the fact that education was completely free in the school. Moreover another source of gratitude was the fact that the community was nearby and allowed girls to walk to school without having to cross foreign tribal territory. Interestingly some community members commented, "We are so very happy to have our own school here because the nearest school belongs to the *Arab* tribe so we could not have sent our children there."

Tribal competitiveness and supremacy often motivated communities to set up additional schools. In Qena, where the schools began in 1994, the Hawara tribe continued to enjoy supremacy in the district of Farshut. In order to avoid sending the Hawara children to be taught by non-Hawaras, additional schools were established. Meanwhile in the Sohag Governorate where the schools were established in 1993, the schools served as a cohesive force in the face of feuding tribes.

Local government officials had been greatly involved in mobilizing the communities with the field team, which led to added trust. Some community members went as far as donating up to six schools in one area when needed.

In al-Akarma, the second community mobilized in Asyut in 1992, community participants and members of the education committee welcomed the school, as they believed it would be a source of empowerment. Being quite poor they viewed the school as a development investment and an opportunity to attract more services to their hamlet, such as decent roads, electricity, water, and sanitation. They were greatly encouraged by the fact that a previous governor of Asyut, Hassan al-Alfi, had visited their school and distributed certificates of recognition for the community work with reference to the establishment of the school. The community had been very willing to participate, but would prefer to do so in labor, intellectual efforts, and in kind, as they could not afford to pay cash.

The community of Abu Risha had been very readily mobilized. The value of girls' education was a clear driving force. Many women in the hamlet had been deprived of an education and so they greatly looked forward to offering their girls one. They were very grateful that the school would provide free education with no hidden costs or private tutoring involved. On many occasions the community recognized the value of educating their girls as it meant that educated men in the hamlet would not be forced to marry people from different communities or hamlets in search of an educated girl. Almost all those interviewed made positive comments on the quality of education in the school.[93] With reference to the later phases of the project, that is, children reaching the fifth grade, the community members and parents commented on how well their children could speak in English.

Like most other sites, community members viewed their contribution to the school as an act of faith; it was a sacred deed, similar to that of building a mosque. All community members interviewed believed that education constituted a very significant investment for the future of their children, their families, and the community at large. This great appreciation of education appeared to be much more pronounced among the women than the men. Again, an important bonus had been the visit of Governor Hassan al-Alfi and the distribution of certificates of recognition to the community members.

Finally, in al-Gamayla, people were again greatly motivated, from their own perspective, by the need to engage in charitable activities for the development of their own communities. Some members were mobilized by the desire to have a place where elections could take place.[94] Other apparently mobilizing factors were the visits by important people to their hamlet, including the village head and governor al-Alfi, and the subtle competition that existed between them and a neighboring hamlet that had already launched a community school.

Clear among all the interviewees' responses was the very high value placed on education. This was particularly evident in the women's responses. They indicated that without the school their children would have continued in ignorance and darkness. They would have been, to borrow their own expression, "like animals." School "illuminated their minds," they believed. All those interviewed were highly satisfied with the quality of learning in the schools and expressed that by drawing comparisons between those children going to regular schools in distant locations, those going to community schools, and those not attending school at all.

During the interviews, future aspirations of the community members for the school were explored. Although some interviewees indicated that the schools were perfect as they were and that they could not have asked for anything better, those who did so were in the minority and were mostly women. The majority of the respondents had suggestions to improve the project. The following are some of the recurrent remarks made:

- The school buildings were not adequate and since the government can afford to build schools as in the case of the one-classroom schools why should the community continue to contribute school buildings. (The MOE launched its one-classroom school project in 1993, so called because many of the schools were made up of single classrooms. The initiative was tailored after the community-school model in certain, but not all, respects.)
- The hamlets required many services that the community-school project should strive to attract to the sites, such as clean and potable water, pit latrines, roads, and most of all, a health clinic.
- The hamlets should have a preparatory school for the graduates from primary schools.
- The schools should expand their literacy classes for women and include men as well.
- The parenting education programs should be increased and accelerated.
- The schools should offer vocational training, particularly for women, around skills such as sewing, knitting, and other home economics skills.
- The schools should continue to expand as more children were waiting in line for an education.
- The community should have income-generating projects around the school to enable them to have full ownership and control over the project's continuity.

By the second year of the initiative, the field teams played a leadership role in mobilizing communities. In the field teams' own view the momentum of mobilization was maintained by closer bonding with the community. This was manifested in sharing the joys and sorrows of community members by participating in weddings, funerals, caring for the old and ill, and other social and community functions. Moreover the field team also took pains to reinforce the idea of the school as the source of benefits for the whole community. Hence, based around the school are literacy classes and vocational training classes that allow women to learn how to wash, cook, and sew as well as acquire other home economics skills. These training sessions are linked to a parenting education program, which empowers families to look after their younger ones, thus making the school the center of a great many community events.

The field teams have also been instrumental in obtaining other benefits around the school, such as medical care from the village doctors on voluntary bases for the children and community members. In addition, communities managed to get free prescribed medicines from pharmacies on a voluntary basis.

In a number of situations, through the school field team's solicitation, the communities managed to get their roads paved and some got electricity and drinkable water. In addition, income-generating activities have been initiated in some of the hamlets, examples of which include:

- A biogas[95] compound in Hawatka.
- A grocery store in al-Kom.
- Artisan works in Abu Zeid and Hamad Ibn Sharan hamlet of straw plates and containers.
- Making pickles for sale in Abu Risha.
- Selling eggs and homemade cheese in Helba hamlet.
- Breeding rabbits in Aliksan hamlet.
- School canteens run by students.
- For-profit agricultural plots run by the school.

The education committees, along with the field teams, were also instrumental in mobilizing new communities. Originally the committees were to meet on a weekly basis with the field team, to look into issues and take decisions regarding the management of the school. Eventually the meetings with the field teams diminished and are now being held on a monthly basis or as and when they are needed. From the records of the committee meetings, the absentee rate is not very high. In most meetings at least half the members or more are present. In numerous cases the attendance reaches 100 percent. The periods when absentee rates are high usually coincide with the harvest seasons for the various crops. The project keeps a lot of data on the members of education committees, which includes their profile (education, socio-economic background, age, occupation, and so on), as well as tracking their progress in meetings. From those documents we are able to design a profile of the committee members. They are on average around seven in number. The total number of committee members by the academic year 1996–97 was 822. The number of female members was 263, constituting 32 percent. In 1999–2000 the number of committee members had increased to 1318, and the total number of women to 337, making up 26 percent of the total. The average age of the members is 40. The age of the men ranges from 20–50 years and that of the women from 20–40. The percentage of educated members is 59 percent for all members, while only 0.9 percent of female members are educated.

Looking at the socio-economic level of the committee members, it is clear that there is a lot of diversity. Although nearly all the members seemed to own property, whether in the form of a house or land, there were a few who were property-less and the amount of land owned varied. The majority owned less than a *feddan* (less than a hectare). There was however a couple of rare cases where people owned fifty *feddans* of reclaimed land. It is not possible to carry out proper statistical analyses on all the members; however it is possible to obtain percentages for those members whose data was complete in terms of the exact quantity of land owned.

The initial conception of the initiative, which was strictly applied in the first four schools, insisted that committee members not all be selected from the most powerful or wealthy inhabitants in the hamlet in question. The project team and support staff selected some of the committee members; the rest was a matter for self selection. Great pain was exerted in the first four sites to include members from different families and from different professions, and possibly residing in different geographic parts of the hamlet; finally women and youth were also included. As the project evolved, more and more participation ensued. By 1998–99, friends of the education committees constituted a new group of people who helped with the community and the school without necessarily being permanent residents of the hamlet or direct contributors to the school.

The way to mobilize communities was first modeled by the project team from Cairo in the first four schools. Later, the process was emulated by the field teams in partnership with the educational committees. The momentum of mobilization was maintained through the strong partnership between the field teams, local authorities, the education committees and the communities. All the different processes followed were quite specific to an existing cultural climate that created favorable conditions for a community approach to schooling. There are, however, many lessons to be learned from this experiment.

Some very significant pillars of this rewarding process are the leadership models that were carefully developed to absorb and act upon a number of profound principles and fundamental skills. Working to mobilize and motivate communities requires leaders who are prepared to be 'mentors' and who are willing to nurture the process at hand. Effective leadership requires a profound respect for the people one is working with, a strong ability and willingness to do some serious listening and dialogue, and an openness and desire to learn in the process.

Above all, the mobilization of communities requires time for external agents and community members to build rapport and cement relations of trust that will transcend simple tribal or family bonds. Communities are very sensitive to sincerity of intention and know when someone has the best interests of their children, and therefore their own, at heart. Compassion, empathy, and strong emotions are part of the mix of qualities desired of project leaders. It is by sharing the cause and plight of those you work with in deprived communities and making their cause your own that allows things to move. Results are also achieved when more and more supporters are invited to join the movement as it expands and grows stronger, and furthermore involves building the confidence of those you work with by empowering them to think for themselves, make their own decisions, and solve their own problems collectively.

Before ending this section on community mobilization a few words are in order in terms of the lessons learned. Even though the above seemed to indicate that each situation and context invites its own particularities, nonetheless some broad directions may be extracted. The mix for success in community mobilization should in one way or the other include the following ingredients:

- Sincerity and a very deep sense of care and commitment on the part of the leadership.
- Consistency of presence by the mobilizers and intensity of the relationships built, particularly in the earlier phases of a movement's development.
- Deep rapport, emotional expression, and trust built between the movement's leadership and community members.
- Manifestation of genuine respect for people and their local culture.
- The conducting of an honest dialogue whereby new ideas emerge that are owned by all.

- A true participatory approach characterized by deep listening to community members.
- Working with natural community leaders and key informants as an initial strategy to learn with humility.
- Showing results in a timely and demonstrative fashion.

The Training Pedagogy

With the purpose of achieving the quality of education so far discussed, a comprehensive training pedagogy was developed over the years. Major characteristics of this pedagogy are that it is based on teamwork and participation, targets diverse members of the educational system, is open to evolution, is activity-based, and is amenable to evaluation.

Teamwork

The initiative's team-spirited approach to training is reflected first and foremost in the make-up of the training teams, which are formed of university professors from the faculties of education, supervisors and practitioners from the MOE, experts in psychology and social anthropology, and finally, the support team from the project and some of its outstanding facilitators.

The team spirit during the workshops is reflected in the roles undertaken by the trainers. Each day of the training workshop the team demonstrates different configurations and a different division of labor. Thus, one day a trainer will be the leading expert on a topic while others are facilitators, while on another day the roles will reverse and the trainer will facilitate and manage the sessions while others will be the experts on various topics.

The harmony and team spirit among the trainers serves as a model for the trainees. It is built over long periods of planning, joint activity, and reflection. The team of trainers began in 1992 with a small core group consisting of the author, the head of the training and planning department at the MOE at that time, and a professor from the faculty of education at Cairo University. Over the years the team expanded and diversified through dialogue, constructivist learning, observation, and apprenticeship programs. The plan is to build on these networks and expand further.

Evolution

The training workshops are diverse, the teams are constantly expanding, and a conscious effort is made to have a dynamic approach to the training. The content is in constant evolution, both with regard to those areas of training that existed from the beginning as well as the topics that were subsequently added.

The evolution and development of the training content and technique are based largely on an ongoing system of monitoring and evaluation, as well as consultations with team members in the field and the MOE. Needs assessments are always revisited and updated prior to the planning of a training event.

The evolution of the pre-service workshops for teachers/facilitators is an example of a vertical evolution wherein the content and format of the training evolved, based on the above. The first pre-service training took place in 1992 with a very limited amount of facilitators and supervisors. This was the foundation of subsequent training programs. Out of this initial workshop a number of outputs were instrumental in shaping the initiative's path. An internal charter and code of moral conduct was produced. The first manual on self-learning and class management was initiated. The objectives of the primary cycle were pulled out of the formal ministry documents to establish a competency-based education. During that workshop the facilitators signed a social contract among themselves and all members of the team to define their own code of conduct. The trainees produced the community school logo. Each of the facilitators were carefully matched with a partner and made responsible for a school as a pair. Finally some important management rules were established.

The training was conducted with the participation of some school children aged 6–12 who resided in the Qaryat al-Amal near the training site. This allowed the newly recruited facilitators to test their own skills and emotions when dealing with children who were their potential pupils. These facilitators had never dealt with a classroom situation or with children in a systematic and structured form.

During this initial workshop, the facilitators were trained on activity-based learning by practicing it with children after some modeling from the trainers. The group was also trained on creativity and the production of learning aids through practical means. They were introduced to storytelling, playing with children, and creating educational games practically, as well as observation and registering their observations.

The major outcome of this first training workshop was to mobilize the enthusiasm and loyalty to the cause of quality education for the hard-to-reach. The workshop also resulted in constructively building a consensual value system and a sense of team spirit. Finally, it succeeded in unleashing positive emotions and bonds toward a movement for quality education with special emphasis on girls and the deprived.

Types of Training Programs

Since the inception of the initiative a diversity of workshops and training activities have been held. The major training workshops have included:

- Pre-service training
- In-service training
- Refresher training
- Innovation workshops
- Teacher/facilitator apprenticeship
- Training of supervisors
- Management training
- Training of the education committees and members of the local community
- Training of trainers
- Training for Total Quality Management
- Training technique and style

The training workshops mainly target the facilitators from the community schools, one-classroom schoolteachers, supervisors for primary education and the one-classroom school, heads of one-classroom school departments, school principals, teachers from preparatory schools, trainers and supervisors from community schools, NGO practitioners, and education committees. Teachers/facilitators are the cornerstone of the initiative. Facilitators go through a series of training programs before being made fully in charge of a school. When a facilitator is first selected she is appended to an existing school for four months as a trainee and observer. She subsequently participates in five training workshops the objectives of which will be discussed in greater detail.

Pre-service Training

Since the first pre-service training which took place in 1992, much has evolved. The pre-service training evolved into three workshops: the first, an orientation, the second, on active learning, and the third, on constructivist learning and schools. This development was based largely on analyses of the need assessments and the evaluation sheet filled by participants at the end of each workshop. Moreover, during the first three years of the project, the training exclusively targeted facilitators from the community schools. Since 1995 the training has combined both facilitators from community schools and teachers from the one-classroom school initiative begun in 1993.

Through constant field observations and monitoring, the other type of evolution also took place, namely adding new topics and new participants, audiences, and partners. Each of the training workshops has specific teams that are not always identical and which are closer to the specialized topics at hand. There are of course team members that cut across most of the teams.

During the orientation and the facilitators/teacher workshop, the participants learn about the principles of community schools. They acquire a great deal of confidence and practice with problem solving, planning, scientific thinking, critical thinking, communication skills, and creativity. They experience participation and teamwork. Moreover they learn about and experience different types of relationships that are quite different from the authoritarian formats they are accustomed to. They are introduced to all the necessary components of quality education, multi-grade learning, the role of facilitation in the classroom, and most important of all, they become familiar with child rights.

During the second, pre-service workshop on activity-based learning, participants gain in-depth knowledge of and practice in creating learning objectives, lesson planning, authentic evaluation, creating learning activities and aids relevant to their objectives, grouping, routines, instructions, classroom management through pupil participation, dealing with learning difficulties, understanding the various learning methods and stages of growth, and finally, working on religious tolerance and the acceptance of the other.

The third pre-service training activity, on constructivist classrooms, is of longer duration. It includes two weeks of classroom observation whereby new recruits are equipped with classroom observation sheets and are asked to write a full-fledged report on the schools designated to them for observation. The facilitators are asked to add meaning to what they experience and to suggest areas needing improvement based on the knowledge gained in the first two training workshops.

The second component of the training consists of four days of presentations and interaction among trainees. The third training workshop sharpens facilitators' observation and reflection skills. It trains the teams to carry out research, censuses, and surveys. Moreover it imparts to the trainees the necessary skills for orienting children and communities to the particular system adopted by the schools and to develop a social contract among all the various actors in the classroom.

An important contribution of the third pre-service training workshop is the development of the necessary skills among facilitators to ask and instigate open-ended questions to allow children to attach meaning to their activities and learning processes. During this workshop, facilitators are introduced to the usage of the child portfolio (see page 87) and to the methods of detecting slow learners and learning problems. They are exposed to a rudimentary introduction to remedial learning.

In-service Training

The in-service training occurred every week for several years through micro-centers whereby facilitators of same grades or same regions met. Recently the in-service micro-center training has been spaced out and occurs every two weeks. It continues to occur on school vacation days that coincide with village market days. This of course does not stop in-service training from occurring on the job through the efforts of the support-staff supervisory teams.

The formalized in-service training has the objectives of strengthening the team spirit and contact between the team members. It is a forum for experience sharing, bonding, and collective problem solving. Most importantly, it is part of the teacher/facilitator practice of empowerment and democratization.

During the sessions the teams also collectively plan lessons for the coming week and month. The supervisory teams, with the help of MOE supervisors and Faculty of Education (FOE) professors cater to the specific needs of the facilitators in subject matters and skills where they need the most help.

A typical in-service day will include lesson planning, presentation of innovative ideas that work in the different classrooms, problem solving of related class, community, and personal issues, manufacturing of teaching/learning aids, and learning of new knowledge and skills. Often, facilitators used the university or public libraries to research certain topics and report them back to the team. On other occasions, a local expert or specialist will be invited to impart and discuss information, based around a specific theme. Both the field and technical support carry out the planning for the in-service training. Specialized support is sought from the local universities and education departments.

Refresher Training

This training occurs once each or every other year. It targets teachers of the one-classroom school initiative and the community-school facilitators who have been previously trained and working for a whole year. The topics and objectives change each year depending on the needs of the project. The overall goal of this training, however, has consistently been the refreshment of learned skills and knowledge as well as the enrichment of the facilitators' knowledge base, with the inclusion of the most recent research findings and best practices.

Refresher training began in 1994. A demand and need was felt for health education and first-aid training among the facilitators, as they faced greater challenges dealing with the "whole child."[96] This very first refresher workshop dwelled on the achievements of the facilitators and the experience acquired since the inception of the project, as well as the problems they confronted. Facilitators revisited methods of identifying learning objectives, defining them according to priority, and monitoring children's achievement at the various levels in question. Moreover facilitators were trained on the various personality traits they needed to develop in children.

The following year, through the assistance of an international expert trainer and the participation of experts from the NCEEE, the team was trained on multi-grade learning and classroom management. The trainees attempted curriculum development to match this new method of learning. This training workshop resulted in the first attempt at reorganizing and integrating activity-based learning materials, which later became the foundation for the development of innovative activity-based materials for multi-grade classrooms by the CCIMD. The training was informed with research on best strategies and practices that enhance activity-based learning. Time was spent on routines, classroom management, grouping, planning for multi-grade learning, presentation skills, and the distribution of instructions and tasks.

In 1996 the refresher training focused on the building and use of a child portfolio for authentic assessment. The workshop, in addition, built in a health and environment component.

The following year the whole team boarded in Hurgada. This was viewed as an added objective whereby facilitators gained greater mobility and were exposed to different regions and cultural environments. They had previously been exposed to Cairo and Alexandria.

Based on the design of the project management team, and with the assistance of a Canadian training expert, the 1997 training workshop focused on games and activities for a multi-grade class as well as on storytelling and writing. A critical health component was added, namely on reproductive health and raising awareness against harmful practices, such as early marriages and female genital mutilation. In fact the overriding theme of the workshop, art, stories, and activities centered around consciousness-raising against harmful practices, namely early marriage and FGM. The talents and creativity of the workshop participants was unleashed and the outcome was a great deal of artistic production in the form of songs, musicals, plays, and short stories to be used as a source of entertainment, fun, and educational campaigns for local communities.

In 1998 both the one-classroom school teachers and facilitators were trained on 'Child Welfare.' During this workshop all the recent research on brain development and Gardner's intelligences (see page 14) was the basis for all the training activities. Trainees were exposed to the research and given tools to identify the diverse ways in which children learn and the various intelligences they withhold. The learning centers or corners—stable areas in the classroom for children to carry out activities related to specific subjects—were developed to cater to learning styles, intelligences, and methods of integrating subjects. The trainees developed measurement, monitoring and evaluation systems.

Both teachers and facilitators were introduced to the concept of a school mission statement and practiced developing several. Moreover the workshop participants were also greatly focused on the various articles of child rights, particularly those emphasizing the classroom atmosphere.

In 1999 the facilitators from community schools and one-classroom school-teachers were again trained on active learning. Original ideas on how to create activities for the learning centers and initiate young children into science were explored.

In 2001, a series of very special refresher training workshops were designed to further develop activity-based learning and multi-grade classroom management. These workshops were special because they were designed to further inculcate the principles of Child Rights in classroom practices. The facilitators worked hard to critique the indicators developed by their supervisors to monitor child rights. They were then asked to synthesize the best five sets of indicators. Finally, they were asked to come up with their own indicators in agreement with the children in their classes. The workshops entailed a great deal of hard work but were a huge success in sharpening analytical and synthetic skills on the one hand, and making child rights a classroom reality on the other. The training also worked on the needs of adolescents and the building of self-esteem.

Training for the Diffusion of Innovations
The first in the series of the innovation workshops was held in 1995. The series consisted of three important encounters that brought together the best educational experiences worldwide. Successes from the Colombian movement *Escuela Nueva*[97] were revealed, as well as best practices from New Zealand, Bhutan, Indonesia, Bangladesh, Canada, and Pakistan.

The planning for Egypt's community education took place during this very lively atmosphere of dynamic audiovisual presentations. The new terminology coined here referred to a closer coming together of community and one-classroom schools to form parts of one movement. The idea was to diffuse best practices from one system to the other. A select group of policy makers and practitioners from both initiatives participated in the workshops, which took place in January, March, and June of 1995.

The main objectives of the workshops were:

- Getting exposed to international experience and successful global models.
- Clearly understanding the concept of active learning.
- Acquiring planning skills for activity-based learning.
- Planning for a diffusion process of best national and international practices.

- Identifying the most appropriate strategies, channels, structures and institutions for a twinning process between community and one-classroom schools.
- Initiating a planning process for educational innovations and reform, to be implemented in phases.

The last workshop of the series was attended by the Minister of Education, Dr. Hussein Kamel Bahaaa El Din, and a group of prominent educational experts, among them the director of the curriculum center, Dr. Kawssar Kochok. Other experts were from the MOE, the NCEEE, UNICEF, the Ontario Institute of Studies in Education (OISE), and other international institutions.

During this last workshop the Education Innovation Committee (EIC) was initiated by ministerial decree. The core function of this committee was to:

- Ensure that innovations in education would be mainstreamed at first in the one-classroom school initiative and later in the traditional educational system at all levels.
- Ensure that innovations continued to be an ongoing concern in reform through dynamic management and partnerships that would ensure sustainability.
- Strengthen a package approach to the reform process that would include the evaluation system, teaching, and learning pedagogies, the curriculum, classroom and education management, school buildings and furniture, learning materials, training and other related policy issues.
- Widen the scope of stakeholders in education by including members of the media and private sector in the education committees.
- Make the EIC a policy forum to facilitate the sustainability of the community school 'seedbed' model, the diffusion process, the democratization of decision-making, and innovations at all levels.

The innovation workshops had a number of impacts and they indeed appeared as a landmark in bringing the community and one-classroom schools closer together. The workshops marked strong beginnings in policy dialogue, with structures in place to do so. The concept of active learning, and methods of planning for it were adopted and began slowly to become a part of the MOE's discourse and, gradually, of their conceptual framework.

A refresher series of innovation workshops took place in 1998. Practitioners and middle-range policy makers from the MOE and the community education programs were invited again. The exchange of experience this time focused on Egypt, Canada, and Pakistan. The emphasis was on innovative educational concepts and practices, such as authentic assessment, multi-grade classroom management, and active learning and global education. A dictionary of innovative educational concepts was produced by the OISE. Both endeavors were useful in introducing to some, and strengthening for others, the critical concepts of educational reform. The concepts were introduced not only academically but practically, through hands-on training.

Classroom-based Training/ Apprenticeship and Mentoring

When facilitators/teachers have been selected, they are invited to partake in participant observation in classrooms. The classrooms thus selected are known for having the best practices and innovations in education. This phase occurs even before formal training takes place, and usually lasts for a period of four months. This gives the project management ample time to evaluate the new recruit and also for the intern trainee to be gradually mentored about the system by an older and more experienced teacher. Mentoring is a crucial part of the training and learning processes. It occurs at every level and between different members of the community school movement. A good part of the work of leaders at all levels is to mentor others. In the initial phases of the project, all levels of the team had direct access to me as the founder of the entire movement. The practice now even occurs between young alumni of community schools and the recently enrolled new learners.

Training of Supervisors

With the increasing rapprochement between the community schools and one-classroom schools, it became imperative to train MOE supervisors and inspectors, as well as directors of the various one-classroom schools across the country, on the core components of the model. Sensitizing the supervisors to the new methods of learning was found to be key in promoting the new pedagogy of learning in community and one-classroom schools and in mainstreaming the concepts.

Five training workshops were held for 275 supervisors in Cairo and Minya in 1998. The objectives of the workshops were:

- To expose trainees to activity-based learning.
- To impart effective classroom management skills.
- To impart mentoring skills to supervisors when dealing with facilitators and teachers.

- Selecting the best twenty-five supervisors during the workshops to become trainers in subsequent workshops.

The workshops stressed a number of values and skills that the supervisors needed to acquire, such as:

- Promoting respect between supervisors and teachers/facilitators.
- Promoting and providing training to enhance teamwork.
- Promoting needs-assessment skills for supervisors.
- Promoting joint and participatory planning between supervisors and facilitators/teachers.
- Promoting problem-solving skills in the professional and personal domains.
- Training supervisors in methods of creating agreement between them and those who are supervised. Writing letters of notification for visits is one method, and jointly recording the outcome of the visits is another.

In December of 1998 a refresher training workshop was held after three months of field observation. The workshop was planned in collaboration with the MOE and were a live-in experience. The objective of this workshop was:

- Training on needs assessment again.
- Identifying major challenges as they undertook a new supportive role in their supervisory job.
- Developing their skills as leaders and mentors.
- Refreshing their knowledge and skills on active and child centered learning.
- Training on how to support the new roles of facilitators in activity-based classroom participatory management.
- Developing their communication skills with teachers and community members.
- Developing field monitoring plans.

Management Information Training

The project adopted a philosophy of leadership liberation by creating leaders at every level. This entailed careful training in a number of topics and skills, among which were flat management—whereby hierarchy was forsaken for a complementary division of labor—and democratic participatory leadership, and creating new forms of relationships for the sharing of authority and power.

Listening and communication skills were among the most important skills emphasized, along with positive and scientific thinking, and problem solving. Conflict resolution and confrontation skills were also dealt with.

Training on the above was mostly tailored to specific situations. Training sessions were devised on the spot when the need arose, and when there were concrete issues that presented cases to be resolved. Early on during the team-building stages and foundation of the project, these sessions were frequent and quite regular. The relationships were carefully nurtured over time, with enormous amounts of time devoted to counseling and mentoring. Modeling participatory relationships was also an important tool in the movement's progress.

In 1995–96, however, a series of three workshops were structured for communication management skills, supervision, confrontation, and conflict resolution. These arose on the bases of demand and needs assessment. The teams suffered from some divisiveness, and conflicts arose as the project expanded. The outcomes of the workshops were outstanding and sustainable. Each workshop lasted for a week of living experience among feuding parties, who ended the training with concrete positive steps for long-term reconciliation and more clearly defined roles and responsibilities, formulated as preventive measures to avoid future conflicts.

The support teams were, over the years, continuously trained on research and data-gathering. The field support staff were trained on how to conduct censuses and surveys of sites that were selected for the establishment of a school. In 1997 this became a regular session of the third pre-service training program called constructivist classrooms. The field support team and supervisors were also trained on how to collect data for ongoing research on oral histories, old traditions and mores, and transformation in the lives of all the stakeholders in the hamlets, including the writing of diaries; they were trained on how to track graduates in the preparatory schools and draw profiles of the education committees with all the required data.

The technical support teams were trained on how to create expansive information systems around the school. They looked at attendance, completion, dropouts, and comprehensive background information on each child with regard to their family circumstances, health and social environment, as well as their performance in school on the academic and life-skills fronts.

Consultants were trained to store and retrieve the information and keep track of the various reports required from team members. The community school project has an intricate reporting system, which, on weekly and monthly bases, covers the following topics:

- Monitoring of the technical aspects of the project and progress of work.
- Progress reports on the technical weekly and monthly in-service training.
- Progress reports on the development of the curriculum and work in the learning corners.
- Reports on the field work including the status of school buildings.
- Regular reporting on the flow of supplies with utilization estimates per child.
- Absences of students and facilitators.
- Progress of the work of the education committees with a record of their minutes.
- Periodic reports on the achievements of the project and the constraints confronting the schools.
- Reports of the annual training workshops conducted in each of the various topics mentioned above and for all the different target groups.

Recently, in 2002, both the supervisory teams and the NGO project staff received a dynamic training workshop on creating their own terms of reference, methods of assessing their work, and effective workflow processes. They also developed formats that would facilitate workflow processes. The result of the three workshops in Asyut, Sohag, and Qena will be developed in manuals to serve as a reference for the facilitation of Total Quality Management, a management concept which began in industry but has traveled to all other types of institutions and organizations. It is a concept which stresses the fact that a whole team or all employees should participate in the process of management by creating an environment in which everyone shares the same vision, and where employees work in teams, and share information and accountabilities, since each individual is responsible for monitoring and evaluating him or herself. A second management training session was held in 2003, which built on the first one. The first session had focused on team building and planning for income-generation activities; the second reviewed the work of the first, and as a result it will contribute to the finalization of the management manual on Total Quality Management.

Training of Education Committees and Community Members

The training of education committees began in 1997–98. This was an extremely significant event, which soon attracted the MOE's attention, and led it to demand that it join the training sessions in 1999, in an attempt to replicate the system. Some twenty training workshops have been held to date. These training workshops were held in Alexandria and Cairo, where the trainees actually stayed for the duration of the training. Moreover in addition to the education committees, governorate, district, and village level officials were invited to attend in addition to NGO management staff. Hence the workshops not only served as training grounds, but were also regarded as channels for communication and problem solving between committee/community members and officials at the various levels just outlined. The workshops were also attended by some of the female committee members who bravely participated, against a background where women are traditionally excluded from participation in public life.

The workshop objectives dealt with the following topics:

- Understanding the philosophy of the project and the essence of activity-based classroom management.
- Community participation and all the accompanying and necessary skills
- The elements of effective leadership.
- Planning at all levels: its steps and methods of evaluation.
- Decision-making at both the individual and collective levels.
- Problem-solving skills and methods of scientific thinking.
- Exchange of experience and creating solidarity within the movement between different governorates and the one-classroom school initiative and the community schools.
- Identifying needs, creating consensuses, and presenting and communicating them to the responsible officials.
- An introduction to the initiation of income-generation projects.

In 2003 the education committees from the various districts of Asyut initiated exchange study-tours and field seminars. The results were very impressive. The exchange of experience proved to be a good method of renewing commitment and mobilization.

Training of Trainers

This type of workshop was tailored to MOE supervisors. It had the objective of building the capacity of the ministry by training a cadre of trainers who would be able to train other MOE staff from within. Once the training of supervisors, mentioned earlier, was carried out, a selection mechanism with criteria was set up to select the best twenty-five of these supervisors to be trained as trainers. Some of the selection criteria were determined by age, others by observation during the workshops, and, finally, through a written examination of their comprehension of innovative educational concepts.

The twenty-five selected candidates attended two workshops. The workshops' stated objectives were that the trainees should learn how to:

- Identify training needs.
- Plan and design a training program, which includes among other things the ability to set goals and objectives.
- Develop the content of the training.
- Deal with all the management and administrative needs of the training, select an appropriate training site for the kind of seating arrangement needed, arrange group activities, and prepare training materials.
- Acquire training, presentation, communication, and facilitation skills
- Develop evaluation and assessment skills for each training session, day, and program
- Become proficient in the concepts of child-centered and activity-based learning, and capable of applying them.

This was one of the most successful and effective training workshops held by the community- schools movement, and took place in 1999. After the first workshop, which lasted for two weeks in Sirs al-Layan, a follow-up meeting, held several months later, indicated that ·the trainees had in fact developed advanced and evolved training plans, which some had applied in the field. Members of this same group, who had been trained as trainers, had later participated in other training workshops for community and one-classroom schools, and had put their newly learned skills into practice.

Many more similar trainers' workshops will be necessary, not just for MOE staff but also for NGOs working in the field of education. In fact great attention should be given to the support and supervisory staff of community schools who have received a great deal of hands-on experience and training, and have observed many models of training. Some now actually conduct independent training workshops.

Training for Total Quality Management

The most comprehensive, innovative, and effective training was training for total quality management in the schools. The training was the result of two emerging needs. The first dealt with adolescents, their educational and other needs, such as the building of self-esteem, and leadership and participation skills. The second dealt with the need to sensitize preparatory schools receiving an increasing number of community and one-classroom school graduates to active learning pedagogies and pupil-centered learning. It was important that the recipient schools understand where the students were coming from.

The workshops aimed at diffusing the concepts and practices of activity-based learning to the preparatory schools. They also aimed at sustaining the efforts made in the community schools to build the children's confidence and self-esteem, increase their participation and self-expression, and strengthen their self-reliance.

The workshop targeted some fourteen preparatory schools in Manfalut and the district of Dar al-Salaam in Cairo. School principles and headmasters were invited, as well as supervisors, district education directors, teachers, social workers, students representing the school student union, and, for future workshops, it was suggested that some parents would be invited to attend. The content of the various workshops allowed for some diversity. Each workshop lasted for a week. In one of the workshops different sectors and departments from UNICEF, representing health, nutrition, water and sanitation, child protection, communication and gender issues, and development were invited. These sectors were invited for the purpose of future planning and coordination. The workshops had the overall goal of improving the quality of schools as institutions responsible for the total and holistic development of the adolescent. The total quality approach not only entailed self-management and effective methods of quality control, but the examination of aspects other than purely educational ones, including hygiene, and the health and well-being of those working in the schools. In addition, building a consensus around key learning principles and school mission statements was also carefully looked into.

The specific objectives of the four workshops held were:

* Learning about the needs of adolescents from observation and current research findings.
* Developing new initiation rites for adolescents' passage from childhood to adulthood.
* Learning and practicing the essence of activity-based student-centered learning.
* Learning about effective schools and the various components shaping the concept.
* Learning about the community- and one-classroom-school initiatives as models for activity-based learning and effective schools.
* Learning about self-esteem and how to develop it.
* Defining participation and looking at best practices while critically examining existing power relations in the school and at home.
* Developing scientific methods of thinking and problem-solving skills.

- Developing creativity among all those active in the school.
- Modeling and developing methods of working effectively in groups.
- Reaffirming critical values for development and cooperative work.

The training workshops were extremely successful, to the extent that some trainees organized similar workshops for neighboring schools that had not yet had the opportunity to attend them. Through this mechanism of diffusion, the training became school based. Moreover the changes in attitude were extremely pronounced and obvious by the end of each workshop, as exemplified by feedback and observed behavior. This training experience was rather special, as, a year after the training, a ministry-led monitoring mission visited the sites which had received the training to measure its impact, and the results were extremely encouraging. Rating systems were developed for attitudinal change and practice. Moreover the MOE expressed the desire to jointly develop a handbook (guide) and a training manual to be disseminated in all government schools.

Training Technique and Style

All the various training workshops, regardless of their content, go through rigorous planning, based on needs identification and assessment. The workshops represent a living experiment that results in deep and sustainable transformations and changes in conceptual mapping, self-concepts, behaviors, and attitudes. The workshops are based on modeling, self-learning, activities, group work, and a great deal of participation for the democratic management of the training experiment. Participants manage the workshop organization themselves. The sessions are fun and include diverse and entertaining methods, such as role-playing, audio-visual presentations, games, field visits, songs, poetry, and case studies. They are usually emotional and intellectual experiences not to be forgotten.

Leadership Styles and Methods of Monitoring and Supervising the Community School Initiative

The community-school initiative has been viewed as a living system rather than a mechanical or static, prescriptive one. It has developed through an iterative process where all the relevant participants have been involved in discovering and unraveling what works in practice, rather than working to a pre-prescribed blueprint of what is right. Most of what worked was discovered and adapted in actual practice. Even though the best educational research and practice informed the founding team, the best pathway was discovered by experimenting and discovering meaning among the various actors of the initiative. Everyone was engaged: the children, the community members, the facilitators, and the supervisors.

In the initial stages, UNICEF carried out the core design work (see page 36). As time went on, however, leaders from NGOs, the MOE, and the local communities became engaged in the dialogue. When schools began and were in operation, children and facilitators joined the dialogue. Issues such as whether one or two facilitators were appropriate was tested and discussed. The school day was changed many times round, both in terms of school hours and class timetables, until the most effective configuration was reached. The old fears of error and missing opportunity were cast aside as the group continued to learn and experiment.

The leadership style was one that allowed for communication in any and all directions. There were no rigid lines of authority. Leadership truly meant mentoring and communicating. The teams on the ground were invited to communicate at any time with the team in Cairo, while project directors continually discovered new methods of management. Relationships were at the core of the kind of positive energy that presided over the teams. Everything was discussed, even the partnering of two facilitators in one school. Working styles and harmonious personalities were matched together in each of the classrooms. An atmosphere of love and care presided whereby facilitators could speak of their personal problems with the manager and leader of the whole initiative, with the project directors and supervisors. When the salaries of the facilitators were delayed from the MOE, they borrowed money from the project directors. Birthdays, weddings, and other happy occasions were celebrated by all the participants together. Sorrows were also shared.

Major pedagogical, management, and training decisions were discussed with the whole teams. There were times when the supervisors changed their title to the support team to signify that they were no longer there to supervise the facilitators but to offer them support. Even though there were senior and junior supervisors, the team called for flat management.

More than sixty young women and fifteen young men were trained as constructivist leaders. They grew with the initiative as supervisors and managers in the three governorates. The technical supervisory teams were responsible for providing technical support to facilitators/teachers and children in the classroom, helping in the production of teaching aids and learning materials, and generally overseeing the sound implementation of all technical aspects of the project. Their most significant tasks over the years have been as mentors, trainers, evaluators, and advocates for the program. Supervisors have become responsible for the regular training of the teachers/facilitators on all the technical aspects of the program. They also visit the schools regularly to train on the job, and to monitor and evaluate the quality of learning, management, and community participation. They write periodic reports, carry out ongoing research, and produce innovative learning guides, materials, and aids. They have in fact been called upon as experts for the development of national multigrade learning materials and guides by the CCIMD.

The field supervisors are responsible for the mobilization of communities. They are the community advocates, who establish and maintain a communication network with the local community through meetings and intensive visits. They maintain very close relationships with the education committees, local councils, local institutions, and parents of school children and facilitators, and are active in terms of awareness raising. Often they conduct community workshops and meetings around topics of concern to the local communities, such as health issues, harmful practices such as female genital mutilation and early marriage, legal matters, and family-related issues. In addition, they may lead discussions on income generation and issues related to agriculture and animal husbandry. Experts will often be invited to talk on each of the topics.

In addition to all the above, the field support staff will participate in solving community-related problems and creating networks between education committees and local authorities in order to solve these problems. The field supervisors coordinate between the education directorate, the facilitators, the education committee, and the program at large. These young women are highly revered in their leadership positions, as they assist in solving problems such as road building or the maintenance of school buildings. They are even called upon to resolve family issues.

The field support staff are also trained to do research. They conduct annual site surveys of households in the hamlet, the numbers of children in and out of school, and the desire of families to enroll their children in school. Moreover they develop profiles of the hamlets they work in, as well as of the education committees which manage the schools.

Both the technical and field supervisors have been engaged in the close monitoring and evaluation of the schools. They carry out periodic evaluations of the standard of children and schools. Both teams have developed creative indicators through participatory training workshops to measure the application of child rights in schools and to assess school performance from a number of angles, including:

- Physical aspects, such as the status of the school building, latrines, playgrounds, availability of clean water, proximity of school to the children's home, and distance from the government school.

- Issues related to the children, such as levels of attendance, hygiene, skill acquisition, the level of participation in learning, self-esteem, and academic competencies.
- Issues pertaining to the facilitators with reference to attendance, their relationship to the children, awareness about child rights, ability to facilitate the learning process, ability to plan, production of learning aids, knowledge of curriculum subjects, relationship with the other facilitator, relationship with the community, ability to solve problems, listening skills, compassion, and general creativity.
- The classroom environment with regards to the existence of learning aids suited for children's individual and group activities, classroom organization, joy of learning, a sense of community, celebration and cheerfulness, and planning and registration notebooks in place.
- The learning process with reference to the existence of active learning, research tools and activities, the perception of the facilitator as not the only source of communication and information, peer- and self-learning, activities that use experience outside the classroom, conducting community-based campaigns and school trips, encouraging hobbies, existence of a library that is being used, and finally democratic practice and open reflective questions and dialogue.

Based on the above, the supervisors evaluated each school and managed to grade them on a continuum of excellent and best-performing schools, good schools, and schools requiring support and improvement. Each governorate managed their own schools. The self-evaluation exercise resulted in a school classification exercise with the objective of remediation. In 2001, of the total of 202 schools 44 percent were deemed excellent by the support staff, 39 percent were alright and 17 percent required improvement and support. The internal evaluation conducted was deemed very effective as a tool for quality management and self-reflection. It afforded both facilitators and support staff the opportunity to take note of their shortfalls and weaknesses and realize that, together, they could do better.

After several years of being trained on 'child rights,' the supervisors of both the technical and field teams were invited to develop child-rights-based guidelines and indicators to both support and evaluate facilitators and themselves. The best five sets of indicators were selected for prizes. The main headlines for the numerous clusters of indicators were: the right to free quality education, respect for the child, practice and acquisition of life skills, the right to play, the right to security, love and care, the right to freedom of expression, and the right to equal treatment. The evaluating committee was made up of the UNICEF team and officials from the MOE one-classroom schools. The sets of indicators were then critically reviewed and challenged by the facilitators in a summer workshop, and then presented to the children for further review. The process is very indicative of the kinds of lines of authority exercised by the initiative.

Supervisors are not alone in their leadership, monitoring, and evaluation roles. They are strongly supported by the education committees who monitor the schools on a daily basis and the UNICEF team that visits the schools regularly. Facilitators and children also support them at times. The teams have been joined by the MOE supervisory teams who also visit the schools, after gaining knowledge and understanding of the pedagogy employed. The visits of the MOE teams, although not as regular due to time constraints and shortages of means of transport, have, however, joined the movement and a sense of trust is gradually growing.

All of the above point to the presence of acts of leadership, which signify that many leaders are at work, and decisions and acts not unilateral.

Within the Classroom: Quality Education and Processes

Classroom practices and management styles are two significant areas where the principles of quality education discussed in chapter one are significantly portrayed. Classrooms also constitute the social space where significant socialization and transformation takes place. It is the very simple practices inside the classroom that lay the foundation for new ways in which all parties to a movement can relate to each other. The teacher is no longer the personification of God. Freethinking, creativity, imagination, and liveliness are encouraged. New possibilities for different forms of gender relationships are unraveled. In addition, a sense of community is built within and beyond the classroom, with a sense of trust and security allowing for mutual respect and cooperation.

The new approach embraced by the community schools is observable in the following domains:

Learner Participation, Self-efficacy, and Empowerment

Activity-based learning is the norm in community schools. Peer and cooperative learning are significant parts of the day. Classroom furniture is particularly tailored to this kind of activity-based cooperative learning. Each child has his or her own private cubbyhole or space to store books, exercise copybooks, and other belongings for daily use. The classroom has stable learning corners or centers. Normally they do not exceed five in number—language, arithmetic, art, general knowledge, and science, and, in some cases, a quiet reflective corner for catching up on missed activities.

Children make free plans and choices about the learning centers they want to be in for most of the day, the projects they will work on, and the best partners with whom to work on those projects. Moreover they exercise the authority of evaluating and assessing their work in pairs or groups. Children in the schools lead a number of sessions and activities during the school day. They take responsibility for their learning by making choices about what they would like to work on during the time spent in corners. They borrow books from the student-run library and write their opinion on the books read. These opinions are discussed in groups or whole classroom activities.

The children are constantly engaged in learning activities that draw on their capacity to understand and organize themselves in groups, in order to fulfill the tasks they select or are asked to do. Learning is done sometimes in games whereby a given arithmetic or language objective will be fulfilled by creating tasks or activities. The tasks are written up in such a way that the students can understand them independently, in the same way that any adult would understand the instructions for an independent activity they are required to do or would like to do. So the first stage is understanding what is required of them. Then the children participate in doing the activity. In many situations the facilitators challenge the children with open-ended questions and problems where many solutions are possible. Often they are even requested to change the ending of a short story in their language curriculum and discuss in what ways this would have different consequences, and to evaluate the pros and cons of such a change. In science classes, children are encouraged to experiment in and out of class. They observe and draw conclusions, and their independent critical thinking is developed. They are also constantly enabled and encouraged to transfer knowledge from one discipline to the next in an integrated fashion, which allows for real understanding. For example, many of the science classes on plants and their patterns of growth are done through the medium of drama and theater. This requires a deep understanding of the concepts in question, to the extent that the abstract may be turned to concrete representations, and vice versa.

Children have reached the highest degree of self-efficacy in specific instances. In Arab al-Kom hamlet, the two facilitators of the school had mistakenly been invited to attend two training workshops at the same time. The children regularly went to school for the whole week. They democratically selected their school leader(s) each day and ran a full-fledged class with activities and lesson plans. They even selected a reporter each day who registered what the class had done and shared the observations with their facilitators when they returned.

In normal days, in all the classes, children select the student of the day who is honored for his or her personal capacity and competencies. In addition a student assistant to the facilitators is also selected and in each of the working groups a child leader facilitates the work of the group.

Community Participation

In those schools that are provided and run by the community, knowledge is sought from different venues. Community members are very often experts on specific areas of knowledge and experience. Children will be guided to approach the knowledgeable and elders in the community in their research endeavors. Community members impart agricultural knowledge and various skills. It is not uncommon for classes to have a community member at any time of the day joining the children for specific activities or even supervising their group work. In one school in Qena in the district of Farshut, a female village elder, who had completed a literacy and adult education course, enjoyed facilitating the work of children working on arithmetic. In Asyut in al Kom School in the district of Manfalut, an elder recounted to the children how their hamlet had come into being. In Sohag, in many of the schools, the community provided the school with old looms and taught the children how to weave some of their traditional fabrics and carpets. Community experts in music, singing, and theater, as well as English and physical training, have volunteered their time, expertise, and at times their personal equipment to the children of the community schools. Very often community members will cook the children a meal.

The library in each of the classrooms is made available to community members. Child librarians keep track of the books loaned out to those interested in reading. The children in the schools learn with their community members. In many cases, adult literacy is achieved through the efforts of school children teaching their mothers or older siblings.

In many of the classrooms the children hang charts and posters of the community members who helped set up their school. They are very much a part of each other's worlds. The children learn songs and games that have been revived and registered by the community, and the art and poetry that they study in the classroom has direct cultural relevance to them.

Children are actively involved in development campaigns within their own community. Theater for consciousness-raising is fairly common, as are posters for health and hygiene messages. Door-to-door campaigns are made when necessary. Finally, children are developed into researchers and are invited to explore and consult with peers and other experts in the community. It is indeed a community of learners.

Objectives of Learning and Instruction

Much of the objectives of learning in these classrooms are centered on emotional intelligence, working in groups, and many of the life skills needed today. Caring is a very strong emotion that is encouraged daily in the schools. The student of the day is honored and cared for. Each child gets to be the student of the day. Children who absent themselves or are late to school due to household chores or other family obligations are cared for through an organized system of house visits, and also by sitting in a so-called 'latecomers and absent corner,' where peers and facilitators help the children catch up. The children have learned that cooperation is essential. They are reminded that what matters is how the entire class is doing; hence there are graphs and measurements of how the classroom 'community' is doing as a whole.

The expression of emotions is officially recognized, systematized, frequent, and functional, with time put aside each day specifically for that. Moreover each month a collective 'birth month' celebration is carried out in class where all the children whose birthday falls during that month will receive small gifts and caring words from their classmates.

Other important life skills, such as problem solving, decision-making, critical thinking, and creativity are practiced and developed daily. Each class has a 'problem' box where children define problems that they confront in their daily lives. There is also a 'suggestions' box for the solutions to their problems that children come up with. These suggestions have been read on numerous occasions by visitors; examples of the problems cited are that the father of a particular child wishes to pull her out of school for early marriage. The children get together and plan multiple strategies to overcome the problem and on many occasions they succeed. Other problems cited have been the existence of stray dogs on the way to school, the need for family income and therefore for the child to work, the existence of garbage around the school, children falling out among one another, children needing clothes, children wanting to go on a school trip and not having the money to do so, the school needing a new door, children having a health problem, and so on. The various problems take their due in discussion and problem solving, and the ingenuity in finding solutions is breathtaking. Solutions mostly depend on collective action and the facilitators and community members are at times invited to join in.

Other skills are practiced daily as we will note from the section describing the daily schedule. At each moment of the school day, different skills are practiced. Presentation, decision-making, and communication skills are constantly and consciously practiced. Other life skills related to health, survival, and hygiene are also developed through daily practice. Each school has a first-aid kit, a canteen created and run by the children, and a small kitchen for preparing small as well as community meals. Some schools even have a tap with running water and a mirror. Facilitators encourage, and inspect for, personal cleanliness. The difference between those in school and those out of it is striking. One international visitor calling on some schools in Manfalut remarked "these cannot be poor children; their appearance, level of hygiene, and mannerisms are that of middle class urban children." Moreover the children running the kitchen and canteen learn about food hygiene, nutrition, and entrepreneurial behavior and accounting.

Other objects of learning involve child rights. The children know of the UN Convention for the Rights on the Child and its main articles. They can express those articles in drawings and stories that are relevant to their own situation. For example, they speak of the right to come to school in their regular clothes and the right to be loved in school and to freely express their opinion. In Manfalut, in Zayed school there is a child rights committee run by the children. The business of the committee is to monitor the application of rights in the school and ensure that they are adequately respected.

In a number of schools the children keep abreast of the news. Newspapers and magazines are used as sources of information and instructional materials. Fulla, a facilitator, from the community schools in Farshut in al Kom al-Ahmar engages children daily in a discussion on current events. During one visit by the deputy executive director of UNICEF, a clipping from *al-Ahram* newspaper with a photo of the visitor was pinned on the classroom board for daily newspaper clippings.

Values are an important object of learning in those schools. Puppet shows, theater, storytelling, and writing are very often used to instill significant values and patterns of relationships. In Sohag in Assar hamlet, Ahmed could no longer go to school because his shoes had worn out. The children collected the money among themselves and a new pair of shoes was purchased. Great respect and politeness is shown to elders in the community. Girls are also treated with care and respect. One cannot miss the collegiality, cooperation, and sense of pride toward each other's achievements when visiting a class. Often a child will display or draw your attention to the work of a colleague in the class. Not once was there ever an incident witnessed or reported during which children made fun of one another, even though some disabled students are included in the classrooms. A great deal of sharing is witnessed during the school day. Sometimes it is food that is shared; at other times, it is the learning materials and equipment. Although all the children are from very modest backgrounds and are indeed taught to be modest, they are meanwhile extremely proud of their achievements and their faces shine with self-confidence and self-esteem. Tolerance is carefully woven into their daily life as they celebrate Christian and Moslem feasts together. They practice peace making by creating their own teams for conflict resolution. Sometimes these go beyond the classroom. In the Helwan hamlet of Sohag, the facilitators managed to build bridges between feuding families. During public examinations run by government schools, a report was written about the behavior of children from community schools. Their ethics were outstanding, as they refused to be helped by or to cheat from neighboring students. Their work ethics are also commendable, and children apply themselves readily to perfecting and mastering their work.

Schools run their own backyards, where plants and vegetables are grown, and birds and animals are kept. These too become objects of learning and a means of ensuring that children relate well to their agricultural communities.

Teacher Use of Time

Teachers/facilitators in the community schools spend an enormous amount of time learning, planning, producing activities and learning aids, and evaluating the children. Facilitators are constantly exposed to training and learn much from their peers, from reading and from the children. They are extremely busy and industrious young women. They often invite family members, husbands, and the children in the classes to help them produce the many learning aids and activities needed as they work late into the night to finish the work.

Each classroom has a planning book which records the facilitators' lesson planning. One hour or more is devoted at the end of the day for the facilitators to review the day and plan for the next one. The weekly and daily plans include minute details of the measurable and observable objectives to be reached during that day, the sequenced course of activities, the tools and aids employed, and, finally, the method for evaluation. The planning books are not only very detailed and useful in guiding the facilitators' work; they are neat, colorful, and artistically produced. In addition, the lesson plans include management directions with regard to when and how group work begins, how each of the facilitators will best manage the multi-ability or multi-grade set-up, and how time is devoted to each activity and group by each of the facilitators.

Each facilitator also keeps an observation book on the children's progress, which she fills on a daily basis. This is later used as material for the child's portfolio. Facilitators also have a record for the children's planned time and work in the learning centers. This record helps them guide the children to rotate through all the corners. Facilitators constantly correct and evaluate the children's work, which they also incorporate into the child's portfolio. They also keep track of children's attendance to share with the field supervisors to follow up on potential dropouts. Another record in the classroom is one that tracks the stationery, utensils, and equipment needs.

Many facilitators have developed learning materials, such as magazines, handwritten encyclopedias, and small dictionaries. Some spend time with the children, decorating the class, and all spend time listening and caring for the children in various ways.

Sources for Curriculum and Instruction

Schoolbooks are not the only source of curriculum and instruction in the community schools. Children write stories that are placed in the school library and become sources of instruction when corrected. Children's diaries are also used as a source of instruction and learning.

In most schools, children learn to design maps of their hamlets and use these as sources of curriculum and instruction. Facilitators and children extract articles from daily newspapers and periodic magazines to keep children abreast of world events and to discuss the content in the classroom. Classrooms are equipped with dictionaries and encyclopedias from which children and facilitators can learn through research.

The curriculum in the community schools is based on activities, and much of the learning is based on research. A plethora of research is conducted by the children, in teams or individually. One girl in Qena won a prize at the governorate level for presenting a piece of research on a famous religious figure. Many research pieces were produced on social problems such as addiction and early marriage. During arithmetic and statistical classes, students drew bar charts based on research they had conducted in their hamlets on the percentage of girls out of school who married before age sixteen. Other teams carried out research on the typical roles of girls and boys in society, and what girls and boys do and don't do.

Teacher Approach to Assessment

Facilitators are in a perfect position to be familiar with every single child's work, abilities, intelligences, personality, competencies, style of learning, social background, strengths, and weaknesses. Not only does the school day and method of classroom management allow the facilitator the time and opportunity to observe and evaluate children, the model has built within it the use of a child's portfolio. The facilitators are carefully trained on its use.

Upon entry into school each child is endowed with a portfolio with her photograph attached to it. The portfolio contains a wealth of information about and by the child. Some of the child's work is selectively included in the portfolio. The content is filled, based on observations made by the facilitators, peers, and the child herself on monthly bases. Obviously the monthly reporting depends on daily and weekly observations. Recently the model has added parent conferencing as a component where the parents' and families' views may be incorporated and added to the portfolio's content.

The portfolio contains information about the child's family (the number of family members, the child's order of birth, professional, and educational status, economic circumstances, and housing). It also contains personal information about the child, such as his or her birth date, previous educational experiences, and reasons for dropping out, if any. Detailed information is registered on the child's and family's health status and medical history. Current information on weight and height is registered. Meanwhile the occurrence of any disease during the school year is carefully registered. Personal hygiene is another area where information is meticulously filled in.

Another area, which is the subject of a great deal of observation and assessment covers the child's social and emotional skills. Hence, detailed reporting and grading is made on: the child's ability to participate, the child's level of commitment, organization, and ability to safeguard school equipment; relating to others; loving others and expressing emotions; talents and hobbies; creativity; planning skills; liveliness and levels of energy, self reliance, self confidence, self esteem; problem-solving capabilities; levels of concentration; memory and the ability to record; perseverance and perfectionism; and the ability to reflect on ideas or actions.

The academic competencies are also carefully measured and graded against specific objectives. Children move from one objective to the next in each subject matter, and in each unit and lesson within, when mastery has been obtained in the preceding objective. This method of evaluation allows children the possibility to be placed within ability groups. This one-on-one method of assessment and learning allows each child to move according to an inner clock and the teacher/facilitator to steer away from vulgarized averages.

The portfolios carry within them a wealth of research information on the children, the schools, and their communities, and are an excellent tool for monitoring a child's growth, learning, and development The model is not a pure one, since children have to sit for standardized tests and examinations set up by the MOE, so the portfolio is not the sole method of assessment. It has however been instrumental in applying flexible promotion and accelerated learning. There is a growing appreciation of the system by the MOE.

Teacher Approach to Discipline

Very early on in the lives of the children in community schools, they learn about the meaning of a social contract. They moreover learn to be citizens. As school begins, during their first year in school, facilitators and children engage in a discussion on desired behavior in the classroom. What constitutes a community and how the interest of the group can be served is also observed. The children not only learn about child rights, but about obligations to their peers in the classroom, their facilitators, and the broader community at large. They learn about looking after school furniture, equipment, and books, so that the notion of public property is absorbed early on. They learn to clear their own mess and to clean the classroom.

Once the children and facilitators have agreed on the rules and regulations they want to abide by, they write them up and hang them on the wall. They also discuss the disciplinary measures appropriate to the breaking of rules. These too are recorded and, in many cases, signed as a classroom charter. Rules of conduct are also signed and observed by the facilitators. A very popular disciplinary measure is depriving children of leadership roles in the classroom when they break rules or not allowing them to present their work to the whole class, measures that constitute real deprivation for some.

Encouragement is a very strong tool in disciplining the class. An honorary tree exists in each school and the names of high-performing students in any of the subjects, skills, or behavior patterns are celebrated by hanging them up together with a photograph of the student. Prizes and written praise are not uncommon rewards for good performance and behavior. In some classes facilitators have a word of greeting and praise each morning for the children as they enter the classroom. The work of the children is proudly displayed on the walls.

Child facilitators are often made to take charge of discipline in the classroom. They have designed posters with frowns and smiles where requests for silence and or better time management are written in colorful letters. Even more impressive is the fact that the schools have their own ombudspersons who are designated to resolve all conflicts in the classroom.

Most visitors to the schools will observe the level of responsibility and maturity manifested by the children. They are true citizens of the world and have learned to be respectful of both their own time, work, and environment and that of others as well. They have moreover learned to regulate their own actions and that of their peers.

School Environment, Management, and Constructivist Leadership

Management in the classroom is shared, decentralized, and participatory. Children are responsible for many of the daily routines that make classroom management successful. Social groupings of children are responsible for looking after the classroom stationery and equipment. Other teams clean the classroom, water the plants, look after the injured, and do the time-keeping. Leaders of the various activities discipline their peers and facilitate sessions. The children are partially responsible for keeping track of attendance and also for deciding how many learning centers they need per day.

The children are responsible for moving the furniture around to match the requirements of each of the blocs in the daily schedule. Although in modest buildings, the classes are bustling with positive energy, industriousness, and learning. They are joyful and safe spaces—a place where a child would want to be.

The School Day

The school day begins at 7 a.m in some schools, and at 8 a.m. or 9 a.m. in others, depending on the convenience of the parents and the community at large. The total hours of schooling and teacher evaluation and planning are six hours per day. Children go to school five days a week, and are off two days, one of which is the market day in their hamlet. Children usually begin their day with some physical exercise with a peer coach, and some schools like to cheer the national flag and have some children present verses from the Qur'an or the Bible, or proverbs with some moral connotations. The rest of the day is usually divided into the following periods, with some variations which are at the discretion of the teacher/facilitator:

Greeting Time

As the children go into class they pick up their name tag, or name symbol, neatly placed in a container and hang it on a board specifically designated to track school absenteeism. It also saves teachers doing the daily roll checking. Once children have entered into the classroom in a very disciplined and considerate manner, they sit on the ground in a circle with their teachers/facilitators among them. It is a precious time when all the members of the class greet each other and notice if there are any children missing. Often, decisions are made to buy a collective present and to visit the pupil if he or she is ill, or to collect money for the child if he or she is unable to come to the school for material reasons. It is also a time when the community is built and certain values and norms are discussed through storytelling or by reporting on community news. This time of the day is also extremely precious and functions as a method of group therapy whereby pupils discuss their daily experiences and draw some lessons from them or simply express their feelings about them. Moreover it allows the pupils to start the day afresh having exteriorized matters that may disturb or distract them from learning. Meanwhile when individual or group problems are raised, this is the time for the classroom community to discuss them and propose solutions. In fact each classroom is equipped with a problem box along with a suggestion box for solutions. Although not the only example, the greeting time is a very good way for children to acquire problem-solving skills.

During the morning greeting time, pupils and facilitators get closer to one another and enjoy indiscriminate attention. It is a time when children are able to enjoy a feeling of security and of being loved and cared for. In some schools, facilitators comb children's hair or wash their faces when necessary, and train older children to do the same for the younger ones.

On some days, the greeting time is used for creating fun. Puppet shows are often used for value education. Humor, singing, and dancing are not uncommon activities during this half-hour period of each day.

Planning Time

During this period pupils are engaged in the collective or individual planning of the kinds of activities they will perform in one or more of the learning corners/centers. Each child is expected to have a plan in mind as to what she will do in what corner, with what materials, with whom, and for how long. Simple material that is easily obtainable in the environment is used. The children usually register their attendance themselves in the corner of their preference, while a peer student of the day or leader writes up the whole plan with objectives for each of the pupils.

During this activity, children learn a great deal about planning and independent decision-making. They are also introduced to the first steps of research and are made conscious of the various steps of their learning. It is significant training for self-learning.

Although the children's independence is greatly respected, facilitators monitor the choices the children make per week. Some pupils are consequently guided into different corners to ensure that all the different intelligences of the child are mobilized. The kind of materials and learning aids in each of the corners usually include possibilities for the stimulation of the various intelligences. Meanwhile records are kept in each of the classrooms on children's developments with regard to the various intelligences and their preferred methods of learning. The process of planning is a half-hour activity each day.

Implementation Time

While children are actively engaged in implementing their plans in their respective corners, facilitators join in to stimulate further thinking, raise open-ended questions, and assess children's progress. Children practice self-learning during that time and learn to work with others. Moreover they are in charge of their own learning. They develop qualities of perseverance and perfection. They also develop a sense of organization, management, and time.

Children may implement their plans with one or more peers and in one or more corners. The activity lasts for an hour and fifteen minutes. The last fifteen minutes are used for clearing up.

The plans may be implemented over more than one day. This is particularly true of those activities that are integrated and that touch on more than one intelligence. For example, some children have worked together on murals or on creating their own illustrated stories. Others have designed plays with script. Still others have designed and manufactured their own learning aids with mathematical games that are later used in math classes.

Presentation and Evaluation Time

This is the most exciting part of the day, at least from an observer's perspective. It is the time when the children manage their own presentation time. Once they have cleared their work, under the leadership of one of their peers, children are asked to present what they have achieved. This is usually followed by a great deal of discussion and critical peer assessment, with many challenging questions leveled at the presenters by their peers. Some are simple enquiries on the processes of work and the materials used, while others test the presenters' depth of knowledge and mastery of skills. Finally, some comments are evaluative, and critical in nature, while others are more supportive. Children and facilitators are trained to point out both the strengths and weaknesses of what they have seen or heard. Often children will make their own self-assessment and point out where they did well and where they could have done better. The whole session is dealt with in an atmosphere of democracy, cordiality, and respect. The dialogue is often remarkable, and, with time, the older children demonstrate that they have truly acquired the skills of listening, communicating, presenting, and accepting criticism. They even distinguish between constructive and destructive criticism. This precious half-hour is full of creativity and the creation of new patterns of human relationships in the classroom.

At the end of the presentation time in some schools, the children will provide feedback on how the session went. They will evaluate the performance of the leader and assistant leader, the group interaction, and the general organization of the session. The leader will in turn do some self-assessment of how she performed.

Break

A half-hour break is scheduled where children play, often with the participation of the facilitators. They may choose to go home for a snack or buy one from the school-run canteen. Some schools have established a school kitchen with the participation of the community. Either during the work in the science and general knowledge corner or through the efforts of some of the community members, meals are cooked and consumed during break time. In some situations the meals are purchased; in others, when the ingredients are donated and cooked by the students, they are provided for free.

Whole-Class Learning Activity

Each day, pupils are introduced to the official written curriculum through games and a plethora of activities. Most of the activities are designed for group work. They are carefully prepared and planned by the facilitators over months, weeks, and days. The technical supervisors often design learning activities and aids over the years. The creativity of the whole team of facilitators, supervisors and pupils is unleashed during this process, as they create learning aids mostly from recycled junk.

The activities are extremely diverse and numerous. They target the various learning objectives in each lesson. The children are grouped according to ability and grade during this time. The facilitators very carefully plan the process, and instructions to the children are carefully spelled out, whether orally or in written form. Older children will find slips of paper with written instructions as to how to proceed with their activities and where to go for more when they have finished. A leader is selected by the children in each group and the activities selected for each level match their ability. Moreover the activities are usually great fun and take account of the different modes of learning and intelligence present in the classroom. Children are allowed to learn at their own pace.

An interesting and exciting example of how children learn and facilitators plan is when, during a modern history class, the facilitator was able to present former president Gamal Abd al-Nasser to her pupils through a sound-and-light activity totally of her creation. She had used a regular torch to light up his portrait, a map, and cardboard reproduction of monuments set up during his rule.

Meanwhile an excellent likeness of his voice was recorded, along with real excerpts from speeches he had made to accompany the images. This wonderful introduction was then followed by a number of activity cards with instructions to be performed by children at various group levels.

The facilitators make allowances in their daily plan for the time spent with each level and group. When children have finished their tasks they may choose to go on to the next one or to put up a red banner (or some other agreed-upon signal) to catch the facilitators attention and wait for their turn. The children become totally immersed in their work. This is very noticeable when visitors enter the classroom: the children hardly glance at them, as they are far too busy with their work. After a certain number of activities, the children or the facilitators improvise and organize energizers—fun exercises, activities, and songs to boost the children's energy. This is usually done to break the monotony of lengthy activities, especially when the children are young. It also adds to the playfulness and the joy of learning.

As the children are mostly self-managed and the flow of facilitation attention is carefully planned, facilitators have plenty of time for evaluation. They observe and test the children's mastery of the various competencies planned for in each activity and lesson. They in addition observe the children during the whole day for other social and life skills all of which are carefully registered in the child portfolio along with the children's self-assessments at times. The portfolios are standardized for ease of application. They are formatted in ways that capture the child's performance authentically and do not consume too much of the facilitators' time. They also contain remedial suggestions. Parent conferencing can only be done orally as the majority of parents are illiterate.

Physical Education Time
One hour before it is time to go home, children practice sports and physical exercise through games. Older girls who are usually most deprived of games and sports have a great time playing basketball. The basket will in most cases be created by the community or the facilitators from recycled waste materials.

Teacher/Facilitator Evaluation and Planning Time
Once the children have cleaned up their classroom and gone home, it is time for the facilitators to reflect on the day that's been. They evaluate one another and themselves, and point to the directions needed for the following day in their daily plan. They reflect on problems they may have encountered and methods of dealing with them. They immediately solve the problems they can manage, and those they cannot solve are taken up during the weekly training

micro-centers. There have been rare occasions when two facilitators had serious problems with one another. If the support supervisory staff were totally unable to resolve these issues, one of the two facilitators was transferred to another school. These instances have however been very rare given the intensive and deeply transformational and penetrating training that the facilitators undergo.

The Planning Cycle for Starting a School

The process of site and facilitator selection begins very early in the year, usually during the months of January, February, and March. Once the field team has negotiated with the local community the possibility of setting up a school, an education committee is established. The school space is built or provided according to certain specifications, and the field supervisory team monitors the completion of the building. The community signs a document to the field team accepting to have the donated space as a school for as long as it is needed. Facilitators are rigorously selected and the team conducts a complete census of the site with age groups, educational status, occupation, economic activity, and other population characteristics taken into account. This is a good way for the team to be introduced to the community, and is also very important for the initiative's information system as a whole. The census is repeated each year.

During this period families of potential students are encouraged to present the child's birth certificate. In case this is not available the team helps the family obtain one. A natural selection process of children wishing to enroll is done through the education committee. Priority is given to girls, followed by the older children who would have missed their first chance of formal schooling. Children are admitted to first grade between the ages of six and twelve. When the maximum number of children have presented their certificates, trained facilitators, with the support and assistance of their supervisors, perform another selection process, through very basic cognitive and physical games, for the purpose of early detection and diagnosis of disability. This time it is based on very pronounced disabilities. Mild disabilities and slow learners are integrated into the classroom. Severe mental disabilities are referred to specialists from the local departments of psychology for specialized diagnoses and assistance. Also, children with severe hearing problems are referred for specialized help, although some classes have integrated deaf and dumb students who have managed extremely well. In most situations, through a spontaneous system of community-based rehabilitation, children are able to manage quite well in the classrooms. A young student from a school in Hawatka village in the district of Manfalut, who had been a victim of severe paralysis, wrote a very moving letter to the project management team. In it he expressed how grateful he was to the community schools and the surrounding community for providing him with a wheelchair. This enabled him to lead a near-normal life at home and at school. He was able to help in household chores and do the shopping for the family. At school the facilitators and all his peer classroom friends treat him with understanding and respect, with the result that he was able to take a leadership position in morning assembly lines and physical training by giving out instructions.

In April, the project management team orders the furniture for the classrooms, with all the necessary measurements and specifications. The furniture is usually manufactured locally and often with locally produced wood. The project management team also begins to order the necessary books, equipment, and stationery supplies.

In the summer months of June, July, and August, newly recruited facilitators receive their first set of pre-service training. By September, the official beginning of the academic year, schools are ready to begin.

The school year normally begins with an orientation period of two weeks. This period is particularly important for new schools. Communities are introduced to the schooling system and are invited to participate. Children are also introduced to their school, with the details of the organization of learning corners, classroom equipment, daily schedule, and routines, but most importantly of all, the social contract is established—children and facilitators work together in establishing the ground rules for social behavior in the classroom and the methods of discipline. These are then written up as charters, signed by all, and hung on the wall. Each classroom has, in addition, posters on child rights principles, which are discussed throughout the school years. With time, the children create their own colorful posters, with their own interpretations of what the rights mean to them. In past years, art and literary contests on the expression of child rights were being launched for all the schools. Recently an application-of-child-rights contest was launched in all the schools.

During the orientation period, social groups are established from among the children. These take the form of rotating committees, the composition of which changes each week. The committees are delegated with certain authorities and tasks. There are committees for the protection of the environment, inside and outside the classroom; they are often also in charge of agricultural experimentation, growing trees, and looking after classroom plants. Other committees include ones in charge of the library and its lending system, committees for school organization, and committees in charge of health and hygiene, both in the school and within the broader community. The latter often organize campaigns to collect garbage or guard against children swimming in the streams.

One interesting committee serves as a conflict resolution system. In some schools children have joined the education committee to have their voices heard there.

In early June, the field and technical supervisory teams are busy organizing for the children's end-of-year examinations. After a brief recess period, summer school begins. Since the very first year of the project, a popular demand emerged for the establishment of summer schools. During the first year the newly trained facilitators could not envisage being away from the children all summer. Similarly the children had grown so attached to their facilitators, their colleagues, and school activities that they requested to continue in the summer.

Summer school had numerous advantages, since it was seen not just as a continuation of the learning experience, but as a fun and entertaining phase of the school year. The project used this opportunity to carry out health-related, social, and cultural campaigns for community awareness- raising. During one such summer, the schools bustled with cultural activities, and drama and story writing to present a case against early marriages. Other objectives were the development of those talents for which there was often insufficient time during the academic year. Music, singing, and theater are therefore popular summer activities. Summer was also a good time for children to practice their hobbies.

Summer schools are relaxed but structured. Programs are developed on a yearly basis by the facilitators and support teams. Careful planned objectives are laid out based on careful analyses of the children's needs and desires. Sometimes the objectives pertain to the acquisition of knowledge; at other times, to the acquisition of skills, and yet again at others, to the development of emotional intelligence and well-being.

In some years, when it is deemed necessary, particularly for advanced and more complex curricula, children might revise the previous years' subject matter to relate it to the coming year and build on it. Facilitators use summer school to create solid and creative learning aids for the whole year round. Children also participate in this activity, and contests are held to revise and review general knowledge and skills, and knowledge obtained from previous years. Moreover facilitators develop their school's mission statement for the following year. They also organize cultural and scientific workshops and meetings.

During summer school, children mostly practice self-learning and develop their research skills. One summer the objective was for children to do research and turn the school into a center for knowledge and information. Action research was mainly centered on community issues. Children also developed their journalistic skills, interviewed important figures in the hamlet, and created a magazine. Diaries and short-story writing is another main feature of summer schooling. Free reading and borrowing from the school library are available for the children and community at large. Crafts are also developed greatly during the summer. Frequently the different crafts will encompass learning aids. Maps are very often produced. Children also manufacture clothes in the summer school, which they are then able to use all year round. Other important areas of summer activities are related to health and the environment. Children learn and practice first aid and learn the basic elements of veterinary practice. Last but not least, children have a greater opportunity to enjoy school trips, games, and sports during the summer. Girls are especially privileged in this domain, as they are not usually allowed to participate in sports, and school attendance gives them the opportunity to do so.

Phases of the Project

The community-school experiment grew and developed through phases. Elements of sustainability were very carefully woven in early on in the initiative's life. This was exemplified by the type of partnership sealed from its inception with the MOE. Between 1992 and 1994, the experiment was in its pilot phase, as it was being implemented in only thirty-eight schools, reaching a total of 1037 students, of whom 655 were girls.

The Pilot Phase

During this critical phase, which lasted from 1992–94, the objective was to design and implement the project in an experimental mode. The critical partners during that phase were the local communities in Upper Egypt in the three governorates of Asyut, Sohag, and Qena, and the MOE at the central and subnational levels. The local communities were partners in a broad sense, but were strongly represented through the education committees established with the setting up of each community school. The immediate counterparts of the core team, which initiated the model and the movement, were the education committees, which were created from the inception phase and were a critical part of the project design. The committees in accordance with the design, were meant to be the actual managers of the school. They were viewed as the future pillars of sustainability. The roles of the committees can be summarized as follows:

- Provide community space for the school.
- Act as the school management board.
- Nominate facilitators to the school.
- Supervise the daily functioning of the school.
- Assist in solving school-related problems, such as the children's absence

or drop-out rate, facilitators' absence, school maintenance, children's health, and other community needs.

- Manage decisions for the schools, such as the start and end of the school day, time off during agricultural peak seasons, student uniforms, and so on.
- Participate in making the daily curriculum relevant by adding items on agriculture, local and oral histories, local traditions and arts, story-telling and legends, and so on.
- Conscientize other community members (make them aware and sensitive) on issues of gender and development, examples of which include avoiding harmful practices such as female genital mutilation and early marriages.
- Solve community-related issues by linking the community to local authorities.
- Mobilize and organize the communities to maximize effective use of their resources, i.e. spearheading innovative economic undertakings to generate income for both the community at large and more specifically, the schools.
- Monitor the application of child rights in the schools and local communities.
- Coordinate all necessary interventions for children aged 1–18 in the local community. These include early childhood care and development, as well as health and environmental, initiatives.

The MOE was very much involved at many levels during this early stage in making the initiative operational. Immediately after the agreement was signed, MOE middle-range managers at the central governmental level were closely engaged in the design and planning of the first facilitators' and supervisors' training workshop in June of 1992. Some key MOE players became closely involved in the numerous in-service training workshops that ensued at both the central and sub-national levels. More depth was brought to the partnership when MOE staff accompanied UNICEF and NGO teams during site selection. This was indeed a turning point in a long-lasting relationship that was to develop between the formal and non-formal participants in the project, that is, between MOE officials and the leaders of NGOs.

Other partners which developed as part of the model during this early phase were the NGOs, specifically three NGOs, one each in Asyut, Sohag, and Qena. The initiative was implemented through those organizations. Although they lacked in educational experience, their capacity was built on a gradual basis.

The local administrative organs in Asyut, Sohag, and Qena were also critical partners that greatly facilitated the establishment of the model. Many of the village heads and district chiefs had joined the alliance and a silent strategy of collaboration emerged. Village heads traveled many kilometers through inaccessible areas to support the core team, select sites, and meet with committees. District chiefs used their authority and resources to support the building of schools by communities, as well as the establishment of productive projects. One district chief in Asyut, Manfalut personally supervised the transport of cement to some of the schools and was there to ensure that the classrooms abided by the criteria for proper learning.

The University of Asyut, and later the branches in Sohag and Qena, proved to be solid partners. Faculties of Education members were partners in the design and implementation of training. Some even volunteered periodic site visits and monitoring. Many of the training workshops took place in the university campus and trainees resided in dormitories. In fact the University of Asyut offered a number of its facilities to the community schools staff. Office and storage space were given to the teams, in addition to the possibility of the use of the university library by the facilitators and project staff. The weekly in-service training workshops were also conducted in the university, which included the use of educational media, aids, and equipment. Finally the university allowed the project to display the various learning manuals produced by the technical teams.

To build the capacity of NGOs and ensure their success, the UNICEF program formed a core team of trained community workers. They were the founding members of the movement. They were a group of devoted people from the three governorates of Asyut, Sohag, and Qena, who had had prior experience with development projects. They were strongly mobilized and challenged by the idea of becoming significant agents of change. A silent conspiracy was in the making. The enthusiasm was infectious and the dialogue for learning had begun. The teams were built and greatly nurtured and strengthened. What it entailed at this very early stage was a continuously present core of committed UNICEF staff on the ground. The leaders were emerging from where the change was needed.

During this pilot phase, much effort was exerted in lobbying and advocacy for the community-school initiative on the national scale. A chartered plane carried 200 invitees including high-level officials from the central government, the governorate, independent institutions, the donor community, and NGOs, to a large gathering in Asyut in 1993 even before a formal airport was established. The purpose of the trip included field visits to the schools, as well as a presentation of the model through the launch of a documentary film and a pamphlet. Many joined the movement at this early stage, and many others who worked for the institutions which were invited adopted the initiative as a source of inspiration to those within the movement.

In 1993 the MOE launched its one-classroom school project, so called because many of the schools were made up of single classrooms. Tailored after the community-school model in certain, but not all, respects, the initiative aimed at establishing three thousand schools as a first step. This was the planned government-led scaling process (allowing the initiative to reach a wider scale of schools) of reaching remote and deprived areas. Some additional NGOs, notably in Asyut, also hastened to launch a replication of the project with support from the Social Fund for Development (SFD).

The Development Phase

The purpose of this phase, which began in 1995 and ended in 1996, was to develop the model further, expand the networks, and consolidate the partnerships. The number of schools was by then 111, reaching a total of 2859 students, 2043 of whom were girls.

Much effort was exerted on human resource development, training, and capacity building. A great deal of emphasis was placed on innovations in pedagogical development and in training. While the earlier phase was one of endogenous development, that is, internally based and inspired 'from within,' this phase was characterized by exogenous development and an opening up to international experience. Great strides were made in this direction and the Canadian International Development Agency (CIDA) became interested in joining the movement, which it subsequently did.

During the development phase, another highly important level of sustainability was established. While in the pilot phase, MOE and community demand had been fostered, in the development phase ministerial commitment became stronger. Even more important was the fact that during this phase the nexus for institutional building and structural transformation became firmly grounded.

Early in 1996, the Education Innovation Committee (EIC) was established by ministerial decree. The committee involved representatives from the curriculum center, evaluation center, research center, school buildings department, training department, planning department, and mainstream educational heads of departments, as well as from media professionals. The goal of the committee was to establish firm linkages between the community-school project and one-classroom school project as a first phase. In a later phase, the lessons learned from those two initiatives would be transferred to mainstream basic education. The philosophy and idea behind the committee was to have it act and serve as a catalyst for broader changes by diffusion of the best practices of the new learning paradigm throughout the overall educational system, both horizontally and vertically. On the horizontal plane, more linkages, both rural and urban, would ensure that a pedagogy similar to that relating to community schools would be applied in more one-classroom and mainstream primary schools. On the vertical plane, as time went by, more demand would appear at higher levels of formal education, reaching all the way to secondary and higher education for the new innovative and activity-based types of learning.

From 1995 to 1996, more of the management and community-related matters took on a clearer shape. It is during this period that a twinning process and an expansion-by-diffusion model was adopted. The community-school initiative began a twinning process with the government-initiated, one-classroom school model. In fact the terminology of twinning was one that was introduced by the Minister of Education when he indicated that he wanted the two initiatives, of community and one-classroom schools, to be regarded and treated as twins. Subsequent first undersecretaries, who headed all pre-university education, later adopted the idea, and one-classroom schools implemented the concept.

The concept of twinning actually meant that the initiatives had to be brought closer together in terms of their core components and that they would have equal access to resources. This triggered a number of joint training workshops for teachers and facilitators participating in these two initiatives for which UNICEF was responsible. It also triggered joint strategic planning between the two programs. The diffusion process went even beyond government-led efforts and attracted the donor community. United States Agency for International Development (US AID) efforts in girls' education and quality learning were largely modeled after the community-school model. Moreover CIDA showed an eagerness to further develop and strengthen its partnership with the model. Finally a number of NGOs demonstrated a readiness to join the movement.

The Expansion Phase

The objective of the project, during the 1997–99 phase was to actively diffuse the model into mainstream formal education. During this phase the total number of schools reached was 202 and the number of children who enrolled was 4656. This phase built on the gains of the previous one. Most of the conceptual effort was carried out during the pilot phase. During the second phase the stakeholders together defined what they meant by sustainability and clearly singled out those minimum components of the model that had to be diffused, namely:

- Strong community involvement and participation.
- Application of child-centered, active-learning pedagogies.
- Innovative curricula in the broad sense.
- On-going teacher education.
- Application of value-based education and child rights (especially for the girl child).
- Addressing the special needs of children particularly working children.
- Educational management excellence (TQM) applied (see page 66).

The main strategies employed for expansion during that phase were:

Training

A great demand for activity-based training by the MOE was met through joint training workshops between the community-school initiative and one-classroom schools. Several training workshops were, in addition, geared at policy makers, heads of department, school principals, inspectors, trainers, and social workers in mainstream primary and preparatory education.

Curriculum

Through a process of genuine participation, the CCIMD, in partnership with the community education project, revised the learning materials for grades 1–6 in arithmetic, Arabic, science, and social studies. The new materials were made to be activity-based and were geared to the management of multi-graded classrooms. All three thousand multi-grade schools at the national level are now utilizing the books. Negotiations are already underway for using the same method to review all schoolbooks.

Evaluation

The community-school project was evaluated nine times between its inception in 1992, and 2004. Four of the evaluations were internal ones, that is, carried out by the UNICEF Egypt office, while the other five were external, led by the MOE or a specialized institution (the NCEEE) within the ministry, the UNICEF regional (Middle East and North Africa) office, and CIDA. The fact that government agencies evaluated the work of an international agency was a significant political statement, as it marked a reversal of the usual power relations: usually it is international agencies that evaluate the performance of government and national institutions.

The evaluations were viewed as interventions in their own right, and as vehicles for advocacy and diffusion. The evaluations' terms of reference were carefully designed and in most instances yielded the results that the project had aspired to. As a result of a study conducted in 1996, the Ministry showed a great eagerness to adopt the education committee model to manage their one-classroom schools. In 1998, the NCEEE conducted an evaluation on the methodology of flexible promotion and accelerated learning in community schools. As a result the ministry endorsed the methodology. The whole notion of multi-ability grouping and learning was being accepted, thus constituting the beginning of very significant improvements in the learning process.

In 2001 a participatory comprehensive evaluation was completed. The evaluation was divided into two main components: one on the quality of learning and effective schooling, with all the various characteristics of the concept, and another on the level of community participation, sustainability, and efficiency. The former was led by the NCEEE while the latter component was evaluated by a hired team of consultants organized by CIDA. Both parts yielded some significantly positive results, which will be drawn upon quite heavily in later sections of the current study.

Community Participation

In 1997–98 a ministerial decree was issued to establish community-based school boards in all schools. Meanwhile the one-classroom schools have sought to establish education committees on the ground. In 1999 the training workshops for the establishment of education committees were also geared to one-classroom schools. Since Phase One, one-classroom schools became increasingly open to community involvement. The school became a multi-purpose center, as is the case in community schools, to deliver and work on other development services such as health.

Accrediting the Children from the Schools

Children from community schools graduate with a certificate that allows entry into regular government schools. In 1997, 73 children graduated from fifth grade, that is, the end of the primary cycle in Egypt at the time. The event was met with national applause and appreciation, both at the official and community level. In a unique graduation celebration carried out through video conferencing in July 1997, the First Lady of Egypt, Mrs. Suzanne Mubarak, distributed prizes and awards to both the children and facilitators of community and one-classroom schools from Asyut. A couple of months later, the governor of Asyut, where the first four schools were initiated, organized a popular celebration where communities participated in acknowledging the efforts of their children and facilitators/teachers. Children performed songs,plays, and dances against the background of music and gleeful cheers from their parents, and in a pervasive atmosphere of joy and optimism for a better future. The following year, in 1998, 383 children graduated from Asyut and Sohag. Again amidst national celebrations and awards, the children from community and one-classroom schools were honored by Mrs. Suzanne Mubarak. A sense of great success and achievement was felt by all. Children from Qena were the last to graduate from the primary cycle in 1999, along with others from Sohag and Asyut, totaling 421 in number. By 1999, a total of 899 children had graduated into preparatory and secondary schooling, 70 percent of whom were girls. By the year 2001, the number of graduates had jumped to 2382, 72 percent of whom were girls. According to more recent (2002) figures from the field, the number of graduates now in preparatory schooling is 2393 and 241 in secondary schools. Through accelerated promotion a number of children are now on the brink of, or have begun a university education. Forty of the graduates of the first cohort of children graduating from community schools are in the final year of secondary schooling, and four have recently been admited to faculties of education and law.

To aid the process of completion, those exceeding the age of entry have applied for and obtained exceptional acceptance from the MOE. Three ministerial decrees were issued: one allowing children who graduate from community and one-classroom schools to join preparatory schooling exceptionally at 18; a second allowing those students to enroll in secondary education at the age of 20, with some exceptions, made on a case-by-case basis, if the student is 21; and, finally, a third decree was issued to waive all school fees and expenses for those same graduates.

Accrediting Community-School Facilitators

A majority of one-classroom schools employ the equivalent of a community-school facilitator. Recently, community-school facilitators have been offered the possibility of permanent employment by the one-classroom schools and were later employed on a freelance basis by the community schools. There have been several such cases already. The community-school facilitators are recognized, with a formalized accrediting system recognizing their years of experience and training already in place. After three years of continuous teaching in community schools, facilitators are eligible for permanent tenured positions, as opposed to mere contracts, within the MOE, once positions are available.

Involving the Civil Society

Largely as a result of the community-school model, NGO involvement in the initiative has slowly become accepted and in fact sought out by the MOE. In 1999 a department for ministry and NGO collaboration was established at the MOE. The Ministry is seeking the help of the community education program to spread the community schools model in both Upper and Lower Egypt. Existing community schools now number 500 if we also include those run by the SFD and the various other versions run by the Co-operative for Assistance and Relief Everywhere (CARE) and other NGOs.

Conclusion

This chapter recounted the story of the community schools in Egypt, placing their emergence within a national and global historical context. It described the fundamental principles guiding the community-school initiative and shed light on the parallels between those principles and the new definitions of learning that have evolved as a result of the paradigm shift in educational theory outlined in the first section.

Through a historical analysis of how communities were mobilized against a background of cultural and political specificity, this section draws some important conclusions on what motivates and drives communities.

Further, this section addressed the question of the kind of investment needed to mount such a movement and in so doing it looked at three main forms of investments—social capital, human capital, and leadership. Social capital refers essentially to community mobilization, partnerships, and networks; human capital covers all forms of training, while leadership, as described in this section, embodies the ideas on management and organic change described in the first chapter.

These investments have yielded the results described in this chapter, as portrayed in the daily activities and planning that make for joyful and meaningful learning. In the next chapter we will look at the long-term impact of this learning experience on the communities.

3
Results of a Movement in Progress

"Never doubt that a thoughtful group of citizens can change the world. Indeed, it is the only thing that ever has."

Margaret Mead

IN THE PREVIOUS CHAPTER THE INPUTS INTO, and processes of the community schools were carefully examined. In this chapter, the results obtained to date will be assessed as the background against which prospects for a successful movement can be examined.

The results to date are examined at three levels—outputs, outcomes, and impacts. The outputs constitute the immediate, quantifiable results obtained as a consequence of the initiative, while the outcomes look at its short-term qualitative results. The impacts of the initiative are a far more important set of results, which normally require more than just a decade to become manifest. Impact in this particular context focuses on personal, societal, and institutional transformations of a far-reaching nature. In simple terms, transformation is the transition or trajectory from one form of existence to a far better one. The critical issue of the twenty-first century, as described carefully in chapter one, is not economic growth but social transformation. The world's collective future depends on achieving a complete transformation of existing institutions (schools included), our technology, values, behaviors, and, most importantly, our relationships.

Real transformations occur when the nature of existing relationships has been revisited, and when members of the revised system(s) share new meanings. Real change occurs when old meanings are questioned in the light of new events and circumstances, and when images of the self and other are changed, making way for new relationships, particularly those concerning power and gender. The extent to which education is a situation where both teachers and students learn, and children's potential is truly fulfilled is examined. As Paulo Freire put it some years ago, "Transformation is not just a question of methods and techniques, the question is a different relationship to knowledge and society."[98] Freire reminds us that education is not a neutral process: it may guide us to either accept and reinforce the status quo, or to question it and produce learners who are able to become active participants in the process of societal transformation and social change.[99]

The aim of the community-school movement has always been to realize change and transformation on both the societal and personal levels through a participatory approach. The fundamental principles abided to by the community-school initiative for change and transformation are:

1. Personal change occurs when one develops a more complex level of thinking and understanding that allows for persons to live in a complex and ever-changing world. It is not so much what they know or do that makes people able to be effective in the world, but who they are. Hence the strong concern for personality development and maturity in the schools.

2. Through learning we recreate ourselves and extend our capacity to be part of the generative process of life and change. As Margaret Mead once said "never doubt that a thoughtful group of citizens can change the world. Indeed, it is the only thing that ever has."

3. Change need not begin with a global fight against abuses in our world of today, important though that is, but requires that we are proactive in creating parts of the new society in our personal and professional lives. This is why role models are immensely important.

4. Change by a process of diffusion has been viewed as the most effective strategy of realizing reform and transformation. Change can begin in any part of the system and diffuse to other parts of a dynamic organism. The agents of the processes of change are those usually viewed as the most vulnerable in society. They are children, women, men, facilitators, and managers in very poor communities.

5. A social movement that is spiritually based in the sense of being founded on love, compassion, inclusiveness, humility, and interconnectedness has greater chances of success than one that is not. It is the kind of movement that is driven by people with a strong sense of commitment.

6. Cooperation, dialogue, and participation by everyone are probably the most effective means of achieving social transformation in today's world. Thus creating social structures that involve these elements is an important force for change.
7. Social transformation happens when a new social consciousness is developed to raise awareness about social issues. These lead first to changing actions by people and policy makers, and then to changing social structures and cultural attitudes and values.

In the following sections we will look at some of the processes and manifestations of both personal and societal transformations, as testified by the writings, accounts, and observations of the actors in the community-school movement. These are the children (the majority of whom are girls), the facilitators (mostly young women), the managers and supervisors (mostly women), education committees (both men and women), and the communities and parents.

The evaluations that were conducted on the initiative will support the above accounts. Nine evaluations were conducted during the span of the initiative from its inception in 1992, to 2004. Two internal evaluations (led by the UNICEF Egypt office) were carried out in 1993 and 1994, and two external evaluations took place in 1995 and 1996, the former led by the MOE and the latter by the UNICEF Middle East and North Africa (MENA) office. Another two external evaluations were carried out by the governmental NCEEE, and a further external evaluation was made by CIDA between 1999–2001. In 2004, an additional two internal evaluations were carried out.

Before we move to the transformations in community schools, a few paragraphs on outputs and outcomes are in order. These are also drawn from evaluations, formal documents, field accounts, and observations.

Outputs
Number of Schools

From the inception of the community-school initiative in 1992 until 2002, the number of community schools in existence has reached 202. The growth process was incremental. In 1992, four schools were established in the Manfalut district in the governorate of Asyut, serving 121 children of whom 74 percent were girls. The following year, in 1993, twenty-one new schools were established, fifteen of which were in Asyut and six in Sohag. The total number of schools then came to twenty-five and the number of students, 701. By 1994 two more schools were added in Asyut, six in Sohag and five in the governorate of Qena. The total number of schools in 1994 was thirty-eight, reaching 1037 children in all. Expansions continued in different districts of the three governorates between 1995–2000 in the following manner:

Table 1: Evolution of Community Schools (1995–2000)
This table traces the annual evolution of the numbers of community schools, the total number of children enrolled, and the numbers of girls, from 1995–2000.

Year	Governorate (Districts)	Number of Schools	Enrollment	
			Total	Girls
1995/1996	Asyut (Manfalut+Abu Tig)	59	1432	1025
1995/1996	Sohag (Dar al-Salam)	37	1007	677
1995/1996	Qena (Farshut)	15	420	341
Total		*111*	*2859*	*2043*
1996/1997	Asyut (Manfalut+Abu Tig)	59	1411	1006
1996/1997	Sohag (Dar al Salam)	37	1007	677
1996/1997	Qena (Farshut)	15	419	341
Total		*111*	*2837*	*1997*
1997/1998	Asyut (Manfalut+Abu Tig)	79	1749	1263
1997/1998	Sohag (Dar al-Salam+Geheina+Saqulta)	52	1292	853
1997/1998	Qena (Farshut)	21	582	459
Total		*152*	*3623*	*2575*
1998/1999	Asyut (Manfalut+Abu Tig)	94	2111	1544
1998/1999	Sohag (Dar al-Salam+Geheina+Saqulta)	67	1636	1100
1998/1999	Qena (Farshut)	26	461	353
Total		*187*	*4198*	*2997*
1999/2000	Asyut (Manfalut+Abu Tig)	104	2213	1549
1999/2000	Sohag (Dar al-Salam+Geheina+Saqulta)	72	1761	1233
1999/2000	Qena (Farshut)	26	682	477
Total		*202*	*4656*	*3259*

Dropouts can be clearly tracked between 1995 and 1996, when the number of schools remained the same and the number of students decreased by twenty-two, constituting 0.8 percent of the total number of students. This marks a slight decrease from the previous situation in 1994–95. In 1994, two years from the schools' inception, the dropout rate was in the order of 2.4 percent, with less than 1 percent for girls alone, the result, mainly, of early marriages. The boys dropped out mainly in order to carry out labor on the farm or elsewhere.[100] Dropout rates decreased as a result of concerted efforts by the field supervisors and anti-early marriage campaigns by the project at large. This was done mostly through theater plays, by the school children, the facilitators, and local communities. These campaigns are ongoing.

School attendance is systematically recorded on a daily basis as a monitoring tool. In 1994, it was reported that the average daily attendance was quite high, in the order of 95 percent.[101] This continues to be the trend except for peak agricultural seasons, which are accounted for within a flexible system of schooling.

With the end of the second phase of CIDA funding, the number of new schools created came to a stop in the year 2000, although the number of children reached by the initiative continued to grow as the number of new starters in the community schools exceeded that of students graduating into the mainstream.

Children Reached

Between 1997 and 1999, 899 pupils completed their primary schooling, of whom 828, or 92 percent, enrolled in preparatory mainstream schools.[102] Of those enrolling in preparatory schools, 96 percent completed the preparatory phase.[103]

The number of graduates has continued to grow, reaching 2393 preparatory education graduates and 241 secondary education graduates in 2001–2002, or a total of 2634 to date. If we add these to the children registered in community schools in 2001–2002, which were in the order of 4745 students, we obtain a grand total of 7379 children.

Girls Reached

In 1994, through the existing information systems and surveys conducted by community-school teams, it was possible to establish that the community schools resulted in a 34 percent increase in access to school for girls in the hamlets reached.[104] The initiative is currently repeating the process to obtain a more recent estimate.

From the initiative's inception until the year 2000, girls in community schools constituted roughly 70 percent of the total number of registered pupils.[105] Of the 4745 children currently enrolled, 3264, or 69.8 percent are girls. This is notwithstanding a large number of older girls who have been reached through non-formal literacy classes based around the community schools. Their number has been estimated at approximately 1000 per annum, or a total of nine thousand older girls over the nine years when those classes were in operation.

Facilitators Trained and Employed

Over the period from 1992 to 2003, six hundred young women have been extensively trained as facilitators for the community schools. Some have migrated to regular government schools, and others to various types of one-classroom schools; and a third category has dropped out. Current estimates of the dropout rate are 2 percent. The number of regular facilitators employed is 404, in addition to the 56 reserve facilitators covering all three governorates, bringing the total number of facilitators currently employed by the initiative to 460. It must be noted that this number constitutes women who were otherwise unemployed, so touching on a category of unemployment that is the most prevalent in Egypt, that of females who are graduates of intermediate education.

Teachers Trained

Through the community-school initiative, some six hundred one-classroom government school teachers have been trained on activity-based learning and multi-grade teaching and classroom management. These are employed on a full-time basis by the government and many of them were receiving training for the first time.

Supervisors Trained

A total of five hundred supervisors from the one-classroom, regular, and community schools received training. The training focused mostly on developing attitudes and skills to support teachers and facilitators and to offer technical assistance as opposed to just inspecting the schools. The supervisors were in addition trained on active learning and best practices for classroom management.

Education Committee Members Trained

Some fifteen hundred committee members have been trained over the years. The training has focused on community mobilization, organization, and participation. It has also trained them on school management and active learning. Finally child rights and gender sensitization has been part of the package.

Communities Reached

The schools had reached a total of 154 communities by 2003; some communities have more than one school, at times reaching as many as five. Each community is made up of about fifteen hundred people, so the schools have touched approximately two hundred and thirty-one thousand people's lives, with women being a specific focus of attention. In addition to school-related activities within the communities, parenting programs have been activated intensively. Health consciousness programs have also been part of the package as have, to a lesser extent, discussions about income generation.

Outcomes

Completion

The rate of completion, as mentioned earlier, is quite high in the community schools, reaching about 92 percent at the primary phase. Meanwhile, it was possible, through a system of tracking, to establish that of those students enrolling in the preparatory cycle, 96 percent completed the three-year cycle. In the coming years, we will be able to track the finalists in the secondary cycle and the percentage of those continuing into higher education.

The Quality of the Community Schools

Despite variation in the quality of school performance and effectiveness, according to the self-assessment of staff participating in the initiative, the schools are on the whole high-performing and fare well by standard indicators of effectiveness. According to the most recent external evaluation of the community-schools conducted in 1999–2001 by the governmental NCEEE, the schools were measured against the following characteristics:

- Student-centered learning and education, with emphasis on self-learning, and cooperative and peer learning.
- Multi-grade class management systems focusing on: flexibility, individual differences, group-work, integrated curricula, learning corners, self-management, and enjoyment.
- Active learning, highlighting educational activities, projects, activity groups, interaction, participation, integration, educational multi-media, low-cost equipment, and local community resources.
- Developing a pupil's mental abilities with a particular emphasis on mental processes, and critical and creative thinking.
- Developing life skills through codes of behavior, as well as the personal

and social skills necessary for pupils to interact effectively among themselves and with the community at large.

- Using various evaluation methods conducive to an authentic, comprehensive, and sustainable assessment of students.
- Making optimum use of the school day through the effective distribution of roles and responsibilities, and the planning of daily program
items and assignments.
- Providing a favorable school atmosphere by ensuring smooth relations
among staff and students.
- Developing all aspects of the child's personality: physical, emotional,
mental, and social.
- Actively developing children's talents.
- Promoting sustainable professional development by providing assistance
for the project's personnel in schools, in conformity with school based
development.
- Creating a sound management system through careful role distribution
among all the stakeholders, the delegation of tasks and responsibilities,
and the documentation of all aspects of performance, in order to build
up a thorough database.
- Enhancing Total Quality Management principles (see page 66) by setting clearly defined goals and using innovative methods to attain them.
- Promoting mastery learning[106] and community participation in ways
that allow for sustainability and the development of positive attitudes
toward community schools.[107]

The verdict on all these was that "community schools have gained experience
and administrative practices incorporating many of the characteristics of the
effective schools."[108] Through rigorous, measurable and systematic classroom
observation in sixteen randomly selected community schools, the evaluation
research team noted that:

- Facilitators frequently encouraged individual and group work, there was
great diversity in classroom teaching methods, facilitators developed and
guided self-learning skills, and pupils worked in groups.
- Facilitators assigned tasks to pupils according to their abilities, responsibilities of classroom management were shared by pupils, concepts were
presented according to the level of the pupils, and facilitators were keen
on having children present their work to the class.
- Many of the activities occurred outside the classroom, pupils participat-

ed in the production of learning aids, the pupils' work was exhibited in class, pupils moved actively in class, expressed themselves freely, were attracted to the learning activities, and enjoyed themselves.

- Pupils engage in a great deal of creative problem solving.
- Facilitators work on developing children's communication skills and self-expression. They elicit discussion through open-ended questions.
- Facilitators assist in developing the children's interest in their own appearance.
- Facilitators assist children in solving their personal problems.
- Facilitators conduct frequent assessments of the children in many aspects, including their academic performance and personality development. However, more effort should be exerted in helping facilitators master remedial activities, which are tailored to remedy the particular weaknesses of children by giving them exercises to help them overcome those weaknesses.
- The relationship between the children and the facilitators is a very special, warm, and close one.[109]

The Children's Performance

Children's performance will be measured in two ways. On the one hand we will rely on the results of official government tests, while on the other hand we will look at the results of achievement testing administered specifically to the schools by way of comprehensive evaluation missions. The latter was carried out on many occasions during the project's lifetime. We will, however, rely on the most recent evaluation performed in 1999–2000, as it was the most rigorous, systematic, and comprehensive of all the evaluations. The tests were based on high-order thinking, that is, analysis, evaluation, synthesis, and critical thinking, as opposed to low-order thinking, which tends to stress memorization. The tests also assessed life skills, such as interpersonal, creative, and decision-making skills.

With regards to the first methodology, it is worth mentioning that the children of the community schools, just like their counterparts in government schools, are subjected to official national tests in the third and fifth primary grades (and soon in the sixth grade instead as the primary cycle lengthens to six years). They will join their sisters and brothers in government schools for the examinations, and will be graded in accordance with a system of anonymity, to safeguard impartiality and fairness. The results are obtained from district-level, local MOE departments.

In the academic year 1994–95 the children of the community schools sat for their first formal government examination for third grade. These were the children from the first four schools. The results were impressive.

Table 2: Manfalut Education District: Third Grade Results (1994/1995).
This table compares the official results of children sitting for the Grade Three government exams—from community schools, regular government schools, and subsidized schools, which are government schools with some private funding. It is clear from the table that children from the community schools outperformed children from the other schools.

Subsidized Government Schools	Regular Government Schools	Community Schools
75%	67%	100%

The district of Manfalut continued to achieve impressive results over the years, although the number of classes increased as did the range of grades achieved. The following tables show the results from recent years for grades three and five.[110] Again, the comparison is between children from community schools and government schools, the results in favor of the former.

Table 3: Asyut (Manfalut) Formal Examination Results

Year	3rd Grade		5th Grade	
	Com. School	Gov. School	Com. School	Gov. School
98/99	90%	60%	81%	48%
99/00	97%	—	81%	78%
00/01	96%	75%	70%	52%
01/02	98%	80%	95%	75%

Table 4: Asyut (Abu Tig) Formal Examination Results

Year	Community schools	
	3rd	5th
2001/2002	86.6%	99%

Not only did the number of schools and grades increase in Manfalut after the first four schools sat for a formal examination in 1994, but the governorates and districts covered also increased. The district of Abu Tig joined the movement in Asyut in 1994 and the governorates of Sohag and Qena joined the movement in 1993 and 1994 respectively.

Table 5: Sohag (Dar al-Salam) Formal Examination Results

Year	3rd Grade		5th Grade	
	Com. School	Gov. School	Com. School	Gov. School
95/96	100%	—	—	—
96/97	100%	—	—	—
97/98	100%	94.65%	94.65%	73%
98/99	—	—	97%	58%
99/00	100%	—	100%	74.7%
00/01	99.6%	94.8%	88.8%	72.7%
01/02	98.66%	87%	96.3%	67%

Table 6: Sohag (Sakulta) Formal Examination Results

Year	3rd Grade		5th Grade	
	Com. School	Gov. School	Com. School	Gov. School
96/97	100%	—	—	—
97/98	100%	—	—	
98/99	100%	91.2%	100%	68.43%
99/00	100%	—	100&	71.68%
00/01	100%	89.86%	100%	72.40%
01/02	100%	88.77%	94.8%	71.40%

Table 7: Sohag (Geheina) Formal Examination Results

Year	3rd Grade		5th Grade	
	Com. School	Gov. School	Com. School	Gov. School
97/98	100%	—	—	—
98/99	100%	—	—	—
99/00	100%	—	96.47%	75.38%
00/01	100%	85%	100%	75%
01/02	100%	84.2%	100%	73.12%

Table 8: Qena (Farshut) Formal Examination Results

Year	3rd Grade		5th Grade	
	Com. School	Gov. School	Com. School	Gov. School
96/97	100%	92.2%	—	—
97/98	100%	94%	—	—
98/99	100%	93.7%	98%	92%
99/00	100%	91.9%	100%	93.6%
00/01	100%	92%	100%	91.47%
01/02	97.7%	96%	98.6%	79.9%

Over the years it has not been uncommon for children from the community schools to rank first in final government examinations. In the academic year 2001–2002, the student to rank first in third grade in the whole district of Dar al-Salam in Sohag was a girl from one of the community schools. Many community-school pupils have also received government awards for the research they presented in contests, such as Amany from the district of Farshut in Qena, who was awarded best prize in a history contest in 1997 when she was in the fourth grade. It is also not unusual for children to succeed in accelerated tests. In al-Shukaliya School in Abu Tig, Nassra, Ahmed and Safaa abu al-Na'im were accelerated after testing from third grade primary to the first preparatory grade in an al-Azhar school. Al-Azhar schools are run and managed by al-Azhar University.

With regard to the achievement tests conducted by the NCEEE, a battery of tests was especially designed to measure the achievement of second- and fourth-grade students in Arabic, arithmetic, and life skills. An additional test for science was designed for grade four. The tests were criterion-referenced, and aimed at measuring high-order thinking according to Bloom's taxonomy,[111] such as applications, analyses, syntheses, and evaluation. The tests steered away from measuring simple recording and memorization. Average marks out of one hundred for the sixteen schools tested were classified in accordance with a continuum of Poor (scoring below 50 percent), Fair (50 to less than 65 percent, Good (65 to less than 75 percent), Very Good (75 to less than 85 percent) and Excellent (over 85 percent).

According to the study the success percentages for both grades two and four were very high:

Table 9: Success Rates of Students

Subjects	Second Grade	Fourth Grade
Arabic	91.3%	100%
Mathematics	98.4%	100%
Science	—	95.9%
Life skills	96%	100%
Total Achievement	*96%*	*100%*

The analysis in the study points to the fact that learning improved over the years. The results from the second to the fourth grade improved.[112] This is not often the case according to other studies of formal schooling, where there seemed to be a deterioration of results as the grades increased.[113]

Moreover the percentage of high-performing students in both grades two and four was remarkable. The percentage of children achieving marks at

Excellent, Very Good, and Good levels were depicted as follows in the two grades tested in the previously mentioned subjects of Arabic, mathematics, and life skills for grades two and four, and science for grade four.[114]

Table 10: Percentage of High Performing Students in Various Subjects

Subjects	Second Grade	Fourth Grade
Arabic	81%	80.4%
Arithmetic	66.7%	65.6%
Life Skills	80.2%	86.4%
Science		77%
Overall achievement	*83.3%*	*78%*

It must be mentioned here that a study conducted in 1994 in collaboration with the NCEEE, examined learning achievements in conventional government schools in three governorates—Cairo, Kafr al-Sheikh, and al-Minya—for a sample of children aged 10–17. The study was based on a household survey; thus the criterion-referenced tests were administered in the children's homes. Home-administered tests are often regarded as a better guarantor of accuracy since one avoids the school administration's pressure to demonstrate high scores. The study notes that the acquisition of basic skills was shown to be generally low, particularly in arithmetic where scores did not exceed a third of the expected mastery level. Reading and writing skills were not that much better. The average score fell below 50 percent.[115]

Two more recent studies, using the same tools and methodology, looked mainly at the performance of adolescents in preparatory schools and came up with similar results. One of the studies found that students in so-called high performing schools scored an average of only 30 out of 100 in arithmetic tests.[116]

Facilitators' and Supervisors' Performance

The NCEEE report clearly attributes the children's advanced performance to that of the facilitators and supervisors, among other elements, of the effective schools: In the above sections on effective schools, positive classroom practices have been outlined. This part will focus on the supervisor's and facilitator's relationship to national curriculum development, the production of materials and guides, evaluation styles, and attitude towards children and active learning.

Supervisors and facilitators of the community schools have been trained on methods of developing activity-based, multi-ability and multi-grade learning materials. Over the years they have managed to produce enormous amounts of learning materials on the different subjects in an attractive and integrated way. Their learning sheets, cards, games, and manuals were borrowed by the CCIMD for two years, to serve as models for the review of national multi-grade curriculum. Both the supervisors of the schools and some facilitators were invited as experts to participate in the review of the work of CCIMD. Their efforts are recognized in the books produced for grades one, two, and three in Arabic and arithmetic. Currently books for grades four, five, and six are being produced for Arabic, arithmetic, science, and social studies.

Facilitators keep child portfolios in the community schools. These have been evaluated by the NCEEE study and the results are commendable in terms of their comprehensiveness, insight, regularity, and diversity.[117] Moreover some years earlier the capacity of facilitators to run multi-grade schools and implement acceleration programs was evaluated by a different team at NCEEE, and the results were again very positive and resulted in the adoption of the system by the one-classroom schools.[118]

The NCEEE 2001 report clearly states that the community-school initiative has over the years been very active in developing staff professionally. Through a process of intensive and continuous education the results have been impressive. The evaluation measured attitudes toward the self, and active learning through very detailed and extensive items in each research tool (reaching ninety items at times). Almost all staff exhibited a profound understanding of the components of quality learning, as spelt out in earlier parts of this work, and of child development. Many had in fact developed tools to monitor children's intelligences, and used the indicators developed by Gardner (see page 14). Moreover they exhibited very positive attitudes toward their relationships with the children, other professionals, and the communities with whom they worked.[119]

The field supervisors have, on the other hand, shown great leadership and an impressive ability to mobilize and build the capacity of local communities. The partnership they have sealed with the communities has resulted in a number of initiatives such as the establishment of a green corner in some schools for environmental education, music classes for children, the establishment of networks with the local 'cultural palaces' (set up by the Ministry of Culture to encourage cultural activities throughout Egypt) and other schooling programs. Traditional skills have been revived, such as the use of the hand-loom and setting up agricultural plots for experimentation. The partnership has also looked at issues of social justice and poverty alleviation by seeking donations and funds from Nasser Bank and local donors.

Performance of the Communities

The very first and clear outcome of the community school initiative is the community's ability to organize and provide space and management for the schools. By 2004 a total of 227 community schools facilities were completely provided for by local communities. Some communities offered as many as five schools when the need arose. The communities have literally built the facilities themselves on that land which was donated. In some instances, women joined in the physical effort of building, and in others they have supervised younger men in the absence of the head of household. Some communities have offered their own living quarters to the schools. An example that stands out is that of two newly wed brides who offered their bedrooms to establish one of the four schools. The communities have in addition provided for the maintenance of the facilities.

Another very clear outcome is the provision of six hundred facilitators over the lifetime of the initiative. Currently 460 facilitators continue to be employed. All the facilitators are women, and most of them have been right from the start of the initiative. The communities have in addition provided for literacy coordinators to teach the older adolescents and women how to read, write, and acquire other life skills.

A third and crucial outcome has been the establishment of education committees as on-the-ground management structures for the schools. These have later transformed themselves into governance, or self-governance structures, as we will see in the last section of this chapter. Some 1318 committee members, 26 percent of whom are women, are organized around 154 committees. The committee's networks have expanded, and a peripheral formation supporting them now calls itself 'friends of the education committees.' The membership of this group ranges from well-to-do professionals, such as doctors and pharmacists, to small business and street vendors. Doctors around the area volunteer free check-ups and medical care to the children and committees of the community schools. Moreover some pharmacists have allowed for a certain number of free prescriptions for community-school members each week. The University of Asyut hospital has on several occasions intervened to perform medical operations on the children free of charge. Early in the life of the initiative a non-formal network, calling itself 'health guardians of the community school children' was established. They collected funds among themselves to support children needing major surgery and treatment. Local friends of the community schools have also provided equipment for the disabled when needed.

The 2001 evaluation revealed that the local communities provided a wide array of services to the schools. Some qualify as maintenance, others take the form of actual involvement in school activities and are a direct contribution to the children's learning and curriculum.[120]

The 154 education committees spend an enormous amount of time managing the initiative on a voluntary basis. They act as mobilizers for the school, contact families and convince them to send the children to the school, collect the necessary documents, such as birth certificates, identify locations for establishing the school and for future expansion, suggest suitable candidates for facilitators, establish the ground rules for admission and the daily functioning of the schools, monitor the school on a daily basis, work on absenteeism and potential drop-outs, and, finally, they engage in problem solving for the community at large.[121]

Impact

Here, we will look at some of the changes to the schools and communities that are more profound and lasting. At times the changes are child-led, at others, community-led. We will be looking at the changes through a child, community, and gender lens. We will be looking at reconstructed selves and transformed relationships, both on the personal and societal levels. We will examine the ways and directions in which the diffusion of ideas and concepts has occurred during the lifetime of the initiative and resulted in transformations of a structural nature.

The whole process and methodology of transformation was centered on the school child; the data and materials used to depict transformation are a reflection of this. The methodology is more ethnographic in nature than psychological methods, which are dependent on measurable cognitive transformations,[122] it relies greatly on self-perceived transformations as well as that of others within an interactive process. The data and materials used consist of:

- Essays written by children where they freely express how things were for them before they started going to school, and what the school has meant to their lives and how they perceive the changes in their behavior and attitudes.
- Collective classroom diaries written by facilitators and children, which include the children's aspirations and some stories reflecting their transformations, as well as the children's development and change as perceived by the technical support team and the facilitators.
- Children's personal diaries.
- Interviews conducted with children of community schools during field visits by the author, project staff, the facilitators, the supervisory staff, and evaluation teams.

- Observations made by the communities, facilitators, and supervisors, as well as teachers and headmasters from the formal preparatory and secondary schools into which the children graduated.
- Observations made by the author and the evaluation teams
- Case studies collected by the media, and the project and evaluation teams

Child Transformation

The materials on children's transformation will be analyzed with regard to perceptions of self and other, relationships, acquisition of life-skills, values, self-esteem, attraction to sustained learning and achievement, and, finally, the part played by children as agents of change for their communities as a whole. Observations and cases used to enrich the description will be drawn from experiences of children currently in schools as well as that of graduates. A system of tracking has been developed over the years whereby the initiative keeps track of its graduates and alumni, while the facilitators, education committees, supervisors, the author, and some evaluation teams conduct regular visits to the children's new schools.

Perception of Self and Other

The children reached in the community-school sites are truly deprived. They have had no prior experience with school. An exception of one child in 50 percent of the sites will have had one year of schooling in the past. A child who had never been to school once told me in the most dramatic way: "Before enrolling in the community schools I truly did not know who I was, why I was born, what my purpose in life was. Day was like night and each day was a renewed ordeal as I asked myself the same questions. I was truly lost and aimless." Admitted to the school at twelve, through a program of accelerated learning, Alaa now ranks first in his secondary school and third in the whole Abu Tig district. He is a member of the education committee in his old community school. He writes the most exquisite poetry on a variety of themes and has been awarded numerous awards for his talent. Recently, during a regional workshop on girl's education, he presented to the audience a moving poem on girls entitled 'A Gift from God.'

What is indeed impressive is the transformation in the self-image of many girls. Awatef, now 13, although officially registered as 15,[123] is in a preparatory school in Manfalut. She was admitted to the community school at 8. The first time I met Awatef in Farouk Na'im school she certainly stood out. She asked me if I would not be interested in reading the stories she wrote, and wanted to publish her work. In her quietly confident and assertive way, she fetched the stories from her cubbyhole to show them to me. The product of a broken home, Awatef was desperately depressed as she watched her brothers and stepsisters going to school. "My life was meaningless," she admits. In one of her former school magazines called the 'Daily Friendship Magazine,' Awatef wrote an article entitled 'Past Experiences.' She writes, "My life before having an education was like having a malignant disease that destroyed everything beautiful in human life and the world. Ignorance is the only thing that always made me so sad and ill. Is there anything worse or as bad? Before getting an education I was indeed this infirmed and disabled person. Education is light and joy, and reading is knowledge. When I entered school I really noticed the difference." Awatef was the star of the most recent documentary film on community schools called 'Our School.' In the film's epilogue she clearly describes her emotions and self-perception before and after going to school. "Before," she says, "I was ignorant and could not speak to people, I feared them. I could make no independent decisions; I always had to ask the family. Now I feel so confident. I communi-. cate with anyone and I go to places."

Awatef has certainly gone places. She represented Egyptian children in Uganda during the Girl's Education Movement (GEM) conference that took place in Kampala in July 2001. Her presentations, performance, and social skills were outstanding. Her levels of maturity, independence, and responsibility were also exceptional. With very little English and a great deal of confidence and communication skills, Awatef impressed the entire conference. She appeared in the media and was one of fifteen children selected by the President of Uganda to accompany him as representatives of African children in the Special Session for Children. On two occasions, Awatef made keynote addresses in the presence of Mrs Suzanne Mubarak, high government officials, and international leaders.

Awatef is a born leader, and has held leadership positions in both her old and new schools. She views herself as an agent of change, and wants to be a writer, in order that she may contribute to cultural and social change. She also wants to be a teacher in a formal government school where she can ensure that the pedagogy she learned in community schools is diffused to the mainstream schools. She already has disciples among the new entrants in 'Farouk Na'im' community school, her old school.

Awatef is not the only star in the firmament. Howaida, a confident thirteen-year-old from Sohag, also after years of depression and feelings of worthlessness out of school, has developed an extremely strong self-image through school. Before an august audience of high-level regional policy makers and agency heads, she delivered a keynote inaugural speech on girl's education in Cairo, in June 2002. She was highly impressive and heartily applauded. Howaida views herself as a role model for other girls, and hopes to be a successful engineer one day.

Amal from Sohag, Dar al-Salam district, in fourth grade in Muhammad 'Ali community school, explains how important and central she feels to her family: "I can read and write fluently. If my father receives a letter, I can read it for him. I know a lot about my country and village. I can handle school registration for my brothers. I know how to fill application forms, create files, and follow all the procedures. I also use the knowledge on first aid, health, and hygiene, which I acquired from school, at home. When my sister was injured I helped with first aid."

Amal's case, like many from Dar al Salam, previously called Awlad Toq, is of particular interest. The area harbored some of the most conservative and strangest practices in the whole of Egypt. Only a decade ago, girls were secluded from the age of twelve, in preparation for marriage. Prior to that they were disguised as boys in order that they may appear in public spaces. Some of these practices still continue.[124] These girls have struggled against strong odds.

Huda, who is in fifth grade in Abu Sunta school in Manfalut stated clearly during a media interview: "I will continue my education to become a doctor. I will first go to secondary school and then to the faculty of medicine until I become what I want to be. I will become a doctor."

There are many like Huda in Asyut, Sohag, and Qena. All the classrooms keep records of the children's aspirations with girls being in the majority, as they are the main targets of the initiative. All the children aspired to continue their education. A number of girls interviewed regarded themselves as 'scientific' individuals because they used logic and proof to analyze facts, they read and researched a lot, and applied the knowledge gained in order to help family and friends. Girls placed a great value on education and vowed to continue no matter what the obstacles would be. Some even valued education more than marriage. They hoped, however, to have small families and marry educated husbands who would treat them well and allow them to continue learning and who would not forbid them from working. Most had ambitions to go beyond university: they wanted to be astronomers, doctors, engineers, lawyers, teachers, police officers, neurosurgeons, architects, and artists. Most of the girls sought careers and vocations in their own communities, and wished to serve the poor and helpless.

When looking at changing images of self and other, it may be useful to look at self-images of girls who had never been to school. On two occasions out-of-school girls were interviewed individually and in groups. In Dar al-Salam, Fifi expressed her depression by saying "I feel very depressed and very dissatisfied, I wish I could go to other places, I wish I could go to school, I wish I could be free." In Manfalut, in a far to reach area, Manga told a media group coming to do a story from New York in March 2001, "If a girl is educated she would be equal to a boy; if she is not, she is different in many ways. We stay at home and the boys go out and bring back so much with them. We have nothing but house chores." Sahar, another out-of-school girl from the same household, explained that they knew nothing and could do nothing, "we wait for someone passing by to read my father's letter sent from Libya."

Contrasting the educated girls' self-image to that of the out-of-school girls, it is clear that the image of the helpless, dependent, and disabled *persona* has been deconstructed by the girls themselves. We will see in subsequent sections how other pupils, their colleagues, families, facilitators, and the community at large have also deconstructed this very image.

The *others* are many for the children of the community schools. They are adults and the elderly, girls and boys, and, finally, people from their own community as well as from other cultures and religions. The students of community schools have been highly exposed to diversity. They have had visitors to their classrooms from diverse cultures: Nepalese, Yemeni, British, Pakistani, Colombian, South African, Iranian, Cypriot, Indian, Norwegian, Swedish, Dutch, French, Lebanese, Swiss, Belgian, and Jordanian, to name just a few. They have been part of international and stakeholders' conferences and workshops, and have been honored in formal celebrations at the national and subnational levels.

Boys and girls are together in school, although the initiative has all along targeted the girls. An assertive majority of girls in the classrooms has emerged, surrounded by a minority of gender-sensitive boys. Many girls no longer wear the veil in these classrooms and in all the schools, girls practice sports. A majority of girls enjoy science and arithmetic, and, in fact, excel in those subjects. Boys are observed cleaning the classroom, often joining in knitting and sewing activities, while girls are in the classroom.

During a regional girls' education workshop, a debate broke out on the advantages and disadvantages of girls-only schools. Awatef, a community school alumni from Manfalut, joined the debate as a participant to the workshop and very cogently expressed her viewpoint, "Seclusion and separation will not help us grow together and understand each other. We need to build different relationships based on mutual respect." During a field trip to Abu Tig, Asyut in April 2000, with a group of National Committee members from different countries, a focus group discussion was conducted with a group of graduates from community schools who had joined government preparatory schools. When asked what were some of the things they missed in their new schools, the boys expressed how much they missed having the girls in their classrooms. They had great respect for them and saw no value in the separation. They were adamant advocates of girl's rights to education, equality, and the benefits of coeducation.

'Ali, a community-school graduate from Abu Tig, believes education is an equal right for boys and girls. He believes women have equal rights as men in all aspects of life. He exerted pressure on his parents to send his younger sister to school, and succeeded.[125]

A class in the district of Farshut in Qena had a discussion on what boys and girls do in their community and the boundaries between both. The discussion resulted in group work and research, and reflected a deep understanding of gender issues. One girl said "never mind what we cannot do that boys are allowed to do, like wearing pants and playing in the street etc., the important thing is we can learn and we will never let anyone take this away from us." Another girl wrote a fictional story about a heroine in her hamlet who spent all her life teaching girls.

The girls from community schools generally maintained that they had acquired several rights. Their opinions and views were sought and respected. They had a sense of control over their lives. They had acquired many freedoms and the possibility of mobility which uneducated girls do not enjoy. Their dress code had changed and they were now able to wear things they had not been allowed to before.[126]

The children have also learned a great deal about one another's religion. Moslems and Christians sit together in the same small multi-ability, at times multi-grade, classroom and learn about Biblical and Qur'anic verses, and the sayings and deeds of the Prophets Muhammad and Jesus. They celebrate feasts from both religions together and learn about them.

The respect for elders in the village has increased. From the children's own diaries and essays it is clear that they are quite aware of their own transformations and their perception of the other. In their writings, the children admit that they had misbehaved in the past and treated the elders and other members of their family badly. They used bad language and swore. Through school, they had vastly changed their behavior toward the elderly to one of great respect in both word and deed. During some focus-group discussions and interviews, community members had described the children of community schools as model children. "They do not use bad language anymore . . . they are extremely clean and overwhelmingly polite . . . they have respect for the elderly, and are caring with younger children and animals."[127]

Relationships

Central to this section on relationships will be the relationship of children, girls in particular, to their families, the development of friendships and networks, and finally the learning relationship at home and in class.

The children's writings and interviews indicate that major changes had occurred in their relationship with their families. Prior to attending school, children unanimously admitted to being exploited and abused by their families. In Roaida's own words, "Before going to school, my family used to treat me badly; they used to beat me. Now no one beats me because I am educated, I have good manners, and I am older. When my father catches any of my brothers beating me, he shouts at them and stops them. My chores have become different now. I no longer do the dirty and unpleasant work. I only help with cleaning the house, and buy things from the market. I visit friends and relatives on my own."

Repeatedly, the children indicated that they no longer carried out difficult agricultural work. Nor did they have to look after the animals. The adults took over. This was indeed regarded as a promotion in status. Rasha from Manfalut, Asyut, is thirteen and states "Before going to school, my family did not acknowledge me as a person with rights; they used to ask me to do lots of things at home and around the house. Now they ask nothing of me during school time. They never ask me to absent myself from school. They show me a lot of respect, and I am able to express my opinions freely." Describing her relationship with her family, Faten from Dar al-Salam makes the point more emphatically, "Our relationship has changed. Before I went to school, nobody listened to my opinion. Now I have an opinion that I express, and they listen to me and are convinced by what I say."[128]

The children had all explained that they had become more caring with regard to their families and more helpful and cooperative. Families on the other hand had greatly supported their children's completion of their education and encouraged their learning. They often expressed this by reserving special spaces for reading and learning in their very modest homes.

Many of the girls had gained much respect among the male members in the family. The latter often relied on them for reading letters and other documents, as well as for bookkeeping and accounts for commerce and agriculture. Rawya's father from Farouk Na'im hamlet in Asyut testified, during the shooting of the second documentary film on community schools, that Rawya was better than ten boys to him. She ran his little shop for him and he acknowledged that before Rawya came to help him his shop had been a mess. It was not organized and there was no system of recording. Now his twelve-year-old daughter from a community school has organized the small kiosk in departments for the various commodities, after school.

Many children wrote about friendship in their essays and diaries, saying that they learned to live those relationships in school. During the monthly birthday celebrations children exchange gifts. Meanwhile each school has a mailbox and a post girl who delivers the daily messages exchanged between them. Some have pen pals from other schools. The children admit to having learned from their facilitators to call on their friends at home, especially when they are late or absent from school. Faten, Azhaar, Amal, Rasha, and Roweida in al-Gamayla School, Manfalut, Asyut, when asked some of the things they liked best in school spoke about friendship. Amal says "In school I learned how to interact with younger and older people, how to treat my father, mother, and older siblings." Faten clearly states that the best part of school is about "friendship, reading, and the teachers."[129]

The 2001 evaluation team observed that, "What remains perhaps the most powerful 'benefit' of the community schools has been its emotional impact on all those who have come into contact with it. Girls, boys, women, and men throughout the interviews repeated words like 'warmth,' 'love,' 'passion,' 'compassion,' 'tenderness,' and 'gentleness' to describe their feelings about the project and it's impact on them. A child in Sohag's Awameya community school expressed her feelings touchingly by saying, 'I learned how to love when I entered the community school.'"[130] These were all significant components of a community filled with *trust*, the true cement of all social organization and social capital. Social capital (as distinct from human capital) refers to the capacity of certain societies to build strong networks other than those of family. This forms the beginning of what some of us refer to as a civil society. For these networks and relationships, or indeed any organization outside the family sphere, to function, a bare minimum of trust is needed.

The leading investigator of the evaluation team called her May 14, 2000, presentation, *Schools of Love: An Egyptian Project*. Several mothers during interviews and studies mentioned that when their children manifested signs of affection to them (like kissing and hugging, and bringing presents for Mother's Day), they had been very moved and learned to love, appreciate, respect, and enjoy their own children more. The foundations of the children's emotional intelligence were being strengthened.

The children's learning relationships are also quite outstanding, both in the community and in the classroom. A very common observation and correlation made in most research on education is one between the level of parental education, particularly that of mothers, and the propensity of young children to enroll in school and complete their education. It is mostly assumed that the education level of the adult parent population will influence the children's enrollment trends. The reverse relationship is hardly ever discussed. In community schools, where the vast majority of the adult population, generally, and the parents of enrolled children, specifically, are illiterate, a prevalent phenomenon occurred whereby young school children were teaching adult and older members of their families to read and write. More interesting was the fact that the children from community schools instigated their older siblings or parents to join literacy classes in those cases where the classes existed.

Community accounts are replete with such instances. In the district of Manfalut, Asyut, where the relations of kinship between pupils and learners in corresponding on-site literacy classes in twenty-two classes were examined, it appeared that 59 percent of the literacy-class attendants were older cousins of the day-time pupils, 30 percent were older sisters, and the remaining 11 percent were a mixture of mothers, sisters-in-law, aunts, and a few neighbors.

In all the community-school classrooms, children and facilitators proudly show off their home copybooks, which are usually the ones they use to teach their mothers and relatives at home. Children are awarded for this kind of work in the form of prizes.

In the classrooms, facilitators and children are learning and being empowered together. In al-Akarma community school in Manfalut, growing tomatoes is the topic of a science/agricultural lesson. In one account, which took place in 1993, Nagwa, a bright young second-grade student, politely, but assertively, corrects the teacher's information on the best environments for growing tomatoes; Nagwa and her colleagues having researched the topic mostly through observation and interviews with agricultural experts in the community. The teacher/facilitator thanks Nagwa and encourages the class to applaud her.[131]

A primary fourth-grade group of children decided to run their own class independently when the two facilitators were on training. Taking over is very normal for the children as they are mostly in charge even when the facilitators are present. Some children even come to school on a Friday when they wish to complete a task or activity they are deeply engaged in.[132]

Two delegations from Yemen visited the schools. This was part of a program of technical support from the community schools, organized with the purpose of establishing and supporting the education of rural girls in Yemen. The delegations were made up of high-level policy makers and practitioners from the MOE. They presented their views orally and through written reports. The following are extracts from their reports and oral comments:

- Children are most unafraid and are proud. They look like they greatly enjoy their work.

- Children are managing their own classroom.
- Children have their own division of labor and responsibilities are distributed among them.
- Children persevere in the improvement of their work; during the performance of a play, they were clearly self-motivated and insisted on repeating certain scenes more than once to make sure they were well done.
- Relationships between members of the team are extremely warm.
- Facilitators are very sad when they have to leave their school for any reason.
- The group of support staff have a weekly meeting called the meeting of 'love and compassion' where they do collective problem solving.
- Mr. Mohamed al-Ghadifi the deputy director of MOE in Ebb, Yemen, at the time stated: "I am in awe of this experience; I am in total admiration to the extent that I fear for its lack of continuation and sustainability."
- Children are learning in an integrated fashion.
- More than one technique is employed to cater to the children's individual styles.
- Children are encouraged to research.
- Children do a lot of self-learning and self-evaluation.
- We observed a lot of creativity and freedom of expression.
- There is ongoing learning and the community is part of it.
- Children are full of confidence and self-esteem.
- The teachers are on a 'mission.' [133]

Traditional power relations between children and adults, students/learners, and teachers have radically been altered. Children's relationship to the whole learning process is one of empowerment.

Citizenship

The dramatically transformed relations with respect to learning have also given rise to the emergence of the elements of citizenship from a young age. Children are conversant with child rights. They are nonetheless also very clear about responsibilities and obligations to themselves, their colleagues, and the community at large.

The children all mentioned in their essays and diaries that they had learned to respect each other and be tolerant of differences. They were aware of child rights and also made their opinions, problems, and complaints known to the facilitators and classroom through a complaint box. Further, class discipline was based on a classroom social contract, and the children took an active part in classroom management and community work through their various committees.

In Zayed School, Manfalut, the children have developed their own child rights monitoring committee. They proudly explained to visitors on numerous occasions that they closely monitor the relationships in school and make sure that their rights are not curtailed and that facilitators will not abuse their authority. They have devised peaceful systems of protest when necessary, and elections take place for committee members. Many of the schools have the same system and all the schools have, in one way or another, practiced voting in secret ballots for one of the many systems of student governance.

The graduates from al-Kom community school, one of the first four established, had enrolled in the nearest village preparatory school. To their dismay, some of the teachers, who were counting on private tutoring, did not spend too much time on regular lessons in class. The children proceeded to sign a petition and requested a meeting with the headmaster to explain their position. They insisted on their right to free and quality education and quoted articles from the Convention on the Rights of the Child to support their case. At a later stage, the school headmaster requested that UNICEF and the community-school team train all the staff at his school for a better performance.

In yet another preparatory school, a teenage, community-school graduate was physically punished by her teacher. She did not drop out, but developed instead a strategy of passive resistance by showing her resentment and ignoring the teacher. Her colleagues and friends supported her. The story was reported to the community-school team by the teacher in question, and the school headmaster expressed his admiration for the girl, and regret for what happened. Apologies were presented to the young girl.

In Assar community school in the Dar al-Salam district of Sohag, the children had been part of the education committees since 1996, and subsequently represented the student viewpoint in the management and running of the school. They struggled to prevent the community from storing junk and garbage in their schoolyard, and managed to lobby for and obtain electricity in their school. The trend soon spread in all the schools. Today, committee membership is made up not just of current students but also of alumni who are very keen to support their old schools and fellow students therein.

Acquisition of Life Skills

Life skills[134] were regarded as covering the areas of health, the environment, hygiene, co-perative behavior, conflict resolution, and basic cognitive skills such as creativity, critical thinking, problem solving, planning, organization, time awareness, and excelling in and perfecting one's work. Other areas such as democratic behavior, and social and emotional skills have already been discussed in the sections concerned with relationships and citizenship.

In terms of health, it is interesting to observe that by the time the children reached fifth grade their physical stature had changed. Information on length and height may be obtained from the child file.

Children admitted to acquiring a great deal of knowledge about health, especially on Bilharziasis, a potentially fatal disease prevalent in Egypt, particularly in rural areas. All of them refrained from swimming in the streams, and launched campaigns in their own communities to prevent others from doing so.

One area in which they felt they had made a great deal of progress in was nutrition. Their eating habits had changed. Both their diets and eating habits had improved for the better, and all the children were very careful not to eat exposed food. Children also researched smoking addiction, sometimes carrying out field research followed by campaigns on the risks of smoking.

First aid is also an area where children acquired knowledge and practical skills. These were transferred to the home. Children often recounted how they managed to help a wounded family member at home. Children also acquired and applied knowledge of physical fitness, with the children carrying out daily exercises during morning assembly lines. Some mentioned that they even learned and did the exercises at home in the evenings or during vacation time.

With regards to the environment, not only was knowledge acquired but many activities initiated by the children were cited, such as garbage collection and the clearing of swamps. Many of the school children planted trees and campaigned against burning garbage, particularly around their school.

Hygiene is an area where significant transformations were observed, on both a personal and general level. In 1995, the joint MOE, USAID, and UNICEF evaluation team remarked, "Children in all the schools visited stood out for cleanliness (hair combed, hands and face washed, dress neat and clean). This was in marked contrast to children not in school, who were very dirty, in torn clothes, with hair uncombed, and had a higher incidence of skin rash and eye problems. This is remarked on by parents, community leaders and visitors."[135] This was further corroborated by the most recent evaluation conducted in 2000.[136]

Children learned new habits, such as cleaning their face, teeth, nails, and hands daily. Some even had baths every day. They also washed and combed their hair. They were careful to wash their clothes and saved special clothes for school outings. These often looked like party clothes.

The children participated in cleaning their own classrooms each day. The practice soon transferred to their homes and streets. The children also practiced what they learned in school in terms of washing their hands before eating and after going to the toilet. They learned to wash the fruits and vegetables before eating them and to cover the food. A group of community-school graduates had been admitted to a preparatory school in Bani-Rafei. They were not pleased at the level of hygiene in the school canteen. Sandwiches were sold uncovered, often attracting flies and other insects. The children organized themselves and volunteered to run the school canteen as they had learned to in the community schools. The headmaster allowed them to do this, and the sandwiches were soon covered in clean cellophane paper.

The children's basic cognitive and creative skills were developed to the utmost at school. Many of them wrote about how they loved to draw and paint, with some hoping to become artists when they grew up and to exhibit in their own community, and others wishing to become interior decorators. Many of the children wrote stories. Some were attracted to theater and hoped to pursue their talents in the field of drama. Most importantly, the children managed to assist the facilitators in creating their own learning materials, often out of recycled garbage.

The children had learned methods of problem solving at both the individual and collective level. For example, when some of the schools wanted to have a uniform they began their own small, income-generating projects by selling cleaning soaps and candies they had made at school, using the revenue to buy the material for their uniforms. The children used the skills acquired not only during the school day, but for other purposes, such as planning their day around their work requirements, and meeting their family, as well as going to school.

The children all claimed to engage in critical reflective thinking, and proceeded to think before they made a decision or acted upon it. They resisted their families' initial pressure to stop their education at a certain stage, enjoyed learning, and thought twice before they were tempted to get married or find employment before completing their education.

The children claimed to have acquired organizational skills, which were used at home and in school. The facilitators' observations and support staff testifies that it is true. This was often reflected in the way their cupboards, furniture, and homes were organized. Some field supervisors reported that children had built shelves in their homes to organize their families' meager belongings. Some were reported to have even organized working space and small bookshelves in their own bedrooms.

All the children wrote and said how time had become an important factor in their lives. They learned to be punctual and to come to school on time, and were now able to use a watch and the school clock. They learned to time their activities, including their regular eating time. Their day was now organized around hours and minutes rather than vague periods of day, such as sunset, noon, evening.

All the facilitators noticed that the children liked to excel in what they did. There was a sense of healthy competition but also a sense of community. Moreover the children did not mind doing the work over again, if it meant improving or perfecting their work.

The children had also learned a great deal of cooperation, both in the classroom and within their families. Essays written about a regular day in the children's life portray young girls' eagerness to cooperate and help at home.[137] Cooperation was clearly evident during group work and in the children's social behavior. Children had a team spirit and learned to share credit and responsibility. On many occasions, the children also shared their food. Many of the children showed a concern for poverty and a large number pledged to look after the poor in their community by becoming community lawyers, doctors, and teachers.

Many of the classes have elected an ombudsperson or a conflict resolution team they call the 'parliament.' The children's and facilitator's activity in this domain often transcends the narrow school boundaries to include the broader community at large. In some instances, severe tribal feuds have been resolved through the schools, with children and their facilitators acting as the peacemakers.

Values

Awatef, the subject of one of our case studies, wants to be a writer and has in fact produced a series of remarkable short stories. These are displayed in her old school library and she also produces copies for sale in her community. Her writing is serious with good plots and colorful character development. A pervading theme in her short stories is the values of poor people as contrasted with those of the corrupt rich. Pride and dignity are clearly emphasized and the value of learning is the most precious of all. Learning is portrayed as a protective shield and a means for infinite development and self-betterment.

Many of Awatef's colleagues attest to the fact that since going to school they place a great value on honesty, respect their elders, treat the poor with compassion, are considerate to others, and behave with good manners. They have learned to pray and to abide by certain moral values and codes of behavior. Further, they have grown sensitive to world injustices.[138]

What has been most remarkable about the observed behavior of children from community schools is their high level of ethics. In 1994, when the children from community schools sat for their first government examination, the support staff and the whole team received a formally stamped report from the education department of Manfalut praising the children's ethical behavior, honesty, and readiness to cooperate with others. They had arrived at the government school fully equipped and prepared to sit for the examination, and offered their pencils and rulers to their colleagues from government schools. They refused to cheat or be helped in anyway to answer the examination questions. All this was formally stated in the district report.[139]

Asked at thirteen about her views on marriage, Awatef explained that she had already had three suitors who had proposed to her through official family channels. One of them was relatively well off, so there were pressures on her to accept his hand in marriage. Awatef emphatically stated that she would refuse and resist, because she hoped to go to university. One day she would choose her own husband, based on his qualities of kindness, understanding, and compassion. This is what she valued most, in addition to ensuring that her husband shared her own values: of honesty, hard work, seriousness, loyalty, and generosity. Most girls in the community schools have made similar statements.

Self-Esteem

Many of the children wrote of how they had learned to look after themselves, and to care about their appearance and clothing. They also cared greatly about their health and future, and took pride in their achievements and work. One could sense their self-esteem from their posture.

Judging from the child portfolios in the classroom, and the various evaluations conducted in the past and more recently in 2000, children's self esteem is high. All observations clearly indicated that the children were goal-oriented, a strong indicator of self-esteem, and that they cared for others. One evaluation stated that children in community schools were self-confident, spoke back eloquently when spoken to, and interacted well with strangers and visitors.[140]

Young girls from the schools have also developed mechanisms of protest at home against abuse and early marriage. One girl threatened to leave the house when discriminated against by her family. Another girl who had been unfairly treated in comparison to her brother had also threatened to jump from the terrace of their modest home. The girls sometimes invite the facilitators to intervene in such matters. Most girls have managed to convince their families and the broader community of the dangers of early marriage.

In contrast with the girls who had never been to school and the feelings of powerlessness experienced by the children in community schools before they had been to school, the above observations depict a marked difference in the development of self-esteem due to schooling. Heba Mohamed from Manfalut laments her fate. She is thirteen, has never been to school, and is too old to be admitted into formal schooling. "I would have liked to read and write," she says. "When my sister, who now goes to community schools, reads something in front of me I envy her and feel embarrassed because I am older and cannot read." She continues "I can do nothing, I just keep silent. When I have children I will send them to school, but I will always be an ignorant mother."

Thirst for Sustained Learning and Achievement

Asked what they hated most about school, children invariably replied, 'vacations.'[141] Their love of learning has come through on many instances. The fact that children read as a hobby and carry out research testifies to that reality. In Qena, in the district of Farshut, fourth and fifth grade students have carried out research projects on a variety of topics, such as gender relations between boys and girls, rural girls, famous Arab scientists, Arab political leaders, the British in Egypt, health and addiction, contemporary world scientists, famous writers such as Naguib Mahfouz, and the dangers of early marriage. Several of the students in fact did some field research on the numbers of out-of-school girls in their hamlet who had married before the age of sixteen.

What is even more significant is the results of the ongoing tracking of the progress of graduates in both preparatory and secondary schools. The tracking system is by no means perfect, and requires more systematization, which is currently being worked on. Final examination results are collected each year, but are not complete enough to allow for proper analysis. However there are records for completion (of school cycles or levels of schooling) and the numbers of graduates per year and at each level, and periodic visits and interviews of children, communities, and host schools have been carried out. Records of awards received by the graduates have also been kept in most of the districts.

From the district of Manfalut, where the tracking system is best, it is clear that the percentages of completion and enrollment into preparatory schools have increased over the years:

Table 11: Enrollment of Community-School Graduates in Preparatory Schools

Year	1997	1998	1999	2000	2001
Percentage of graduates from community schools enrolling in preparatory schools	85%	90%	98%	99%	99%

Meanwhile, in terms of performance, eleven graduates from community schools received awards in the year 2000 from the preparatory schools in the mother villages, where village heads and local councils preside, and nineteen in 2001. The awards were for proficiency in the Arabic and English languages, science, arithmetic, and social studies, while four of the girls received general awards for achieving the first rank in school. In the district of Abu Tig, the graduates from Abu Wulad were in the first five positions in the Bani Sami' preparatory school, which they had joined.

Back in Manfalut, schoolteachers, social workers, and headmasters of the host schools were interviewed and asked to write observations of the children in their schools. The results were impressive and indicate that the investment in those first years of the children's lives reaped dividends that were beyond all expectations. Strong resilience had been developed and all the learning skills acquired early on in the community schools allowed the children to pursue self-learning. They were high-achievers, in most cases without the help of private tutoring, relying instead on their own personal resources and the loving support of their facilitators and their communities.

Through an examination of some fifty formal written reports from social workers, teachers, and school headmasters, it appears that the behavior and performance of the community-school graduates in government preparatory schools was highly commendable.[142] The children are singled out for their enthusiasm to learn, their capacity to self learn, their high levels of participation in class and in the student unions, their eagerness to help others, their leadership qualities, and, finally, their high level of maturity. Only on three occasions have the school headmasters advised that more attention be paid to developing the children's English-language skills and that they might need private tutoring in the subject.

The headmaster from Mostafa Kamel preparatory school of Umm al-Kussur village in Manfalout wrote in his report "The girls who have graduated from the community schools are outstanding in their behavior, discipline, cooperation with others, and relationship to the teachers. They also shine academically."

From the headmaster of Muhammad Hamad preparatory school the report indicated that "the graduate girls from community schools were exceptional models in all the academic subjects. They also did very well in sports." The social worker from the same school supported the opinion and added that Ne'mat Nossier Omar had ranked third in school and received an award for best behavior. The sports teacher was very proud of their achievement in sports tournaments.

The coeducational preparatory school of Abd al-Awad also had something to say about the performance of the boys and girls from community schools. "The children are very well behaved and are academically very advanced. They are very talented and have learned to rely on themselves. They are very expressive and loving. This is true of all the grade levels. Moreover the children participate in many of the school and community activities. They organize school trips, are part of the student union, are activists for the preservation of a safe environment, and have formed a group to fight addiction among youth." The two Arabic language teachers, the English language teacher, an arithmetic teacher, two social workers and the school headmaster signed the report.

Preparatory school headmasters were so enthusiastic about the community-school graduates that they often went out of their way to admit them for free, even before the exemption policies were obtained from the MOE. In 1997 a decree was signed by the Minister of Education waiving school fees for all graduates from the community and one-classroom schools. Another decree was obtained raising the age ceiling for student admission at the preparatory level. Children aged up to eighteen were allowed to enroll in preparatory schools, in order to complete the compulsory basic education cycle.

As earlier mentioned, in the academic year 2001–2002, 241 graduates from community schools were enrolled in secondary education. The tracking of students' lives and performance continues to be carried out by the field and technical support teams of supervisors. The children remain deeply attracted to sustained learning and the levels of achievement remain high. A third of the students are expected to complete higher education.

Amana, a young community-school graduate completed the preparatory cycle at age twenty. Full of ambition and a love of learning, she enrolled in the nearest village secondary school. Her performance had been remarkable throughout her basic education school years. Two months after starting the academic year, the school administration informed her that she was beyond the legal age of admittance and therefore needed to return her schoolbooks and work from home. Unable to cope with the shock, Amana fainted and had to be taken to hospital. When she was better, her positive attitude drove her to write a letter to the Minister of Education seeking a solution. Project staff made sure that the letter reached the central team for the initiative in Cairo and the Minister signed an exemption. A month later, another student, Amer, faced the same problem and he too was admitted. Both have ranked first in their first year of secondary education, as has Abul Hassan, also a student.

When Amana passed the examinations for her first year in the secondary level, she wrote a thank-you letter to the Minister of Education. The objective of the letter, however, was to turn the exception made for her and her colleagues into a general policy for all the graduates from the community and one-classroom schools.

Reports have also been obtained from the schools where the children and youth are enrolled. The content of the reports is impressive, in terms of both personal and intellectual growth. The Umm al-Kussur secondary school headmaster from Manfalut wrote in an official report: "Male and female students from the community schools are a thousand times better than other students. I observed the high level of responsibility among these students, their commitment to learning, and their impressive academic achievement. Even though a few of them are slightly past the legal age of admittance to the school, I have been flexible and accepted them as I admire them and have great respect for their achievements." A second report from the Nozat Qarar secondary school stated that the level of comprehension manifested by graduates of community schools was outstanding and far surpasses that of the others. It attested to the fact that the students had developed wonderful relationships with their colleagues and schoolteachers. The report concluded by saying that they greatly welcomed more such students. The economics and technology teacher from the same school observed that graduates from community schools asked many questions and their level of concentration in class was very high. They had a great deal of confidence and were very assertive when asking for additional explanations in class. They acted like this was their natural right. They are not at all intimidated or afraid.

Agents of Change

In addition to engaging adults in education, school children have become role models for the entire community.[143] They have taught their families the value of learning, freedom, and progress. Nagat Abd al Moneim, the forty-five-year-old mother of a community-school graduate now in secondary education, says, "It is my daughter who has taught me not to be afraid and be brave in life. When I observed how strong and assertive she had become, I became determined to support her all the way to the highest levels of learning. She developed a strong personality at home and expressed her own opinion. Her father and I consult her for everything. She has enlightened us. Today I aspire to educating all my daughters like her and I advocate for girl's education in the neighborhood."[144]

Nassreya, a young mother in Saad Abu Gayed literacy class, is encouraged to go to class by her young daughter, a pupil in the community schools. Many parents like Nassreya have learned to write a few basic words, including their names, from their daughters. Nassreya and her daughter are able to write and receive private letters from Nassreya's husband working in Saudi Arabia. The husband sent his daughter a new dress to reward her for learning to read and write. Nassreya says that she now feels she has acquired her full humanity.[145]

Other interesting developments led by the children spread a taste for reading in the community. The library in each school is organized and maintained by the children. They are responsible for library loans, which are not limited to the students in school. The community is encouraged to come into the schools and borrow books. This is a natural post-literacy initiative. Some books cater to adult tastes, and many parents have taken to reading for pleasure.

Earlier in the life of the community-school initiative, a study had been conducted to observe changes among mothers of school-goers in two of the hamlets in Manfalut. The study revealed that mothers had acquired many skills from the children at home, among which were organization and time management.[146]

Through the children, communities have begun a spontaneous community-based rehabilitation process (CBR) to integrate the children in school.[147] In al-Gezira School, Gamila, a disabled child broke her walking stick while trying to run away from stray dogs. Children arranged a collection and used the money to have a new stick made for her. In Arab school, Hala, a mildly mongoloid child, is the daughter of the donor of the school. Her parents have been advised to put her in an institution. The children have however greeted her in the school and made some games for her. They deal with her with great care and she is learning some skills. Milad, from al-Kom School, has had two operations on his leg for serious bone problems. The children and all the teams involved in the initiative helped. The children were particularly good at visiting him and catching him up on lessons he missed.

On health and hygiene, in both Helba hamlet and Sa'd Abu Qayed, children pledge never to swim in the stream after their friends have been cured of the symptoms of worms. The children then create teams and start a campaign and succeed in stopping others from swimming in the streams.

One of the most remarkable of the child-led changes in the communities where schools were set up is the age at which girls marry. Many campaigns have been led and initiated by the children of the community schools, mostly through drama and theater, against the dangers of early marriage. Although comparative statistical analyses are still not available, the students are currently constructing it. Judging from extensive interviews and observation over the life of the initiative, the practice is on the decline. Not only have children led the campaigns, but have also, on numerous occasions, resisted community and family pressure themselves to marry young and interrupt their education.[148]

Moreover as a result of the schools, some parents have formalized their marital relationship under civil law. In the district of Abu Tig, the parents of a graduate from a community school were, not unusually, married according to customary law. As a result, when applying to the village preparatory school, the student was missing some formal documents. The parents rushed to formally register their marriage contract and formalized all other related documents to enable their son to pursue his education. Birth registration is also becoming much more regular as parents do not wish to jeopardize their children's opportunity to get an education.

Community Transformations

The transformations recorded in the community are particular to families, education committees, and facilitators. In this section we will be especially concerned with transformations that depict changes with respect to the relationship to learning, women's empowerment, and governance.

Relationship to Learning

A truly radical transformation occurred over the years in terms of the community's support for girls' education and demand for quality learning. During the early years of the initiative a number of focused group discussions with the girls at community schools had revealed that they were at risk of not completing their education due to family opposition, from fathers in particular. In 1994, in al-Gezira hamlet in Asyut, fifteen of the girls in the group discussion maintained that their families had refused to let them pursue their education any further. Suzanne, who was nine at the time, informed us that her father believed it was improper for her to continue her education. Her mother, however, was on her side. Basma, who was ten, also sadly informed us that her uncle and older brother did not wish her to go to preparatory school. Shereen, Refqa, Hanaa, and Asmahan all shared the same problem. In each case, an older brother, a father, or a grandfather had raised objections, although the mothers had been supportive. They all in fact continued to preparatory school, the men's change of heart brought about by the quality of learning they had observed in the schools.

In 1998, the two delegations from Yemen that had visited the schools (see page 123) had come back with some very different observations. In their report they wrote, "The fathers and male leaders of the hamlets they visited were extremely enthusiastic about their daughters going to school. They have great trust in their girls, and the barriers of seclusion have been broken."

Two years later, during a field trip with a headquarter CIDA delegation, fathers of the hamlets visited declared their strong support for girls completing their education. One father was asked to which level he hoped to support his daughter. "To the highest" was his reply, and when asked where he hoped to enroll his daughter for university, he responded, "It is not up to me to decide. It is where she wants to be. Even if it means traveling anywhere, I will sell anything and find a way to support her."

The education committees and the children have, over the years, become the strongest advocates of girl's education and quality learning. From the recent evaluations it is clear that the committees at first had a tough job convincing communities. Moreover, the very extensive and expansive interviews and focus-group discussions of the most recent evaluation revealed that the education committees had a very clear understanding of quality learning and the high demand for it. They knew about active and peer learning. They had an appreciation for group work and learning corners. They also had a taste for democracy and how it was cultivated in the schools.[149]

During one of the focus group discussions in Sohag, Dar al-Salam district, in the presence of CIDA representatives and the director of the MOE one-classroom schools, the committee members were asked what they would do if the funding was withdrawn. They responded to say that they would never give up the schools. They might suffer from a sudden withdrawal of funds, but they would persist with the movement, as they now knew what quality education meant and were not willing to give up on it. They have indeed, throughout the years, proved the sincerity of their words by truly supporting the provision and management of the schools. They are constantly initiating the expansion of the schools. Abu al-Wafa from Dar al-Salam in Sohag has contributed five schools in his hamlet. Committee members are very frequently on the phone requesting that we allow them to set up a new school. Recently Abd al-Malaak from a hamlet in Geheina pursued the possibility of building a third school as he noticed at least thirty children who were out of school.

Members of the education committees have, in every single one of the training workshops they attended, requested that the initiative cover more than just the primary level. They wanted the schools to cover the preparatory phase and insisted that daycare centers be established in the hamlets, and that the preschool level become a priority in the education of their communities. Community daycare centers were in fact established in Farshut, during the pilot phase, and will spread to Asyut and Sohag. A father of one of the students voluntarily runs one of the community daycare centers in Farshut. The demand for quality learning is growing strong in these communities.

The quest for learning has spread out in many directions. In 1993 the communities pressured hard for literacy classes, particularly for women. The classes spread very quickly to all the sites and had, by 2003, reached some ten thousand learners, 40 percent of whom have in recent years gone back to formal schools, once they had reached the necessary level of schooling equivalence. Although UNICEF has recently stopped supporting the classes financially, communities in partnership with an NGO and the state-run General Authority for the Eradication of Illiteracy and Adult Education, continue to run the classes in Asyut and Sohag. The model has proved sustainable and merges very well with an NGO-run parenting education program supported by UNICEF in the same sites. Through the community-school libraries a natural post-literacy initiative has evolved whereby community members borrow books and are beginning to enjoy reading with their children or on their own.

The facilitators have also experienced vast transformations in their relationship to learning. Seventy percent of the facilitators recruited have enrolled in some form of learning to upgrade their skills. A vast majority has gone to calligraphy institutes to improve their handwriting. No small number have taken a secondary certificate degree again in order to enroll in university. Even more impressive have been the five facilitators who have registered for graduate diplomas. Tahany from Qena, Farshut has been with the community-schools project since it began in her region in 1994. From her intermediate education she has moved to graduate studies. She first graduated with a BA in commerce and is now taking a graduate course in education. She has also been promoted from a facilitator to a supervisor/trainer, in order to support other facilitators.

An analysis of the feedback from the very many training workshops organized as a result of the community-school initiative over the years reveals the transformation process at its inception phase; namely through training. Some poignant remarks were often made after the training workshops. One facilitator burst into tears during the last part of an oral evaluation session. This had been an intense, soul-searching emotional experience in which facilitators were required to critically reflect on and reproduce old learning experiences. They had been exposed to some aspects of child psychology, learning styles, and child rights. Amal from Qena confessed in tears that she wished so much she had known more about all these theories of learning and the needs of the child before. She felt guilty of the possibility of having harmed some children in the past when in ignorance. Fatma and Adl, two facilitators from Sohag, burst out crying during a weekly micro-center training session for having lost their temper with the children in class, and solicited the help and advice of others on how to control their temper.

Art, poetry, singing, and deep emotional communication are the norm in each of the training experiences where trainees board and live together for several days or weeks. The training reports are replete with statements from the heart, from the many facilitators who are in the process of learning to learn. In every single one of the workshops, facilitators mentioned they had become truly liberated and had understood the meaning of freedom of expression. Most spoke of the self-confidence they had gained. All had been inspired with the passion to learn.

Many of the facilitators have acquired analytical, writing, and research skills, and keep diaries. They prepare intricate materials for learning that require much research and independent reading. They have access to university and public libraries but also use newspapers, magazines, and classroom encyclopedias as references.

Facilitators are partners in the ongoing experiment of the community-school initiative. Much of the creative development of the classroom practices has emanated from them. Although a prototype daily block-class schedule had been developed in 1992, the Asyut field team decided, after some testing and analyses, to change it. In 1993–94, after some consultation, the new schedule was implemented, which did a better job of coordinating the acquisition of basic life skills and the formal syllabus requirements. The facilitators in all three governorates had been trained on an intricate set of evaluation indicators for pupils on cognitive, emotional, and social skills. After some attempts to implement authentic assessment, they came up with an improved system to allow for more manageable and in-depth observation.

Women's Empowerment

Learning has been one clear avenue to women's empowerment and participation. The second level of analysis in the Women's Equality and Empowerment Framework (WEEF), a framework that springs from UNICEF, is that of access. Clearly the community-school initiative has been seriously concerned with this particular level of a gender gap and has been positively biased to girls and women. A gender audit conducted in March 2000 states that the initiative has definitely been mainstreamed and made resources accessible to both genders. The report states, "in *ezbas* where the project has supported the community to establish schools, the effort has markedly reduced the gender gap by increasing girls' access to education and potentially, employment." On the teaching methods, the report states that "the teaching encourages critical thinking, self-reliance, and growing self-esteem, and other characteristics, which traditionally are not encouraged in girls. The teaching approach overcomes gender stereotypes through the encouragement of positive behaviors, independent of the sex of the respective child. Girls and boys learn to share, to lead, to openly voice their opinion, to respect themselves and others, to care for their appearance and the environment of the community. Through equal treatment and encouragement, girls and boys learn to see the respective other sex as equal."[150] Thus on the level of conscientization (becoming aware, sensitive, and conscious), the third level of analysis in the WEEF framework, women and girls are being empowered.

On yet another level of the WEEF analysis, participation, women have been especially privileged by the initiative. Great efforts were exerted to pull the women out of their seclusion and encourage them to participate in public life. They currently constitute 26 percent of the members of the education committees who control, run, and manage the schools. The percentage has fluctuated over the years, reaching at times a peak of 30 percent. They have been initiators and part of critical community decisions. In fact, the decision to contribute two of the first pioneering schools in Asyut to the initiative were made by women. They have participated in workshops and many diverse training sessions. Many have stood out as leaders in the sites and training workshops.

Fayza, a woman of forty-five from Saqulta in Sohag, is unmarried. When her parents passed away, her three brothers inherited a very small plot of land from their families. Because all the siblings were married and settled in different homes, she inherited the small family house. In fact her father sold it to her on paper before passing away. As is the habit in most rural areas, male members of the family have a sense of entitlement to all property. It is customary for sisters to willingly give up their inheritance to male members, brothers in particular, or to be pressured into doing so. When Fayza decided to donate part of her home for girls' schooling, her brothers obstructed the decision and brought all kinds of pressures, some of which were violent, to bear on her to reverse her decision. Fayza was supported by the whole community, and in 1995, she inaugurated the school. She is in control of her life and has earned everyone's respect.

Women in Manfalut, Asyut explained that since they joined the education committee their voices have been heard and respected. They are consulted during the decision-making process, and their self-esteem and confidence have been greatly enhanced. They also claim to have gained a great deal of independence. From Abu Tig distirct in Asyut, Om Kawssar recounts how her participation in the training workshop in Alexandria had been invaluable. She had, for the first time, traveled away from her village, gained a sense of freedom and mobility, mixed with strangers from other governorates, made a public presentation for the first time in her life, and freely voiced her opinion. Other participants had listened to her carefully and respected her opinion.[151] In another training workshop in Cairo a year earlier, a male member of the education committee had lent great encouragement and expressed respect to his female colleagues. During the last session of the workshop he recommended that they develop strategies to encourage more female participation, as he felt that some women had learned to be shy and subsequently found it difficult to express themselves publicly. He suggested an incentive system whereby a woman would be presented with a bouquet of flowers whenever she spoke up well. The young man then proceeded to offer the older woman who had just spoken earlier a bouquet of artificial flowers, which he had made himself.

A committee member in Sahara school stated that "education for girls has opened the door for them to know who they are, understand their potential, and have a goal in life. Girls now have a say in their marriage arrangement and some, with the support of their mothers, manage to persuade their fathers to complete their education before marrying."[152] Women and their daughters are slowly gaining positive control of their lives.

Even those women who are not in the education committees have benefited through the parenting program. The program looks at gender relationships, with the aim of creating a safe, harmonious, and loving environment at home for the young child to fulfill her full potential. Safaa Ahmed Ibrahim, a forty-two-year-old housewife, and Fatma Mahmoud el-Sayed, forty-five, both recount how they gained immense confidence and experience from the parenting education workshops which they attend with fathers and other male caregivers. The progress reports from the implementing NGOs observe that the relationships within the family have indeed changed over time. Both women state that during the workshops they were told how important it was to have their own opinion and to express it at home. and how it was important that decisions were shared. They were trained on negotiation skills. Both said they practiced the advice and felt greatly respected and empowered as a result.

Facilitators have been critical agents of change during the course of the initiative. Their whole lives have been transformed as they have moved from a situation of powerless unemployment to one in which they have discovered a life purpose through the teaching vocation. According to the gender audit report of March 2000, "the community schools have clearly changed the life of the facilitators and empowered them in different ways. Mostly young unmarried women with at least a diploma, they have gained access to crucial resources like employment, income, mobility, training, and status in the community."[153]

During a large meeting with forty facilitators, an interesting series of observations was made by them. One facilitator expressed her new sense of being by saying, "There is freedom now, I am free of constraints." Another went even further by saying, "I was restricted before, now the sky is the limit." A third one said, "The world has opened up for me now, there is no depression and sadness anymore." Augustine, the author of the gender audit report notes, "The facilitators have gained control over their lives and a self-esteem that enables them to make their own decisions and stand up for them."[154]

Augustine is quite correct in her observations. Many facilitators have either decided to postpone marriage or include clearly in the marriage contract their right to continue their newly found vocation. Most have selected sensitive and refined young men as husbands. The relationship between the couples in nearly all the cases is one of respect and mutual understanding. In fact many of the facilitators' husbands have, in their free time, become voluntary assistants to the community schools. They spend time with the children while their wives work hard at night, preparing teaching aids. Many of the facilitators returned to work two weeks or a month after giving birth on account of the support they were getting at home. Many of the men are reported to bring food, tea, and drinks to their wives as they prepare lessons and materials at home. Many more help in the making of the materials. One male science teacher from a village government school who participated in the education committee training workshop openly admitted that he had not only assisted his wife but had in fact borrowed ideas from her creative work. He proudly stated that when he used her teaching methods, it was the only time his students understood the subject matter and performed well. He also showed off the photograph of his newborn twins, who were looked after mostly by him.

Governance

Against a background of traditionally tribal forms of organization and authority common to many of the communities targeted by the initiative, and in the absence of formal governance at the hamlet level, communities have taken their political lives in their hands. The lowest formal level of administration is the mother village, where village heads and local councils preside. At the hamlet level, the education committee has evolved as the hamlet's ruling body. They have ownership of the central institution in the community, the school, and have managed to forge an alliance with the next level of rule, that is, at the village level. A highly significant indicator of community ownership and local official support is the very close relationship now developed between the village heads and district chiefs with the local community members. This relationship has been carefully nurtured over the years, in training workshops and in praxis.

An example of this relationship can be seen when official documents were produced by village heads to solicit help from health clinics for children in the community schools. The village heads then delegated the responsibility of following up to the education committees. Two village heads, Mr. Mohamed Nabil and Mr. Nadi, who have proved to be very strong supporters and friends of community schools since 1992, wrote an essay on community schools and their organic relationship to the local community. They also submitted a two-page evaluation note to the district chief, commending the work of the education committees in developing the local communities through the school. The then district chief, a Mr. Sirs, allowed the committees direct access to him. Over the years, the education committees acquired legitimacy as the official spokespersons for their constituency, to local government. The channels and networks were acknowledged and the hamlets now had access to decision-making bodies. The committees have been trained to delegate members for different missions and follow-up activities. They have gained legitimacy at the local level of administration and governance, and at the MOE central level, as partners in the management of the schools. The committees are being institutionalized, and we will see how in the last section on structures.

According to the support field staff, the committees have evolved greatly from simply asking for solutions and being observers during the committee meetings to becoming active problem-solvers and participants in their political lives. The committees had at first a relatively narrow focus, limiting themselves to the management of the schools. Judging from the minutes of the committee meetings, they first functioned rather mechanically, but with time their interests widened. The records and minutes of the committee meetings of December 1996, and January and February 1997 show that the following issues were tackled and discussed:

1. School and Academically Related Issues
   • Prolonged absences by children from school, and incentives to encourage them to attend, such as awarding prizes to the most regular school-goers. The committees also thought of incentives for the parents, including offering home economics classes to the mothers of regular school-goers. The possibility of having sewing machines in school was also discussed, as an incentive to the mothers.
   • Children's academic level was commended, and methods of continuous improvement discussed.
   • The need for special attention and care for slow learners was discussed.
   • The committees were eager to ensure that the children pursue their education by enrolling in nearby preparatory schools, and creatively made provisions for that to happen.

- The committee felt responsible for evaluating and monitoring the performance of facilitators.
- Problems of punctuality were discussed.
- Ways of solving the problem of the late arrival of schoolbooks was discussed and solutions suggested.
- Much discussion was centered on the methods of self-reliant school refurbishment and maintenance. Suggestions on how to obtain cement and wood were made.
- The children's high standards of hygiene were recognized and methods of spreading these habits beyond school were discussed. The committees also discussed ways of improving and maintaining the high level of school cleanliness and hygiene.
- The education committees invited children to participate in the school maintenance sub-committee created by the community.
- The committee discussed the possibility of replacing those children who dropped out during the year by newcomers on the waiting lists.
- The committee members also discussed whether or not to accept non-enrolled children halfway through the year, as observers.
- The selection criteria for admitting children to school was reconsidered.
- The approval of the date for the mid-term examination was discussed. According to the committees, it had to fit the children's needs and agricultural seasonal needs. They also expressed the need to work out an annual school schedule that would indicate best times for vacations.
- The committee participated in organizing for pupil's contests in academic subjects on the governorate level.
- The committee discussed how to organize the community-school children's participation in local and national children's festivities.
- The committee discussed organizing school trips for the children.
- The importance of school meals for the children was discussed.

2. Community Services
- A recurrent concern for the committee members was school health services. They discussed ways of having access to medical insurance and providing regular check ups for the school children. They also discussed how best to coordinate with the local unit to establish health posts. Many were in fact prepared to donate extra space to set up health posts.
- Other services of significance to them were road-paving, renewal of electric wiring, cleaning existing water containers, obtaining potable water and pit latrines. The discussions mostly centered on the best methods of

linking up with official authorities, projects such as Shorouk,[155] and how best to catch the attention of local authorities for action.

- When it was within their means to handle the relevant service, the committee organized itself to handle it. One such example was when the committee recognized the need for environmental protection and decided to organize for the cleaning of a nearby stream and to plant trees.
- The committees organized vocational training for the women in the community. The skills offered were limited but the concept was recognized.
- The committees organized the collection of contributions to expand and build new school sites to absorb more children.
- In those sites that still had no literacy classes the community had organized temporary classes in homes until the schools were set up and regular literacy classes held.
- Many of the committees had thought of ways of linking the school and education committees to local networks of NGOs.
- The committees discussed the need to establish cooperatives, and ways of organizing them.
- Some committees had linked and networked with local youth centers and had gained access to a great many services.
- The need to organize for micro-enterprise activities and possibly acquire loans from Nasser Bank was expressed.[156]
- The committees also discussed ways of linking up with development agencies and international NGOs such as CARE, with the purpose of maximizing their gains.
- Organizing health-awareness programs and campaigns was another area of concern to the education committee.
- The facilitation of access to birth and marriage certificates was also seen as an important priority for discussion.

3. The Concern for Child Rights and Social Equity
- The committee members showed great concern for the plight of poor disadvantaged children. They planned to contact the Ministry of Social Affairs for scholarships, pensions, and aid programs. Some committees established their own poverty safety nets through donations made to the poorest families.
- A remarkable and significant concern of some committees was child abuse at home. They were aware of a number of such cases and hence arranged for home visits and campaigns.

4. Political Empowerment
- The education committees had become adept at organizing collective demands on behalf of their community, and at demanding their rights, often in writing, and addressed to the relevant executive or administrative authority, sometimes even a governor or the minister of education, at the most opportune time.
- The committee had managed to build the appropriate political networks to obtain their requests.
- The committee members had also acquired the art of lobbying for their rights.

According to the most recent external evaluation in 2001, the committees were described as "lobbyists and advocators" for the project and other services for the community. They dedicated time and effort to network and organize, and solicited the support and assistance of local authorities. The latter regarded the local committees as their natural counterparts and often as their advisors for less developed communities. Through a partnership between the local authorities and the committees, electricity was often extended, water pipes connected, footpaths dug, and roads paved.[157]

Along with the empowerment gained, democratic behavior and consensus building had developed as norms among the committee members, who deliberated until agreement was reached on most issues. Sometimes they resorted to voting on issues by a show of hands.

Another rather remarkable trend is the level of transparency and accountability manifested by some of the committee members. On several occasions committee members would evaluate a facilitator negatively even if she were a daughter, sister, or niece of a school donor. In one case the daughter of a school donor (in this particular case, the only one) was asked to leave the school and the father agreed that her performance with the children had not been good. In another case a husband respected the communities' desire to replace his wife with another facilitator, as her performance was not satisfactory. There were of course many other instances when it was difficult to tackle cases of this kind. However, the members of the education committees have been a part of several of the selection panels for facilitators, have been very wary of nepotism, and have showed great maturity, objectivity, and a concern for the ultimate school objective, namely the well-being and best interests of the children. One elderly man from Aliksan hamlet in Manfalut very clearly told us, "We cannot afford to select untalented or uncommitted facilitators for our children because the program will fail if we do that. It has given us so much, we cannot afford to let it fail."

In the district of Abu Tig in Asyut, Kawthar had performed very well in her community school. As a result the mother decided to send the younger daughter to the same school. Kawthar's father had donated the school. However when the family was ready to send the younger sister to the school, other children had filled all the places in accordance with the priority criteria set by the education committee members. Kawthar's father complied with the rules and his young daughter had to ride a donkey to get to the nearest school some kilometers away.

Financial management is also done very transparently. Accounts and expenditure items are presented to the whole community. In some cases, the committee will have established a treasurer to handle donations; in other instances they will have formed a small sub-committee for finance.

The facilitators are no less empowered than the committee members. In the academic year 2000–2001, the salaries of the facilitators in Manfalut were delayed. For nine months the young women worked devoutly with no pay. Their patience and economic tolerance had come to an end. Wishing to make a statement, the facilitators went on strike and actually closed down the schools. Because of their deep emotional attachment to the children and the cause, they received the children in their homes and held activities in ways that would not allow the students to drop out of school. The salaries were paid and the schools quickly resumed once again. They had, however, made their voices heard. The Minister of Education had personally intervened and the bureaucratic obstacles rapidly removed.

On many occasions, facilitators had manifested a great sense of solidarity. In Qena two facilitators from feuding tribes were working together in the same school. The conflict between the families grew and one of the two facilitators was about to suffer and be transferred to another school. All the facilitators stuck together and pressured and lobbied at the community and management level to allow their colleague to stay in her old school. Functional solidarity is also not uncommon in the project. Hannan in Manfalut is part of the technical support staff. Her mother heads the field support staff. On many professional discussions, Hannan's loyalties were clearly to her colleagues in the technical support team.

Both the facilitators and the supervisors have shown exceptional examples of self-motivation and total quality management, where they themselves control the quality of their work. There have however been times where, in certain locations, the quality of performance temporarily declined. In one such instance, during an intensive monitoring field trip which I carried out, displeasure had been shown with regard to the performance of four of the schools visited in Sohag, and comments of a critical nature made. This led to deep self-reflection on the part of the team members as evidenced by the several letters of analyses and apology received. This was then followed by a phase of strong positive energy and reactivation.

Challenges are nonetheless quite significant in this quest for change. The empowerment of the actors is not a seamless process, nor is their commitment unquestioned and uninterrupted. The initiative is after all embedded in a culture of robust hierarchy. Moreover, sustained innovation and quality learning is no easy task.

There have been times when the commitment of some of the actors faltered. Facilitators reverted to old habits at times and fell back on their own educational and cultural heritage. There have been instances when supervisors and leaders exerted authoritarian practices. Finally, on some occasions, communities have been dependent on the NGOs and UNICEF and lacking in initiative.

Sustained innovation and commitment to quality learning requires ongoing efforts in dialogue, education, and mobilization. Creating safe spaces for empowerment and democratic practices can be quite challenging if the surrounding social formations and structures have not moved at the same pace. A 'safety net' of ongoing support, mobilization, and dialogue must be in place to prevent lull periods from possibly developing into total reversals. For the dialogue to result in deep-seated sustained transformation on the personal and collective levels, the anchoring period and incubation of the new ideas must be given time, and strategies to overcome resistance to change will have to be created at many levels. Some will be at the grassroots level, some at the middle-range policy level, and yet others at the broader cultural level. Time is an important ally that can only help deepen the impact of such movements incrementally and permit for learning along the way. Development often takes place in exponential leaps. One should not be discouraged at the first hurdles or shy away from closed doors and resistance. Many doors have been closed at different points in time and many more will continue to do so. The strength of any movement lies with time, faith, and the ability to enter into multiple alliances with key actors, organizations, and groups.

Diffusion of Concepts

The community school model has been conceptualized as a 'seedbed' model. The 'seedbed' model is based on a metaphor that implies that the beginnings of change and innovation are best nurtured when situated in the 'grassroots' of a system. All research on the best models of reform and change indicates that the successful adoption of change in complex systems is best achieved when the persons who deliver and receive the fruits of reformed services are closely involved in the change process and advocate for it. Moreover the process of change in the overall system does not occur through replication, but through inspiration. No act of development, social change included, can be achieved by replication or crude imitation. Change is, for the actors, intensely lived as an experimental, unfolding, and incremental experience.

Meanwhile the community-school model has aimed at catalyzing systemic innovation and change through a process of diffusion that is supported by certain elements of the State. It is important to emphasize the heterogeneous nature of governing states in most social formations. Alliances have and can often be made with those parts of a governing state that represent its most progressive elements and that are in favor of change. As mentioned earlier in the first part of this work, it is our belief that change is an organic, not a mechanical, process. It does not occur sequentially or as the result of an act of legislation. Nor does change occur at an equal pace in all parts of a system. In complex, living, human organizations there is a great deal of symbiosis at work. The webs of relationships make it quite ephemeral to predetermine how and where the change begins. Normally once a movement has developed into a critical mass it will work its way to other parts of the system.

In the following paragraphs we will trace the ways in which concepts have been diffused and adopted. We will look at high-level policy discourse, as well as policy discourse at the middle-range levels. The community grassroots levels have already been discussed earlier. We have seen in earlier discussions how the diffusive process began with a core team who diffused the concepts to the facilitators, supervisors, and children. These in turn continued the diffusive process to the families and communities. Since 1995, with the adoption of a twinning process with the one-classroom schools, the concepts have traveled and snowballed, reaching parts of mainstream regular schools and the broader educational system.

Many of the one-classroom schoolteachers in Asyut, Sohag, and Qena have attended training with the community-school staff. Those attending the training indicated that they had gained great insight into the concepts and practices of the schools. They singled out the learning corners and aids. They had in fact replicated the very same methods and techniques in their schools. Moreover the teachers from the one-classroom schools had gained a great deal of confidence from the training sessions, which greatly empowered them and enabled them to foster strong relationships with the local communities and local authorities.[158]

The supervisors also maintained that the training workshops they had attended had changed their concept of supervision and the nature of their relationship with the teachers and local communities. They had adapted their teaching methods to incorporate the constructive sharing of experiences as opposed to the traditional, and potentially overbearing, approach of fault-finding. As a result of the dramatic change in perspective and relationships, the performance of the teachers had vastly improved. Their creativity had been unleashed and their teaching had become far more child centered.[159]

During the feedback session of an inspector's training workshop conducted by the community-school team, the participants had made dramatic remarks. One inspector said, "We used to be looking out for criminals, now we have acquired new ideas for monitoring." Another remarked, "Through this training I now feel like an added force in this new movement for learning." A third participant admitted, "This training resulted in personality changes and altered one's concepts of learning." Finally another inspector cheerfully noted that, "through the training we have gone back in time and re-learned to be playful and young again."

These comments are not uncommon in many of the training sessions. In that same year, as a result of the graduates' performance in preparatory schools, UNICEF was requested to train a number of the host schools. Representatives from forty schools were reached with a training package on Total Quality Management for effective schools. Included in the package was a youth component to meet the needs of adolescents. Many of the participants came away with changed concepts and visions. Several had commented that their confidence and self-esteem had improved greatly; others asserted that they had lived out a true democratic experience. More impressively, several of the schools had replicated the training in their own school for those who had not attended, and in neighboring schools. The following year, the MOE sent a monitoring team with indicators, and methods of measuring and observing the impact of the initiative on the schools, and had been very impressed by the results, both in the change of attitudes and in practice. The director of basic education, Ms. Fayza Khalil, accompanied one of the monitoring missions. In a public speech on the diffusion process and the relationship between the community-school initiative and mainstream education, she remarked, "This is an initiative built on love and it is creating miracles."

The director of the one-classroom school initiative, Mr. Samir Ibrahim, made it quite clear on several public occasions that the community-school seedbed model had had a deep impact on the educational system at large and more specifically on other initiatives that followed the same path, such as the one-classroom schools and small schools. Mr. Ibrahim was particularly keen on diffusing some of the concepts and practices, notably those of active learning and the deepening of community participation. He wished to establish education committees in the one-classroom schools. The committees have been formalized and legitimized over the years. Officials from the one-classroom schools have been trained by UNICEF and the community-school team on how to establish education committees. The concept and practice is fully adopted by other initiatives that have been shaped after the community-school model, such as the small schools.

Early in 2002, the department of the one-classroom schools at the MOE hosted a large ceremony to honor some four hundred committee members. Mr. Ibrahim was the master of ceremony and the Minister of Education was the keynote speaker. The minister's speech was a real testimony to the adoption of the education committees as critical partners to the ministry. Earlier in the life of the movement that particular concept and practice had met with much resistance, as seen in 1993 when one undersecretary made his conservative views known by saying that "surely, illiterate members of education committees cannot lead, manage, or inform us of the needs of their communities."

During a workshop hosted by the Curriculum Association in 1999 and in the presence of some of its distinguished members[160] the first undersecretary at the time, Mr. Ragab Sharaby, stated, "We have been following in the footsteps of UNICEF in teacher training. We greatly benefited from them and are now adopting the whole idea of community participation." He then went on to say, "There has been a remarkable paradigm shift in the training and preparation of teachers." During the 2001 evaluation, the same first undersecretary is quoted to have said, "With the adoption of the community school concepts, most of the groundwork for policy reform has been laid, and the actual transformation of the system will inevitably take time. Policy is not something that you discuss and then write down: it is a process. The decree itself is but the final step in that process."[161]

The whole notion of an important paradigm shift is not Mr. Sharaby's view alone. The special advisor to the Minister of Education, Dr. Sidhom, used those same terms. She maintained that the MOE, due to the community-school model, had experienced a paradigm shift. The special advisor has been performing this function for thirteen years and is in a perfect position to observe the changes. She recounts that when the model was first initiated, it was met with lukewarm interest. Little was expected in the way of large-scale impact. She claims it moved out of the periphery into the center of attention, and became a catalyst for change. The model created a forum for policy dialogue. It provided a practical demonstration of a vision and a model that can be applied nationwide."[162]

The director of the Curriculum and Instructional Materials Development (CCIMD) center also indicated that a major breakthrough had occurred in curriculum development as a result of the community-school model. She maintained that curricula had always been traditionally treated through a top-down approach of specialized experts. When the center worked closely with the community-school model, the ministry was exposed to an alternative method, which was child-centered, relied on community participation, and adopted a total quality approach to management (see page 66). The facilitators from the community schools became the CCIMD's most dynamic and relied-upon consultants for the development of activity-based, multi-grade materials, since they had the relevant hands-on experience. The director expressed her gratitude to the community-school staff and UNICEF experts for the production of multigrade materials in arithmetic, language, social studies, and science, and the accompanying teacher's guide. It was her belief that this was a first step to widespread reform, as mainstream schools and teachers would also be introduced to the principles of self-directed learning with the use of the new learning materials and guides.[163] The books have been produced for up to third-grade level and are in use in all the community and one-classroom schools nationwide.

An incredibly important contribution of the model, according to the same special advisor mentioned earlier, is the fostering of partnerships between the ministry, NGOs, and communities. In the advisor's own words, "By bringing in the NGOs and linking the school with the community, the community schools have created an unprecedented partnership between the NGO, this community, and the ministry."[164]

In 2000 a department for NGO collaboration was set up at the MOE. In March of that same year a conference was held at MOE, presided by the Minister of Education in partnership with the Ministry Of Insurance and Social Affairs and the NGO confederation, to announce the new department. The first undersecretary made a statement in which he said, "We are in need of an innovative program of educational reform. To attain Education for All (EFA), we absolutely need the participation of NGOs. They have always played a role; however today is the birth of a true partnership and the beginning of self-help. Today is also one of the opportunities to celebrate innovations and to establish the many things we need to learn from the community schools and the one-classroom schools."

On that same occasion the Minister of Education made an eloquent speech, which essentially held that education is everyone's business even if the MOE takes the leading role. He cited the private sector, the NGOs, the media, intellectuals, and families as important stakeholders. He maintained that the great effort needed for education could no longer come from the State alone. Although the budget for education had· increased greatly in absolute terms, more support in the form of human capital and effort was still needed. The minister went on to assert that the efforts of others would be accepted on egalitarian terms. "We want equal partners" he said, "we need the participation in decision-making. NGOs are our partners and we do not just want money, but also their conceptual participation and help in many other domains. We have seen great examples of such a partnership, we only have to look at the community-school model." The minister cited the areas in which he hoped NGOs would participate, such as:

- Supervise the work of the ministry at the school level.
- Participate in parent associations.
- Provide services to the schools.
- Offer possibilities of projects to the schools..
- Facilitate school feeding, including helping children and their families to cook the food they bring into school.
- Attend to the needs of children with special needs.
- Link the school to the community.
- Support the initiative for clean, beautiful, and effective schools adopted by the ministry.

Early in 2002, the National Council for Childhood and Motherhood (NCCM)[165] hosted UNICEF's launch of the *State of the World's Children* report and showed a recent documentary on the community schools. The lead investigator on the NCEEE team working on the evaluation of the schools remarked during the discussion session, that the initiative constituted "a pioneer project and one of the best we have ever seen or heard about . . . it is a valuable experience which needs to be mainstreamed in the whole of Egypt." This was in fact one of the main recommendations of the final evaluation report.

The secretary general of NCCM, Ambassador Moushira Khattab, had herself visited the schools in Asyut a few months earlier, in November 2001. She requested the assistance of UNICEF for the expansion and replication of the model. That same year, liaison officers from NCCM were trained on components of the methodology of community schools.

The relationship between NCCM and UNICEF grew even closer as they jointly led the UN Girl's Education Initiative (UNGEI). After a series of preparatory meetings and conferences an agreement was signed between the NCCM and the UN family, led by UNICEF, to foster girls' education in Egypt. The partnership led a participatory process of planning in the seven most at-risk governorates with regards to the gender gap in education. The process was a truly exemplary one where local communities, NGOs, families, schools, and out-of-school girls planned with local government officials on how to decrease the gender gap in their respective geographic areas. Much of the community-school concepts were prominent in the process. A national task force on girls' education, which integrated the efforts of all the ministries, supported community empowerment. This in fact set a precedent for national planning, both in terms of grassroots involvement and in terms of coordination/integration between line ministries. The plans, which were an outcome of the participatory democratic process, were incorporated into the national five-year plan. The community-school model was being mainstreamed through the Egypt girls' education initiative coordinated by the NCCM.

In 2002 the new first undersecretary of the MOE Dr. Bellawy visited the community schools in Asyut. He returned a strong supporter of the movement. When debriefing the minister on his visit, he remarked, "I saw in one glimpse every thing you would have dreamed of for Egypt's educational system." A month after his visit he organized a lecture and a public screening of the most recent documentary on the community schools entitled, 'Our School.' Many of the MOE middle-range leaders attended the event, and from the discussions and feedback, the outcome was very encouraging and positive in terms of the diffusion of ideas. The first undersecretary was deeply encouraged by the visit and decided to strengthen the role of the EIC. The committee members were reviewed with the purpose of making the committee more effective. During the first meeting of the committee, six of the community-school core components (see page 36) were selected as the driving force for the work of the EIC during the first year. The components were written up in a concept paper, shared with the minister, and cleared. Among the critical components were community participation, authentic assessment, active learning, relevant activity-based curriculum, and dynamic transformational training, all within the context of democracy. These later became the founding principles and guidelines for the national educational standards set in 2002–2003.

During a presentation on educational reform by the Minister of Education to the opposition left-wing Tagammu' Party in June 2002, the minister made the case for democracy in education. He also cogently elaborated on all the above issues, including the need to reform assessment. He spoke of authentic assessment and the diversity and complementarity of the various methods of evaluation. As the overall discussion touched on the broader issues of underdevelopment, which included the cultural crises of values, the minister in fact pointed to the need to include values for education. Others spoke of a 'cultural revolution' to support educational reform.

The policy-making allies have indeed moved from the periphery to the center and have even moved all the way up to the First Lady of Egypt, a strong supporter of girls' education. In 1997, the community schools graduated seventy-three children from the end of the primary cycle. The event was met with national applause and appreciation, both at the official and community level. In a unique graduation ceremony carried out through video conferencing in July of 1997, the First Lady of Egypt distributed prizes and awards to both children and facilitators of the community and one-classroom schools in Asyut. A couple of months later the Governor of Asyut organized a popular celebration where communities participated in acknowledging the efforts of their children and facilitators/teachers. Children performed songs, plays, and dances against a background of music and gleeful cheers. An atmosphere of joy and optimism for a better future was pervasive. The following year the same level of celebration took place for the graduates of Sohag.

The First Lady of Egypt not only honored the first cohort from those schools, but in June of 2000 she was quoted by the *al-Gumhuriya* daily paper to have said during an international meeting that "the community schools were an important successful example of community participation. It is in fact the closest to my heart. It enabled deprived communities to get an education, with special emphasis on the girls in the Sa'id. It has established 200 schools since it began in 1992, through a partnership between the MOE, UNICEF, and NGOs. There must be a real balance and sharing of authority and responsibility between the central government, the local councils, communities, and NGOs. The local councils should coordinate between the central government and the beneficiaries. Decentralization will not occur unless the central government strongly encourages the local councils to enter into negotiation with it. It is only then that the local councils will become agents of real change."[166]

The diffusive engine has certainly been set in motion. In addition it had a clear impact on international agencies and other donors working in Egypt. The SFD supported a number of community schools in Asyut. Another clear example is the development of the USAID girls' education program in Egypt, which developed its version of the community schools, called the "small schools" and "new schools." These came about as a result of dialogue between the agencies and several field visits conducted by high-level decision makers from Washington.

The Canadian CIDA supported the community schools since 1994. It has developed into a full-fledged partner in the initiative since 1997 and has contributed significantly to the expansion of the movement. The World Bank and European Union have, through their Education Enhancement Programme

(EEP), supported second-chance education, yet another version of initiatives in this movement. Most recently, the Swiss Fund has also joined the movement.

The major vehicles selected for the process of diffusion have been training, curriculum development, field visits, and advocacy and policy dialogue. The process has resulted in some structural transformations. In the following section we will look at some of these structures. In the final chapter we will be examining how the diffusive process and the resulting structures can be deepened even further to sustain the movement and result in educational and social transformation.

Structural Transformation

The first structure created, following the establishment of community schools, was the one-classroom-school department in the MOE in 1993. The department was set up by ministerial decree 255 on 17 October 1993 for the establishment of one-classroom schools for girls. The schools would be set up in deprived hamlets and in remote rural areas. They would be multi-graded, extended to admit thirty-five girls, seven in each of the five primary grades. Two or three teachers would be responsible for teaching academic subjects, as well as vocational training, to enable the girls to acquire income-generating skills. Classes would be held five days a week, with Fridays and an additional day coinciding with the village or hamlet market day, both designated days off. The school would be built on donated or government-owned land. The governmental General Authority for Educational Buildings (GAEB) set up the building according to a specified model.

Although the one-classroom school department was part of the MOE, it somehow developed a less bureaucratic and cumbersome style of management. Each of the new department's directors have shown an openness to innovation and change, and the department as a whole has managed to set a number of precedents in terms of non-conventional problem solving. Moreover it became the legitimate umbrella for the ensuing models that expanded the numbers of similar schools and became part of the movement. A clear example is the small schools, fashioned and modeled after the community schools. These schools are being set up in three governorates that also have out-of-school girls and deprived areas.

The second important structure created was the EIC, which was the result of a long process of national and international consultations and exchange of experiences occurring in 1995–96. In October 1996, by virtue of ministerial decree 357, the committee was established. The official document uses as its basis the former agreement signed between UNICEF and the MOE in 1992 and the ministerial decree of 1993 for the establishment of the one-classroom schools. The function of the committee, as it was spelled out, was to find mechanisms of diffusing and mainstreaming the lessons learned and best practices from the community and one-classroom schools to the broader educational system. The membership reflected an integrated package approach to education. Represented were the media, private sector, civil society, evaluation, curriculum, training, school buildings, and management leadership.

Despite the frequently interrupted functioning of the committee, between 1997 and 2000 when it was most active, it managed to issue a number of facilitating and supportive policies for the effective functioning of the community and one-classroom schools, among which were:

- The creation of innovative specifications for small schools' buildings allowing for more than one variety of building and more cost effectiveness in building them.
- Waiving school fees at the preparatory and secondary levels for graduates from the community and one-classroom schools
- Allowing the pupils of both these initiatives the privileges enjoyed by other students, such as health insurance and a daily snack
- Facilitating the admission of graduates from both initiatives into preparatory schools by allocating space for them and by increasing the age limit upon entry.
- Formalizing the flexible promotion and accelerated learning programs applied in community schools and applying them to the one-classroom schools.

A third critical structure established in 2000 through decree number 30 was the 'Department for NGO and Ministerial Collaboration.' The decree stipulated that NGOs would be allowed to establish schools like the community, one-classroom, and small schools. This was a first in any of the ministries. The partnership between governmental and non-governmental organizations was being strengthened and formally recognized.

A fourth, interesting development was the establishment of departments for multi-grade education in some faculties of education. One such example is the university of Zaqaziq.

In this chapter we have examined the results of the community-school initiative. Some impacts are in fact even more obvious at the national level and amenable to measurement. The decrease in the national gender gap (the gap between male and female rates of school enrollment) is a case in point. It has been vastly attributed to the expansion of community-type schools, including the one-classroom school. This will be discussed further in the following chapter. The remaining part of this chapter will be devoted to the issue of cost. Education does cost money, but if learning is priceless what then can be said about transformation and change through learning?

The Cost of Community Schools in Egypt

A true measure of sustainability should no longer be the narrow project-oriented concept of cost-effectiveness. As will be discussed more elaborately in the last chapter, all stakeholders can only safeguard sustainability through a growing public taste for quality and a strong demand for it. Quality in its transformational sense is indeed priceless, and developing a model for the improvement of sustainable quality education is an expensive and intensive endeavor. This is precisely why the endeavor is needed, otherwise average performance would have attained the status of acceptablity and quality. Paradoxically, the cost of a poor or average education is often far greater than that of a high-quality one. The cost of ignorance and bad quality is high. Moreover, the allocations of limited resources in some systems are often not ideal and may require some reconsideration. These may not always be controlled by traditional education sectors.

Cost analyses of the community-school initiative were carried out in three of the several evaluation studies undertaken. The results are presented here chronologically and supplement the analyses with additional information where necessary. The cost of setting up and running the schools, it must be remembered, is shared between the communities, the MOE, and international organizations, essentially UNICEF and CIDA. Most evaluations have only looked at the cost carried by the international organizations. On two occasions, UNICEF carried out a comprehensive cost-analysis exercise that accounted for all the partners in the community-school initiative: once during the initiation of the Master Plan of Operations in 1995, and on another occasion during the preparation of the governorate-level five-year plans within the girls' education initiative.

The 1994 Internal Evaluation[167]

According to the cost analyses carried out by the consultant, the cost of one community-school to UNICEF at the time was in the order of US $4000 inclusive of furniture, equipment, stationery, and training and supervision/quality control. The cost of the land, buildings, books, and teachers' salaries were not included. The pupil unit cost was calculated at US $120, or 384 Egyptian pounds (L.E.), per year, based on the then dollar exchange rate of L.E. 3.2 to the dollar. The consultant compared this to the L.E. 200 per year, which was the government's unit cost per pupil at the time. He argued, however, that as the community schools expanded, the unit cost would drop. Meanwhile with cost analyses, internal efficiency needed to be factored in. Dropout rates or students repeating their school year would decrease or increase costs. Moreover the future success of acceleration programs would contribute to the reduction of the cost. In 1994 there were only two dropouts from a total of 708 pupils. From the examination of UNICEF books, the evaluation concluded that the costs had already been reduced between 1992 and 1994, from L.E. 384 to L.E. 248.

The 1995 External Evaluation[168]

The evaluation had begun to look at the question of cost comparability with government schools, stating that it was a complex matter requiring attention to three categories of recurrent cost: base, start-up, and developmental.

The unit cost per primary pupil for government schools was estimated at L.E. 264 compared now to L.E. 248 for community schools. According to the new suggested method of cost analyses, the government schools had a higher unit cost if the community schools' development recurrent costs were omitted, the latter largely being the cost required to establish the knowledge base, and to build organizational and personal capacity. The cost of activities related to advocacy were also part of the development costs.

The 2001 External Evaluation[169]

The analyses made by this evaluation at least acknowledged the fact that the costs were shared between three partners, and ranked them in the order of contributions made. The largest contributor was the local community, the next largest were the international agencies, UNICEF and CIDA, through their support of NGOs, and lastly, the MOE. The community funds land, buildings, and school maintenance. UNICEF and CIDA support the NGOs, who in turn fund the supervision of the schools, training, and some supplies and equipment. The ministry funds the schoolbooks and the salaries of the facilitators.

The evaluation team then goes on to analyze financial documents of a sample NGO in Sohag for the years 1998 and 1999. The document essentially reflects donor support to the project. The line items of the project document do not however give a clear idea of the purpose of the expenditure or the nature of the line item. An analyses of the 1998 project agreement document with the Association for Women's Development and Training in Sohag shows how the money was spent in one year of the life of the project:

Table 12: Allocation of Expenditure According to Type in Sohag

Expenditure items (realigned according to their purpose and combining categories together)	Actual expenditure for the year in Egyptian pounds (this is different from the allocations made early in the year)
Supervision (Salaries + transport)	245,251
Training (all types)	323,385
Administrative expenses	10,558
Supplies	200,285 (managed directly through UNICEF)
Grand total for 72 schools	*779,479* (NGO total = 579,194)

The start-up cost of a community school, according to 1998/1999 estimates, is L.E. 11,000. The cost per pupil was estimated at L.E. 364. The evaluation team compares this to the cost of basic education per child in government schools, estimated to be in the order of L.E. 560.

Cost analyses based on actual UNICEF/CIDA, MOE, and Community Investments[170]

According to the most recent cost analyses for 2002, conducted by UNICEF, the communities, and the MOE, the cost of setting up one community school is L.E. 33,650, shared in the following fashion between the three critical partners:

Table 13: Comprehensive Cost of a Community School

Partners	Investments in L.E.
Communities (Land + Building + Maintenance)	15,000
UNICEF/CIDA/NGOs (Training + Supervision + Furniture + Supplies + Administrative Costs)	12,341
MOE (Salaries + Books)	6,309

The analyses conducted by the evaluation reports have in a sense tended to compare apples and oranges. The correct reference point of comparison for the community schools is the equivalent, governmental, one-classroom schools, which are special types of initiatives that not only aim at accessing the hard-to-reach, but also include innovative quality components, including the involvement of communities. They should not therefore be compared to conventional schools in mother villages or towns.

The cost of a one-classroom school is estimated at L.E. 97,505, not including the cost of land, which may be government or community owned. The investment and current cost items may be broken down as follows:

Table 14: Comprehensive Cost of a One-classroom School[171]

Items	Investments in L.E.
Buildings and equipment (exclusive of the land donated by communities)	80,000
Salaries(teachers and inspectors)	5,796
Training	9,000
Books	2,709
Total	*97,505*

The above is a much reduced estimate of what the one-classroom schools might cost in reality. The per pupil cost was very high, since, in an earlier version of the model, only seven girls were admitted during the first year. Each year an additional seven girls were admitted. Fortunately the model has changed and moved closer to the community-school model. Nonetheless the fact remains that this model yields a unit cost that is more than triple that of the community-school initiative.

The costing of such an initiative is a classical exercise required of any documentation, but although not entirely futile, it is not central to the philosophy of diffusion and sustainable structural and social transformation, which will be discussed at greater length in the last chapter of this work. Since the aim of the movement is not to replicate endless numbers of community schools but to diffuse best practices in the broader educational system, the cost effectiveness of catalyzing a movement is not essential to its sustainability, and is often a fallacious and potentially misleading criteria of a movement's success or otherwise. Many more elements appear to have greater relevance and depend far more on an understanding of the context of the movement than on how much an initiative costs. In fact, as mentioned in the first chapter, if we are serious about educational reform and development, we must steer away from the project approach toward a movement approach, one which requires a different mode of analysis and assessment. One must carry out a cost analysis, however, simply because it is an issue that is very often raised by those opposed to innovative approaches. It is nonetheless clear that such analyses neither resolve the existing opposition nor explain the initiative's potential for success or failure. To do so requires a political economy approach in analyzing the structures, concepts, and values that can create the environment for sustained educational reform.

Conclusion

This section has looked at the impact of the community-school initiative on the personal lives of those involved, as well as the broader national educational scene. It depicts how the community school experience has allowed for and facilitiated dialogue between all the actors in the movement, from schoolchild to policy maker, to create an environment for learning and serious transformation.

Although it at times reads like an evaluation, it actually simply means to show how far-reaching the impact of such an initiative can be, and how inter-related are the trajectories of individual/personal transformation and the creation of a reform environment and a culture of change and innovation. It also serves to show how valuable models on the ground can be in catalyzing and creating a national dialogue on change and reform, and how permeable systems can be to innovations when 'seedbeds' are established on the ground, thus drawing both proponents and opponents into a serious dialogue. In the end it becomes clear that the "proof is in the pudding": it is what works that counts. The visible successes of the children and the learning processes vouch for the strengthening of such initiatives. The center and the periphery of the educational system are thus engaged in a dialogue where both innovative and more traditional actors can recognize a niche in such an initiative for themselves. The dialogue cannot be stopped. It has set in motion a whole dynamic, which I describe in the last part of this work.

4

The Way Forward:
The Road to Sustainable
Learning and Reform

Organizational change starts anywhere and is to be followed everywhere.
Margaret Wheatley and Myron Kellner-Rogers

I N THIS LAST CHAPTER I AM INTERESTED IN ANSWERING some significant
questions that were raised in the first chapter, namely, has the community-school initiative served as a catalyst for deeper social and educational
transformation? Has it contributed, even in a small way, to educational reform?
And, finally, does it look like a movement that is here to stay and expand in all
kinds of directions? These are the kind of assessment questions one poses with
regard to movement-based education as opposed to isolated educational programs or projects.

At the heart of reform within a movement approach is the concern with
changes in structures and relations as opposed to just material conditions (the
number of books or teacher training courses, or enrollment rates) at a given
point in time. Moreover, in line with the analyses of the first chapter and the
definition of learning adopted by the initiative, reform is not just about better
learning achievements in reading, writing, and arithmetic. Nor is it just about
preparing individuals for a competitive labor market. Reform is about return-
ing to the fundamentals of what it means to be human, and tackling the root
sources of worsening inequalities, poverty, powerlessness, and destitution. It is
about reviving the essence of learning in its most noble form, by fostering
democracy and teaching children how to live together. The aspired to reform

movement is one that regards education as a public good that enhances justice and people's ability to bond in solidarity and compassion to make this world a better place to live. Educational reform is in essence a liberating force that unleashes the highest potentials of learners in the affective, cognitive, social, and physical domains. It transforms schools into safe spaces where relations are redefined, as opposed to institutions that reinforce existing relations of power and oppression. It is the sub-culture of classrooms, the practices and webs of relationships therein, that truly reflect a paradigm shift in learning and a reform in motion, or not.

In a well-developed argument, Arthur MacEwan (1999), in fact shows how social programs, particularly those relating to community education, can lead a nation not just to educational reform, but can be the entry point for huge democratic transformations. This is provisional on the existence of some room for democratic dialogue that can later be enlarged. I argue, however, that in most countries of today's world, whether democracy is a mere façade or much more, there is substantial room for negotiation, for innovative programs, and for different ways of doing things. A virtuous circle is then established whereby the space for negotiation expands and the pillars of democracy become deeply anchored.[172]

It is precisely at those spaces for dialogue that I will be looking when attempting to answer the question of how the community-school initiative has contributed to the creation of a reform environment. As to the question of the depth and sustainability of the initiative's impact, this will call for an analysis of the political economy and landscape of educational reform in Egypt. Finally, with the insights obtained from the story of the community schools, I will discuss current theories and ideas around educational reform.

Community Schools and the Multi-level Dialogue for Reform

What the community-school initiative has most certainly done is to help trigger and facilitate a reform dialogue at many levels, in many directions, and with many stakeholders since the early nineties. Like the concentric ripples caused by a pebble cast into a pond, the effects of the initiative have spread further and further, the circles representing not just how deprived or physically remote children could be reached, but also how community participation could become a reality, as well as an active learning step toward educational democracy, and the empowerment of deprived communities and of girls in particular, a sure step toward the achievement of equity and justice.

The reform dialogue took place at many levels—at the grassroots and intermediate levels, at the institutional level, and at the level of policy-making. The grassroots level represents the local communities; the intermediate level includes governorate officials or middle-range government policy makers; and the institutional level covers those experts or managers with more technical expertise of policy implementation, such as universities and specialized institutions including the CCIMD and the NCEEE. The level of policy-decision makers includes the First Lady, the Prime Minister, the Minister of Education, and the First Undersecretary on the local front, and donor agencies and international organizations on the international front. The reform landscape was touched everywhere and the ripple effects experienced by all. The dialogue did not only take place between external and internal forces but between two Egyptian cultures, one representing the forces of change and progression, the other the forces of resistance and regression. A tolerance for a critical mode of education was developed in Egypt, with clear examples of how things could be done in alternative ways. The environment for reform was strengthened, and the pedagogy for empowerment demonstrated. In the following lines I will narrate the progression of the dialogue at all the various levels.

At the Grassroots and Intermediate Levels

It is clear from the previous chapters and sections that this is where, in fact, the dialogue began. The possibilities of a new learning paradigm, with community participation, child centeredness, empowerment, and participation at its heart, were discussed endlessly at an early stage, with local communities, facilitators, and staff belonging to community associations and NGOs. The dialogue took the form of open-ended conversations, workshops, research, and praxis. The ideas took root in the three governorates of Asyut, Sohag, and Qena at first, but soon traveled fast to other geographical locations.

Dialogue did not just take the form of words and intellectual exchanges, but was concretized in a model and in praxis whereby structures ensued on the ground, schools were created, and reality was transformed. The landscape had indeed changed as education committees, as earlier described, had been created. The multiplier effect of the dialogue at the community level was great, and showed that although over two hundred thousand people had been reached, millions more could, over time, be engaged in the dialogue. NGOs began to have an audible voice and to realize that they too could play a pivotal role in educational reform. The dialogue extended to both national and international NGOs. Many were now ready to begin playing their part.

At the Institutional Level

The dialogue at the university level was extremely powerful. It was not without difficulties at first, but it promises to render significant results. When the faculties of education in Asyut, Sohag, and Qena entered into dialogue with the community-school initiative early in 1993, they were skeptical. Although many of the faculty members had been exposed to some of the model's ideas through their research and graduate studies abroad, these had retained the status of theoretical study, the province of books and articles that could not be visualized in practice. Many faculty members at first resisted but later joined the reform movement.

Members of the faculties of education had been invited to join the training workshops and become part of the training teams. The first encounters were painful. Professors arrived with their briefcases, ties, suits, and a screen to maintain a distance with the trainees. They lectured for hours, were forceful, authoritarian, and maintained their position as the sole source of all knowledge. They had in fact secretly thought of a name for the community school group; they called us the "circus team" and clearly ridiculed the participatory training methodologies practiced. Fortunately the core team had been trained for a year, and could stand their ground and enter into a dialogue, which resulted in visible transformations. Those very same trainers became staunch advocates of the movement and have continued to support the mainstreaming of the process. They have volunteered work for community schools, the girls' education initiative, and the national standard setting program (see page 171). They also encourage their students to join the initiative and carry out action research in the schools. This type of research is geared toward taking action as opposed to just descriptive or academic knowledge. It is essentially participatory and allows both researchers and target groups to come up with concrete plans of action.

On the national level, there is an ongoing dialogue with respect to the possibilities of reforming the curriculum of faculties of education to allow for more teacher classroom practice, coaching, and mentorship so that students get more hands-on experience before teaching. In addition, some faculties of education have introduced a department for multi-grade teaching.

The MOE departments at the district and governorate levels have also been part of the dialogue from very early on. Supervisors have participated in training workshops, both as trainers and as trainees. They have learned about self-learning and active training. They visit the schools regularly and their hearts are clearly with those classes and the way children are learning. Many of them have expressed their appreciation in writing when visiting the schools; others have made public comments during seminars or field visits. They have often commented that what happened in those classrooms was possible because the community schools did not have to go through the various bureaucratic layers of management in the mainstream system. Through the dialogue they came to the realization that the community schools are using the government books and curriculum materials, and that the schools come under the ministry's supervision. However, they also realize that there is certainly greater empowerment of teachers/facilitators, not through higher salaries, but through greater autonomy and freedom in the ability to plan and make classroom decisions. The administrative constraints and management guidance are certainly less imposing.

Schools have been another institution obviously drawn into the dialogue. The one-classroom schools were twinned and clustered with the community schools since their inception in 1993. The training between the two initiatives was done jointly and it is instructive for those interested in processes of decentralized reform to observe how one culture transferred to the next. Whereas the one-classroom school teachers could initially not speak up before getting the approval of their supervisors through a submissive process of eye contact, the community-school facilitators were totally empowered and easily contributed to the dialogue even if at times in ways contradictory to the trainers and their supervisors. The multi-dimensional transformational training packages offered by the community-school initiative has proved very effective in one-classroom and conventional schools. It not only targets teachers but all other related actors in the educational ecosystem. It is very much on demand by teachers and supervisors. One trainee from a mainstream regular school remarked after the end of a training workshop, "At first I used to look out for training as a way of supplementing my income through stipends and daily subsistence allowances; after attending these workshops I am actually prepared to pay fees to enroll in future workshops." Training is supplemented by field seminars where teachers, supervisors, and other players are able to observe a whole new culture of learning.

Since the first cohort of community-school children graduated into conventional schools, the latter became aware of a different culture of learning and being. Through the interaction with the children, conventional schools developed a taste for inquiry, being curious to understand why the community-school graduates were so different from anyone they had dealt with before, despite the fact that they came from a similar socio-economic background of poverty and deprivation. As a result, schoolteachers and administrators were eager to establish contact with community-school children and start a dialogue. The first group of schools was approached through training in 1996–97. The forty schools selected were primarily preparatory schools (grades 7–9) that had been recipients of the community-school graduates. All the players and stakeholders in the school were invited. Teachers, principals, directors, supervisors, social workers, and students were included. The training workshops extended over three years and the level of engagement was phenomenal. Teachers were for the first time able to speak their minds before the whole school and administrative hierarchy. The school principals were listening and making commitments. The pattern of interaction was markedly changing as the hierarchies were gradually flattening and all the stakeholders entered into a dialogue that even involved the students. It was interesting to observe how much the experience was enjoyed and appreciated. Even more interesting was the fact that those who had attended the workshops had made attempts to extend the experience to others in their neighboring communities. Follow-up missions from the MOE picked this up. Teachers were learning that it was far more gratifying and enjoyable to forsake traditional, authoritarian methods of teaching for more activity-based, democratic ones. Once basic relationships take a different turn, it is remarkable how both the oppressive and the oppressed in any given situation will understand the enchantment and fulfillment inherent in democratic dialogue.

Another venue for the engagement of schools in the dialogue for empowerment is an initiative begun in 2003 whereby nine conventional schools in the Governorates of Asyut, Sohag, and Qena were clustered and twinned with the community-school initiative. The dialogue was a truly interesting one whereby teachers and school principals were trained, mentored, and coached to introduce activity-based learning in some fifty first-grade classrooms. After a year of dialogue and training, the schools opened their doors to members of the community-schools initiative to become part of the scene and help them turn their bare and hostile classrooms into child-friendly spaces. Very simple changes were made to the classroom arrangement to allow for more interaction and group work and already there was a sense of comfort and ease. The children's eyes brightened and the behavior patterns revealed more confidence, joy of learning, and participation. A new culture is being introduced and new concepts such as "child rights" and "child-friendly classrooms" are coming into play. Moreover the teachers are slowly learning about all the fine and intricate strategies that must be in place to allow for activity-based learning to happen. The dialogue is still young, and already a bright-eyed teacher with a glow in her face was telling all the participants in the meeting how she had just been introduced to magic: "My daughter is in my first primary grade and she hated school in the past and I always had to exert a lot more effort when I went home on a one on one basis. Since I have started to use the activity-based methods in class and children are working together with some minimal facilitation it is just like magic! On the way home my daughter is reading every single poster or sign we encounter; I cannot believe she is willingly learning so much on her own initiative. I did not think I would be able to enjoy teaching; it is actually so much fun creating learning aids and playing with and observing those children working together."

Other institutions have been the set of specialized centers appended to the MOE such as the CCIMD and the NCEEE. The dialogue with the two institutions has been very intensive from a very early stage. Both centers have developed strong partnerships with the community-school initiative, participated in training, monitoring and evaluation at various stages.

Facilitators in the community-school initiative, through the many training and creativity learning opportunities received, managed to use the existing school textbooks as guidelines for learning objectives and standards at each level. They did not limit themselves to the content and/or the activities in those books. Cards, sheets, learning aids, and games have been produced en masse and objects and materials for learning are endless. Competent teaching and effective classroom management is at the heart of the creative utilization of textbooks as guides for activity-based learning.

In partnership with the CCIMD, the community-school initiative has offered a bottom-up approach in which teachers have been deeply involved in the creation of new learning materials, textbooks and guides. This resulted in newly produced multi-grade textbooks with more activity-based self-learning materials nationwide. The teachers/facilitators from the community schools were relied upon as experts by the CCIMD. Learning guides and books were produced for all six primary grades and were made available for all multi-grade classrooms. Meanwhile a letter of cooperation was signed by the Minister of Education to further diffuse this methodology of developing materials and content to mainstream conventional schools.

It has frequently been argued that one of the main reasons for the spread of private tutoring in Egypt is the nature of the country's national examination and evaluation systems, which have traditionally relied heavily on the measurement of low-order thinking and rote memorization. Hence the role afforded to private tutoring in imparting the necessary skills to pass such examinations. Although the community school pupils do compete on national examinations like all other children, they have not been victims of private tutoring, nor have literate and educated parents tutored them at home. There is therefore a lot to learn from the methods of assessment employed in those schools. The child portfolio is one of the most important methods used and has proven to be extremely versatile. It has expanded to include teacher evaluation, peer and self-assessment and parent conferencing. All of these are very dynamic and authentic means of assessment.

The NCEEE was on several occasions engaged in assessing community schools. This partnership introduced innovative methods of conducting evaluations. The evaluation was viewed as an intervention in itself as it created indicators and criteria for effective schools that could become national standards. It moreover used classroom observation and in depth interviews to come to grips with the complete educational scene and the actors therein. It also devised ways to measure these. This was coupled with a more ethnographic approach. Meanwhile the evaluation was a comprehensive one which clearly emphasized the package approach to reform and quality improvement.

One special evaluation mission focused on the method of assessment in those schools and the ensuing system of flexible promotion and accelerated learning. The evaluation was very positive and the Minister of Education issued a decree to allow other mainstream schools to use the acceleration model developed in community schools.

The 2001 NCEEE evaluation of the community schools, discussed in chapter three, clearly recommended that many components of the initiative be transferred to the mainstream system. In 2002/2003 the ministry began a nationwide reform process in its evaluation and assessment systems. Thirty percent of the schools nationwide are to employ authentic and incremental assessment. The use of portfolios is being introduced in those schools.

Although the NCCM was a latecomer to the dialogue, in 2001/2002 it developed into a major channel for the mainstreaming of the community-school integrated conceptual package and, indeed, became an important player in the reform movement. The Girls Education Initiative in Egypt, which was discussed in the previous chapter, has been a very significant forum for a widespread consultative process and has been viewed as a model for the entire MENA region. Based on a strong partnership between the National Council for Childhood and Motherhood and the United Nations family, led by UNICEF, a unique process of participatory planning has been put in place. The global goals of parity and equality set out for 2005 and 2015 respectively are to be reached through this democratic process. In 2001 a national task force was established at the central level composed of sixteen ministries, four NGOs, the UN family, and other information-related agencies. The composition of the national task force was a clear message that the stakeholders in education needed to be enlarged and those educational concerns depicted should not be limited to the MOE. Through a process of consultation and integrated planning seven governorates were selected as the most at risk and where the initial phases of implementation would begin in order to reach the parity goal of 2005. Consultative participatory workshops were conducted in the seven gover-

norates, emphasizing the importance of community participation, which resulted in the identification of problems and needs, in designing broad strategies and
in the creation of seven voluntary local task forces. The workshops included a
vast array of stakeholders including educators, parents, communities, and in-
and out-of-schoolgirls. The capacity of the local task forces has been gradually
built to enable them to actively participate in the development of action plans
for their governorate and to monitor their implementation. These have been
mainstreamed in the government five-year plan and additional resources have
been allocated for the girls' education initiative. The process of consultation and
participation in the implementation, monitoring and evaluation of the plans
will continue at all three levels of governorate, village, and hamlet. An
immensely significant process of consultation has been unleashed and if not
perfect at first, it certainly is introducing new concepts and practices in the
landscape of reform.

At the Policy Level

Donors are key players in the policy dialogue. Although they do not represent
a large percentage of the investments in education, they have flexibility, however, in how they can use their funds—and these are often in ways that can make
a difference. When the community-school movement was in its infancy in the
early 1990s, there were hardly any donors on the educational scene.

One of the main players at the time who had been engaged in the educational sector in the 1980s, namely the United States Agency for International
Development (USAID), was on its way out of that particular domain. It had
been unable to enter into dialogue with the various players and was in fact on
the verge of closing down its education division in Egypt. When the dialogue
with community schools began, a long-winded process to draw USAID back
into the policy arena was put in place. The agency got a close-up of the initiative and was given the opportunity to observe, learn, and come into conversa-
tion with it, all of which resulted in the creation of a joint group of donors
wishing to support education and an $80 million dollar program for girls' edu-
cation. After a number of iterations the program developed into a much wider
source of support for educational reform. It built new schools and in addition
established the equivalent of community schools, the "new schools" and "small
schools" in a number of governorates. USAID has also been engaged in quality
education through the multi-level training of teachers, middle-range policy
makers, school principals, and supervisors. It furthermore established models of
community participation and developed an early childhood intervention institution, the Egyptian *Sesame Street*.

CIDA has developed into a critical partner of community schools over the years. It has supported the expansion of the community schools in the first phase and is developing into a partner for reform in the second phase. It is currently starting the endeavor with the early childhood phase (pre-school programs).

The European Union and the World Bank became major players in the community-school initiative in 1996, when they initiated a joint Education Enhancement Programme (EEP) managed by the Programme, Planning and Monitoring Unit (PPMU), which reports directly to Egypt's Minster of Education. The program has supported community participation and teacher, principal, and supervisor education. They have also built new schools.

UNESCO has of course been instrumental in assessments, in establishing, in partnership with the World Bank, Educational Monitoring Information Systems, and in leading the EFA planning processes. The UNDP and other UN agencies have joined UNICEF in supporting the UN girls' education initiative and have supported female literacy. The Japanese International Co-operation Agency (JICA) has been assisting in the improvement of learning materials, particularly in science and arithmetic

Finally, all the agencies coordinate through a sub-group for donors. UNICEF and USAID originally put the group together and jointly chaired it. It now has a rotating chair. Although the group began coordinating as a form of experience exchange, it is now eager to become part of the policy dialogue. It has as a group the potential for acting as a forum for additional support to the reform infrastructure. The group members do not necessarily constitute a homogeneous entity. There is however a clear interest in reform and in supporting strategic planning toward that reform. The alliance between those willing change, educational reform, and progress toward human development becomes that much more potent when it has a globalized voice. Just as the forces of national regression and repression seek external allies and protection to maintain and sustain the unjust status quo, described earlier, in the first chapter, so must forces of change, development, and progress seek external allies to break a number of vicious circles obstructing human development.

Even more significant than the impact of community schools on the donor's role in policy-making is their impact on major national policy initiatives and the dialogue held with two of the most prominent national institutions. A national initiative of immense significance has been the National Standards program by the MOE introduced in 2002/2003, the standards of which have provided a vision for reform.

Through an intricate consultative nationwide process that took place in 2003, standards for quality education were established. The standards span five critical and intertwined fields: the curriculum and outcomes of learning, the teacher and educator, the effective school, educational organization and management excellence, and finally, community participation. In each field several standards have been set for a number of critical domains. Each standard is in turn amenable to measurement through a set of specific indicators. The standards have been negotiated among a wide array of participants spanning communities, educators, administrators, and parents; they purport to be culturally sensitive, doable, and focused on the best interests of the student. The process, which lasted for a whole year has resulted in, agreed upon documents, which are very quickly disseminated to schools, directorates and training workshops.

Strategic planning has begun to point out ways in which this vision may be turned into reality. There have been different attempts at policy and strategic planning from a variety of stakeholders. The challenge is to streamline those attempts and consolidate the efforts into a package approach that should bring about deep-rooted and sustained changes to the educational system at the national level, very much in line with the learning paradigm delineated in chapter one. The outcomes of learning promise an empowered student who has actively acquired the skills of life-long learning and all the skills necessary to learn to be and to live with others. The standards for educators point to the advent of a facilitating leader in the classroom, a thinker and a planner who can relate to students in empowering and democratic ways. The school is to be effective, meaning a place where any child would flourish and want to be in. It is privileged with a team of educators who can work together for the best interests of the child, her family, and community. The community is vastly empowered and its relationship to its school an open and participatory one. Finally, the culture of learning and schooling is enhanced by a flat management style that allows for excellence, connectivity, communication, innovation, and production. The vision embedded in the standards opens the way for the creation of a community of learners and for the democratization of education. It points the way to school improvement and the professionalization and empowerment of teachers.

The standards are setting the measures against which reform and quality learning will be assessed. It is a true challenge that will require much in the way of policy change, systemic reform, and a willingness to challenge the existing culture of education. It already recommends school accreditation and teacher licensing through a professional academy of educators, called the Professional Academy for Teachers (PAT). It is making all the players accountable and moving toward better school governance. Meanwhile the standards are also making more space for the dialogue to continue and for strategies and structures to further enhance the humanity of the system.

Critical Structures for Supporting Reform

The broad consultative processes defined above will further enhance the creation of a reform environment and will strengthen the possibilities of building alliances and coalitions that can support the reform process. Meanwhile a number of critical structures have been established as the beginnings of building a true reform support infrastructure (see page 5), which promises to further broaden the democratic and participatory base. Examples of such structures, which promise to play a leading role in replicating the conditions of innovation, are:

1. The Education Innovation Committee (EIC), which has been instrumental in shaping educational policy to support innovations (see page 62) and will continue to do so by acting as the think tank and technical support for the implementation of standards. The Committee began its work by tightly linking the community schools and one-classroom schools together to generate a process of diffusion in favor of the innovative activity based learning strategies developed in the 'seedbed' model. The next process the committee undertook was to generate another diffusive flow from the 'seedbed ' to the mainstream conventional schools. With the development of standards, the terms of references of the committee have evolved to enable it to oversee the piloting and implementation of standards along with all the necessary policy and structural changes.

2. The Coordinating Committee which is set up to align all educational initiatives around a ministry strategic plan for reform. This committee will have representatives from the ministry, NGOs, donors, and the business sector.

3. The NGO department at the MOE, which will broaden the scope of stakeholders and foster strong partnerships between educational initiatives by the ministry and those supported by the donors.

4. The Professional Academy for Teachers (PAT) which will be charged with the licensing and certification of teachers. It is meant to be an institution for the professionalization of educators and a forum where their voices will be heard. It is an institution, which will empower educators and allow them to develop to their full potential both on the level of competencies and on the level of their profession.

5. The CCIMD will be engaged in mainstreaming activity based learning, supplementary materials and kits for child-centered self-learning, and

developing manuals for teacher education and guidance. It will also rein-vent its functions to allow for more participation in curriculum develop-ment. The focus of its main function will be one of curriculum service and certification.

6. The NCEEE is engaged in developing alternative assessment techniques and has, in cooperation with the community-school initiative, developed indicators of effective schools that can serve as guidelines for accredita-tion. With some development and enhancement the NCEEE can devel-op into the national accrediting overseeing body with decentralized arms and departments at the local and school levels. It can also lead a school improvement plan starting from the school level at the village and dis-trict. The NCEEE is already being restructured to act more as an Office for Supervision and Technical Educational Assistance.

Lessons Drawn from the Dialogue

What is interesting about the dialogue just described is the fact that it is one that cannot be described as exclusively bottom-up or top-down: it is in fact a mixture of both. The strength of the dialogue stems from the fact that it occurred at all levels at once—at the grassroots level, at the institutional and intermediary level, and also at the policy and political level.

Another interesting dimension of this particular dialogue is the fact that it took place over a long span of time. What makes it even more special is the fact that while newcomers joined the dialogue, a significant group of core leaders initiated it and stayed with it over time. Critical policymakers and leaders such as the Minister of Education gave the dialogue continuity, and the resultant changes and evolution have been visible. Leaders from the community-school initiative have also been part of the process over time, which has allowed for the main actors in the dialogue to nurture the process and ensure it does not come to an end.

The dialogue has also tackled a wide range of possibilities—from classroom improvement to curriculum development, assessment methodologies, commu-nity participation, and finally, to management styles and governance. It has therefore approached educational reform through a multiplicity of entry points substantiated by both local and international examples.

Finally a truly critical characteristic of the dialogue is the fact that it was based on and informed by theoretical modeling. A 'seedbed' model (see page 147) was firmly established as the dialogue began and continued to evolve and improve as the dialogue developed in all kinds of directions.

I believe that it is all the above-mentioned characteristics that have given the reform dialogue strength, opened doors to change, and created a reform environment. Change and reform must occur through 'multiple stream' models and not 'stage' models, where a sequence of activities leads to change. These are streams whereby people identify problems, seek solutions, create a receptive environment, and work closely together. Meanwhile the entry point of change and reform can be anywhere as long as it is facilitated to reach everywhere through advocacy, analysis, information, and commitment.

The Political Economy of Educational Reform

In this section I will be examining the political economy of reform in Egypt. The players in the political economy of educational reform are many and varied. They include teachers, politicians, bureaucrats and civil servants, textbook manufacturers, technology brokers or salesmen, businessmen, families and communities, the economy at large and the way it is organized, and the different cultures and ideologies within which the players operate.

In most countries in the world, the general constraints that have obstructed the scaling of reform conditions for the furthering of innovation and change have been:

- Widespread knowledge gaps. These appear both on the side of the general public, and with educators and bureaucrats working in the education sector with regard to quality education, the way people learn, and the nature of educational reform.
- Conservative modes of thought. These, too, stand in the way of educational reform. Parents and educators tend to want to stick to how things were always done. Policymakers tend to prefer piecemeal solutions to counteract crisis situations as opposed to adopting whole new visions.
- Rigid laws, statutes, bureaucratic rules and regulations, and union contracts. All these will impede change.
- Bureaucratic inertia and reform fatigue. These often make it very difficult for motivation to be sustained and become system-wide.
- Governance arrangements. In certain systems these appear to be so authoritarian leaving very little space to teachers in classrooms to individualize the curriculum or make meaningful decisions in the classroom. All decisions at all levels are highly centralized.
- The absence of clear and high academic standards along with assessment systems that are owned at the local and decentralized levels. These are the

kind of systems and mechanisms that would allow schools to be accountable and know exactly what they want to achieve and how much of the objectives defined they are achieving. Moreover these systems and mechanisms need to be accompanied by incentives and normative structures that reward innovative high-standard achievements by both student-learners and teacher-learners. In many systems, in fact, it is lethargy and inertia that are rewarded, while innovation is often times penalized.[173]

Moreover in the neo-liberal globalized context of today, the role of states is rapidly changing. Centralized states are encouraged to relax their control of market economies, and areas of dominance overlap between state and civil society in many instances.

Effective schools are one arena where state and community clearly come together in the same political space. The state in its centralized and decentralized structures affects the operation of schools. Communities, parents and pupils also maneuver and affect the way a school is run.[174]

States, whether strong or weak, are not homogenous entities. They carry within them forces of both progression and regression and embody different factions that represent dissimilar interests,which in turn may form alliances with varying segments of the broader society. Fostering the appropriate alliances for change and reform is not only an art but also a prerequisite for sustained reform movements. The choice is no longer one between a top-down approach or a bottom-up approach, but between striking the right alliances and coalitions for change or not. These coalitions and alliances cut across all levels.

In the current age of globalization, transnational alliances are often particularly effective. Movements can no longer be confined to national boundaries and in fact should not be, nor should they necessarily be confined to the grassroots level. Partnerships with factions of the state are sources of strength given the greater space awarded to civil society, and hence the new roles and boundaries assigned to them.

The silent conspiracy emerging among those willing change, educational reform, and progress toward human development can become that much more potent when it speaks with a global voice. Just as the forces of national regression and repression seek exogenous external allies and protection to maintain and sustain the unjust status quo described in chapter one, so must forces of change, development and progress seek allies to break a number of vicious cycles obstructing human development.

What is at stake in educational reform is much more expansive than just the improvement of the quality of learning. Educational reform has strong political, economic, and social implications, and the most significant guarantees that any change is moving in the right direction are popular participation and consultation in the formulation of policy and experimentation.

The essence of educational reform is not so much to replicate in detail the various successful pockets of innovation, but to spread those core components and conditions that allow, promote, encourage, and reward innovation. What is at stake here is the need to restructure the rules, organizations, and relationships that govern educational sectors. Widespread educational reform is not just about the acquisition of new technologies and techniques of teaching, but all the political, economic, and social transformations that go with that. For example, it is not just about equipping teachers with new skills, but also giving them the necessary space, freedom, and incentives to actually employ those new techniques and create new ones all the time. Reform is by its very nature a never-ending process in education, as we are indeed in the business of life-long learning. It has everything to do in fact with instilling and spreading a culture of innovation, knowledge, freedom, and creativity.

In Egypt for some time there has been a mix of all of the above-mentioned impediments to change, alongside growing forces for change and reform, operating in those spaces in which innovation and democracy may take place. The momentum for educational reform in Egypt took on a very serious dimension in the early1990s. The third five-year plan (1992/93–1996/7) clearly reflects the concerns for education. The plan states that, "education is no longer seen as an ordinary service, for it has a critical role in ensuring progress and national security." It further suggests that "the state should give top priority to education in working out the coming five-year plan."[175]

Recognition of a sector in crisis has been expressed at the highest level of the political system. During a meeting of the people's assembly and Shura Council on November 14,1991, President Mubarak said, "We've to be frank with ourselves concerning the crises that education in Egypt is facing today. It is reflected by the school, the teacher, the student and the curriculum. Though it exhausts the resources of the state and the family, the final output is feeble and humble."[176] Education was earmarked as the foundation for national security, and the 1990s as the decade for educational reform and the eradication of illiteracy. In 1993, the President said there was a need for "comprehensive reform of the educational system at all levels and stages in order to cope with a new epoch that depends on the continuity of information and the efficiency of using and investing this information to serve the society."[177] Another presidential quote emphasizes the links between education and development: "Updating education is our access to the New World map. Education is the major pillar for our national security on a broad scale and comprehensive view and also our economy, our policy and our cultural role for interior stability, prosperity and development. It is our way to world competition in interior and exterior markets."[178]

The third five-year plan purported to focus on education for all with an emphasis on basic education; improving educational quality with emphasis on those sciences with the greatest impact on future development; expansion and upgrading of technical education; the teacher; and educational administration. It highlighted in more detail some of the areas of concern and pledged to promote educational democracy through:

1. Achieving Universal Basic Education, UBE, and reducing dropout rates and wastage (repeated years or underperformance).
2. Improving the quality of both education and the graduates.
3. Providing educational services in all the governorates.
4. Collaborating with the General Authority for the Eradication of Illiteracy and Adult Education to put an end to illiteracy.
5. Ensuring educational democracy and equity and closely supervising private schools.
6. Allowing for the development of the full potential of all students while giving special attention to the talented and disabled children.
7. Combating private lessons.[179]

A clear delineation of problems was made early on and at the highest political level. The public reiterated the problems and issues on endless occasions. The media has been replete with debates on components of the reform such as the status and performance of teachers, the prevalence of private tutoring, violence in schools, the relevance of curriculum, and the adequacy and authenticity of assessment systems.

Popular and political demand for reform is certainly secured as one of the major prerequisites for sustainable educational reform. The visions are also articulated extremely well in some instances and at certain levels,[180] but are not clear at certain other levels. Knowledge is still lacking on both the demand (students and teachers) and supply (governmental) levels.

Against a background of pervasive educational crises during the 1980s, punctuated by low and declining investments, a dilapidated infrastructure and a heavy brain drain of educational personnel,[181] educational reform in the nineties managed some outstanding achievements. Investments in education have steadily increased reaching L.E. 22 billion in 2002. Education's share in the government budget reached a high of 20 percent in that same year.[182] The number of schools has increased phenomenally. In one decade 12,350 schools were built. In 2003 the number of schools built in eleven years amounted to 13,163 schools.[183] Enrollment at the pre-university stage including pre-primary, primary, preparatory, and secondary levels increased from 12.1 million in 1991–92 to 15.4 million in 2001–02.[184] Enrollment in primary education alone increased by 19.68 percent, from 1992–93 to 2002–03.[185] By 2002, the pre-university education system in Egypt consisted of thirty-five thousand schools, eight hundred thousand teachers and 15 million students. Egypt in fact has the largest educational system to manage in comparison with Africa and other Arab countries.[186] The gender gap decreased from 8 percent to 3 percent. Egypt won many awards regarding the numbers of learners whose illiteracy was eradicated during that decade. Impressive strides were made in the area of technology and its expansion. An expanded program of in-service teacher training began in 1993/4, which aimed at improving learning processes and introducing interactive pedagogical approaches. Many teachers and middle-range policy makers have been sent for exposure to first world countries. Between 1993/94–2003, a total of 9806 teachers, supervisors and school principles were sent abroad for training.[187]

The learning content has witnessed considerable progress as earlier mentioned. A specialized CCIMD was established in the early 1990s after which the curriculum was completely revised and new textbooks and teachers' manuals were developed, tested and published. Moreover new issues were introduced in the curriculum such as human and child rights, globalization, tolerance and education for peace, life skills, education for citizenship, health, and the environment. Supplementary educational materials were also produced through multi-media channels. The curriculum center in partnership with the community-school initiative produced activity-based learning materials, which will be mainstreamed. These aim at promoting critical and creative thinking, problem solving, cooperative and individualized learning.[188]

In 1996 an international team representing UNESCO and UNDP conducted a sector wide evaluation of the educational system in Egypt. The outcome indicated that a reform environment was gradually being put in place:

By all standards, the initial phase of the basic education reform in Egypt (1991–1996) has been successful. Actions taken have created the dynamism for a sustainable and long lasting reform process. Political commitment, public responsibility, and broad-based partnership of major stakeholders and reform actors are present. The establishment of a conducive reform climate with nation-wide consultations through conferences, seminars and work-shops on major initiatives of the reform was vital and decisive. National centers and implementation agencies at central, governorate and district level were set-up to support and service the reform process. Resources were mobilized (local and external) to assure the quantitative growth and qualitative improvement of basic education.[189]

The content of the report then goes on to show how some of the space-clearing and space-filling activities were beginning to be put in place, examples of which include the acceptance of initiatives such as the community schools to support the one-classroom school initiative. Space clearing refers to the ways in which an environment conducive to reform is generated. This takes in policy dialogue, legal changes, lobbying, networking, and coalitions. Space filling, on the other hand, is about promoting large-scale on-site school management and classroom reform, and making them mainstream. Other examples were increased qualified teachers, revision of curriculum, expansion of a national technology program, initiating new assessment procedures, and finally establishing structures and committees to effect future collaboration and institutionalize the reform.

Generally the prognosis for reform was good. The report however ended with more challenges to be tackled on the qualitative side. Seven years later an almost identical UNESCO mission returned to observe the progress in reform and remarked, "The vision of the Egyptian educational reform has become a reality. The emphasis is now turning to how to improve its quality, relevance and efficiency. This may require structural, procedural and management mechanisms that are somewhat different from those in place during the initial stages of the reform. This is the basic challenge for the coming decade: how to continue to develop an educational management system that continually adapts to a revitalized and continually improving education reform process."[190]

Although some of the reform infrastructure is there, and the political discourse reflects great commitment, there is enough evidence to show that the challenges are still quite big with regard to bringing the learning paradigms earlier described in the first chapter and all along the rest of the book, to the majority of classes in schools. Ethnographic studies have shown how school and classroom cultures can be oppressive. The studies also show that although education is a national priority and fares very high on the country's development and security priorities, educators do not. Teachers and other educators, in those studies, either become powerless state employees or profiteers who are making money through illegal channels and thus deeply hurting the status and profession of teaching.[191]

It is clear from the public debate and also from attempts at implementation that there are clear forces of resistance to change. Moreover the political debate between the various parties also portrays a debate at a different level, namely one between the privatization of education and market needs on the one hand, and equity, social justice, and state responsibility on the other hand.

Political parties have been consulted on matters of education and have been actively engaged in the debate. In the summer of 2002 the Minister of Education visited the opposition Tagammu' Party mainly a leftist party, to hear out their concerns on Egypt's educational strategies and practices. The discussion was extremely democratic, animated and controversial. Many of the points raised by the education committee in the party coincided with the Minister's vision. At the end of a very long-winded debate and heated session, the Minister of Education presented the education platform of action, which was largely based on the principles of social justice, participation, democracy, active learning, authentic assessment, teacher education and relevant curriculum. He elicited the help of the party to educate the public on innovative thinking and to spearhead what some in the audience defined as the need for a 'Cultural Revolution,' whereby values need to be revisited and enhanced to support the reform movement. It was clear from the discussion that culture and ideology had a real role to play in supporting reform.

Recently the ruling National political party has gone through a process of expansive consultations to produce an innovative and daring vision for educational reform. Many stakeholders and party members have been engaged in the process. The outcome of the consultations has been written up in a document which is being presented for voting and consensus building to six thousand party members in the presence of the president and prime minister of the country. The document represents a strong demand for reform through decentralization. It considers the classroom and school as the main arena for implementation. It set up guidelines for decentralized management. It also calls for community participation and the fostering of strong partnerships between the state and civil society. The document very critically analyzed the constraints and challenges in the educational sector and came up with key reform strategies which includes teacher education, curriculum relevance, revisiting examination and assessment systems, and finally, establishing accreditation systems of international standards that can match the international market competition and that also makes room for a strong private sector role.

The broad consultative processes defined above will further enhance the creation of a reform environment and will strengthen the possibilities of building alliances and coalitions that can support the reform process. Meanwhile a number of critical structures have been established as the beginnings of building a true reform support infrastructure, which promise to further broaden the democratic and participatory base.

To counteract the obstructions and complexities of educational reform a number of requirements and strategies need to be in place. Reform does not just happen nor do initiatives automatically grow and replicate themselves in the absence of a favorable reform environment. There must first of all be a clear recognition of a problem, which manifests itself in the dissatisfaction of people with current educational practices.

There is a need therefore for agents of change and permanent political salespersons and/or what some have called 'sellers of education reform' to facilitate the process.

Hence a reform environment and infrastructure is created when techniques, institutions, and mechanisms are established to:

1. Generate widespread demand for reform.
2. Facilitate decentralized discussions and consultations over the profile and substance of that reform.
3. Create a policy environment that is friendly to change.
4. Ensure that learning and change are on-going activities.
5. Establish a reform support infrastructure, which refers to organized networks of individuals, institutions, and organizations working together to effect widespread, ongoing, learning-driven reform. It is this coordinated effort that creates the infrastructure of reform that allows for space clearing and space filling.

The mechanisms and techniques normally employed to bring about an educational reform support infrastructure are grouped into four components:

1. Data and information, which usually involves Education Management Information Systems (EMIS) for accountability and dialogue, in addition to research, censuses, and needs assessments, the results of which are used for analysis and public discussions, and finally meetings and discussions for political mapping and policy making.
2. Analytical approaches which are mostly sector analyses for internal and external efficiency, budgeting and financial analyses, school funding, simulation, projection and planning models, analyses of salary scales and cost implications, and finally, analyses of governance options.
3. Communication strategies, which focus on policy dialogue, policy mar-

keting, social marketing, advocacy, negotiation and mediation, public communication campaigns, and political-economic discourse.

4. Institutional development and capacity building for analyses, communications and advocacy, which will involve networking, building of coalitions, funding of advocacy groups, and strategic planning for public sector and non-governmental organizations (NGOs) in policy development and policy advocacy, in addition to environmental mapping, organizational capacity building and technology transfer.

All the above does not necessarily happen in the most organized of ways, nor is it an easy and uniformly successful pathway. However, the chances of success are vastly increased when a sufficient number of credible institutions are involved in policy issues in the sector, and when NGOs are engaged in the dialogue and supported by an umbrella organization and/or a collaborative structure of some kind.[192] This is gradually happening in Egypt despite the continuing contradictions and struggles between forces of resistance and change.

Although I am tempted to leave the reader on this optimistic note of a good prognosis for change, some cautionary remarks are in place in the end. Yes, the reform is in motion but it will require a great deal to sustain it and to continue to direct it in those ways delineated through out this work. Some of the risk factors are reform fatigue, serious knowledge gaps and political interests.

One important way to counteract these risk factors is to continue the national dialogue and campaign on educational reform, and to continue to enlarge the democratic spaces for the dialogue. A multi-layered media strategy for knowledge and consensus-building on the components of quality learning would undoubtedly raise an informed demand for reform. A campaign, 'a la Cardozo'[193] in Brazil would certainly sustain the reform momentum. The campaign called 'Awaken Brazil, it is time for school,' mobilized society at large to support educational reform in the 1990s. The results with many segments of society were outstanding. A social communication plan was designed to inform all citizens of their rights and obligations to quality learning. Demand was on the rise and a toll-free telephone line called 'Speak Brazil' was set up so that people could register their views. Hearts and minds were won over to the cause of education through journalism, advertising, and good media programs.

A similarly vast campaign is needed in Egypt for education and mobilization. Informed policy debates should be presented to the public to draw more participation. Meanwhile best practices in classrooms, and teachers' and children's views should be captured by the media and introduced into people's homes. Positive deviant behavior[194] should be glorified and better understood, and bad practices such as private tutoring and violence in schools vehemently fought through diversified media strategies. Viewers and media audiences should be treated respectfully, as learners capable of absorbing advanced knowledge and innovative ideas. Educational reform is everyone's business provided it is truly led by children—the learners for whom it is intended.

The stage must be set for some deep-seated structural and relational transformations in the classroom, but only as a reflection of the society at large. Teachers and educators need enhancement programs to allow them to have a voice, and to live respectful, honest, and professionally productive lives. Oppressive relations between teachers and students must be reversed as a prerequisite for all other relations in society. There is a clear need to empower both the educator and the learner for the pedagogy of the empowered, as described throughout this book, to prevail.

Conclusion

In this last chapter I have narrated the story of the dialogue between the community-school initiative and a vast array of critical players in the Egyptian educational reform endeavor. What I have shown is that, despite the many prevalent theories of reform and the literature pointing to the linearity of the movement, the case in Egypt demonstrates that the process of reform can start in the most unpredictable and chaotic of ways. Dialogue can precede structural changes, and reform environments can emerge in ways that are not willed or terribly systematic and strategically planned for. Moreover, the dialogue can begin in any part of the organic system and end up affecting all other parts of it. When movements that allow a voice for people begin, they tend to have a ripple effect that empowers more people than just the direct actors. Like a great windstorm, the reform travels a long way and unfolds over time in a never ending fashion.

Finally, the situation in Egypt as in many other parts of the world, calls for a disaggregated and analytical approach to political blocs and groups, which can lead to alliances between the unlikeliest of partners. Governments and most political blocs are not homogenous: there are factions within these blocs willing to ally themselves with the forces of change and to help in creating an institutional environment conducive to reform and change. It is only through strong alliances across different levels and borders that movements can take off and gain energy. The spaces for a democratic dialogue expand, and the pedagogy of empowerment gets underway.

Notes

1 'Iterative Incremental Development' is a mathematical term used by software engineers, and increasingly by management experts, to describe a process of development that does not simply mean re-work or repetition, but evolutionary advancement. The basic idea behind iterative development is to develop a system incrementally, allowing the developer to take advantage of what was being learned during the development of earlier, incremental, workable versions of the system.

2 Jacques Delors et al, *Learning: The Treasures Within: Report to UNESCO of the International Commission on Education for the Twenty-first Century* (Paris, UNESCO, 1996).

3 The four pillars of learning being: Learning to know, Learning to do, Learning to work together, and Learning to be.

4 Sheldon Shaeffer et al, "The Global Agenda for Children: Learning," paper presented at the ninth UNICEF Innocenti Global Seminar: Basic Education: A Vision for the 21ˢᵗ Century, Florence, Oct–Nov 1998.

5 See statement by Carol Bellamy, Executive Director, UNICEF, at the opening of the first regular session of the UNICEF Executive Board, New York, 26 January 1998.

6 UNICEF, *A New Global Agenda for* Children (New York, UNICEF, August 2000).

7 UN, *The Copenhagen Declaration and Programme of Action, World Summit for Social Development, United Nations* (New York, UN, 1995), 5–8.

8 UNDP, *Arab Human Development Report* (New York, UNDP, 2002).

9 UNICEF, "Medium-term Strategic Plan for the Period 2002–2005," unpublished internal document, October 2001.

10 Joseph Kahne, *Reframing Educational Policy: Democracy, Community and the Individual* (New York, Teachers College Press, 1996), 1–34.

11 *Ibid.,* 43.

12 The external component of which would include democratic behavior, i.e., preparing individuals and communities to live in a democratic environment.

13 *Ibid.,* 153.

14 http://www.alternativeeducationindra.com/transform/dlc

15 The Global Alliance for Transforming Education was established in 1991 and includes such organizations as the Northwest Regional Facilitators and the New Road Map Foundation, Washington University. Their role is to create a forum for dialogue through the worldwide web and other Information Technology forums. The subject of the dialogue is how to attach new meaning to one's existence and reform eduation. See Carol Flake, *Holistic Education: Principles, Perspectives, Practices* (Brandon, VT, Holistic Education Press, 1993).

16 http://www.resilientcommunities.org

17 F. Henry Healey and Joseph DeStefano, "Educational Reform Support: A Framework for Scaling up School Reform" (Research Triangle Institute and Academy for Educational Development, June 1997), 13.

18   See, R. G. Paultson, "On the Limits of Educational Alternatives Seeking
     Individual and Social Change" in R. G. Paultson, *Other Dreams, Other Schools:
     Folk Colleges in Social and Ethnic Movements* (Pittsburgh, University Center For
     International Studies, University of Pittsburgh, 1980), 156–268.

19   Ralph Turner and Lewis Killian, *Collective Behavior* (Englewood Cliffs, NJ,
     Prentice-Hall, 1957), 308.

20   Jack Levin and James Spates, *Starting Sociology* (New York, Harper and Row
     Publishers, 1976), 223–53.

21   Kenneth M. Roberts, "Beyond Romanticism: Social Movements and the Study of
     Political Change in Latin America," *Latin American Research Review*, 32: 2
     (1997), 138, 139.

22   On the concept of the relative autonomy of the state, see N.Poulantzas, *Classes in
     Contemporary Capitalism* (London, Verso Publications, 1978), 165–89.

23   Michael Kaufman, "Community Power, Grassroots Democracy, and the
     Transformation of Social life," in Michael Kaufman and Heraldo Dilla Alfonso
     (eds.), *Community Power and Grassroots Democracy* (London, Zed Books, 1997),
     1–3.

24   Dependency theory emerged in Latin America in the late 1960s and early 1970s
     as a political economy approach to the histories of the Third World and an alter-
     native to the classical economic theories propounded by Adam Smith and others.
     It used historical analysis to show how the countries of the Third World had
     become dependent on those of the First.

25   Eduardo Canel, "New Social Movement Theory and Resource Mobilization
     Theory: The Need for Integration," in Kaufman and Alfonso (eds.), *Community
     Power*, 189–90.

26   *Ibid.*, 191.

27   *Ibid.*, 196–98.

28   R. G. Paulston and D. Lejeune, "A Methodology for Studying Education in
     Social Movements," in Paulston (ed.), *Other Dreams, Other Schools*, 26–33.

29   *Ibid.*, 35–45.

30   D. C. Davis, "An Argument for Humanistic Education and Ethnic Revival," in
     Paultson (ed.), *Other Dreams, Other Schools*, 251.

31   Paultson, "On the Limits of Educational Alternatives," 268.

32   Andy Hargreaves, *Changing Teachers, Changing Times: Teachers' Work and Culture
     in the Postmodern Age* (London, Cassell, 1996), 3–9.

33   Daniel Keating, "Habits of Mind for a Learning Society: Educating for Human
     Development," in David R. Olson and Nancy Torrance (eds.), *The Handbook of
     Education and Human Development: New Models of Learning, Teaching and
     Schooling* (Oxford, Blackwell Publishers, 1996), 462–81.

34   Renate Nummela Caine and Geoffry Caine, *Unleashing the Power of Perceptual
     Change* (Alexandria, VA, ASCD, 1997), 5.

35   *Ibid.*, 6

36   See J. Madeleine Nash, "Fertile Minds," in *Time*, February 24, 1997, 29–36;
     Sharon Begley, "Your Child's Brain," in *Newsweek*, February 19, 1996, 43–46;
     Lynnell Hancock, "Why Do Schools Flunk Biology?" in *Newsweek*, February 19,
     1996, 46–48.

37 Janet Wilde Astington and Janette Pelletier, "The Language of the Mind," in Olson and Torrance (eds.), *Handbook of Education*, 608.

38 Robbie Case, "Changing Views of Knowledge and their Impact on Educational Research and Practice," in Olson and Torrance (eds.), *Handbook of Education*, 82.

39 Keating, "Habits of Mind for a Learning Society," 470.

40 Rosa Maria Torres, "Learning: 12 Common Assumptions," presentation made at the ninth UNICEF Innocenti Global Seminar: Basic Education: A Vision for the 21st Century, Florence, Oct–Nov 1998.

41 Socio-cognitive theories are ones that recognize the importance of social factors as pupils learn.

42 'Multiple intelligences' was a term coined by Howard Gardner who argued that people did not have one type of intelligence, measurable by IQ tests alone, but several types, including emotional, logical, linguistic, spatial, musical, social (intra-personal), reflective (introspective) intelligences, and so on. See Howard Gardner, *Frames of Mind: The Theory of Multiple Intelligences* (New York, Basic Books, 1983).

43 Caine and Caine, *Unleashing the Power*, 26–28.

44 Daniel Goleman, *Emotional Intelligence* (New York, Bantam Books, 1997), 224.

45 *Ibid.*, 21.

46 Carol Flake, *Holistic Education: Principles, Perspectives and Practices*, http://www.great-ideas.org

47 Caine and Caine, *Unleashing the Power*, 77, 85, 92, 96, 97, 101, 104.

48 Barbara Rugoff, Eugene Matusov, Cynthia White, "Models of Teaching and Learning: Participation in a Community of Learners," in Olson and Torrance (eds.), *Handbook of Education*, 388, 391, 396, 398, 399.

49 Sheldon Shaeffer, *Participation for Educational Change: A Synthesis of Experience* (UNESCO International Institute for Educational Planning (IIEP), 1994).

50 Carl Bereiter and Marlene Scardmalia, "The Language and Culture of Schooling," in Olson and Torrance (eds.), *Handbook of Education*, 491.

51 David Wood, *How Children Think and Learn* (Oxford, Blackwell Publishers, 1997), 140–46 and 147–65.

52 Bereiter and Scardamalia, "Language and Culture of Schooling," 493.

53 Goleman, *Emotional Intelligence*, 279.

54 Brahma Kumaris, *Living Values: A Guide Book* (New York, Brahma Kumaris Office of the United Nations, 1995).

55 Rachael Kessler, *The Soul of Education* (Alexandria, VA, ASCD, 2000), 17–35.

56 Waterloo Region Roman Catholic Separate School Board, "Teaching Tomorrow's Thinkers," Ontario, 1992; Robert Marzano and others, *Dimensions of Thinking: A Framework for Curriculum and Instruction* (Alexandria, VA, ASCD, 1998).

57 Vinayagum Chinapah, *Handbook on Monitoring Learning Achievement* (Paris, UNESCO, 1997), 26–28.

58 Amaya Gillespie, Draft Concept Paper on Life Skills, UNICEF Education Cluster, New York, 1999.

59 Gill Nicholls, *Learning to Teach* (London, Kogan, 1999), 85–115.

60 Michael Connelly and Jean Clandinin, *Teachers as Curriculum Planners: Narratives of Experience* (New York, Teacher's College Press, 1988), 3–10.

61 See, Heldi Hays Jacobs (ed.), *Interdisciplinary Curriculum: Design and Implementation* (Alexandria, VA, ASCD, 1989); Marzano and others, *Dimensions of Thinking*; L. B. Resnick and L. E. Klopfer (eds.), *Toward the Thinking Curriculum: Current Cognitive Research* (Alexandria, VA, ASCD, 1989); G. Zindovic-Vukadinovic and S. Krnjajic (eds.), *Towards a Modern Learner-Centered Curriculum* (Belgrade, Institute for Educational Research, 1996).

62 See Joan Herman, Pamela Aschbacher, and Lynn Winters, *A Practical Guide to Alternative Assessment* (Alexandria, VA, ASCD, 1992); Marion Cross, *How to's in Getting Started with Assessment and Evaluation using Portfolios* (Ontario, Exclusive Educational Products, 1995); Carol Rolheiser (ed.), *Self-evaluation: Helping Students Get Better At It* (Australia, Clear Group, 1996).

63 David Johnson, R. Johnson, and Edythe Johnson Holubec, *The New Circles of Learning: Cooperation in the Classroom and School* (Virginia, ASCD, 1994), 76–105.

64 Margret Wheatley and Myron Kellner-Rogers, *A Simpler Way* (California, Berrett-Koehler Publishers, 1996), 3, 13, 14.

65 Bruce Joyce, James Wolf, and Emily Calhoun, *The Self-Renewing School* (Alexandria, VA, ASCD, 1993), 3–38.

66 *Ibid.*

67 Stephen J. Ball, "Better Read: Theorizing the Teacher," in Justin Dillon and Meg Maguire (eds.), *Becoming a Teacher* (UK, Open University Press, 1997), 247–48.

68 *Ibid.*, 155, 156.

69 Ira Shor and Paulo Freire, *A Pedagogy for Liberation: Dialogues on Transforming Education* (South Hadley, MA, Bergin and Garvey Publishers, 1987), 33 and 35.

70 *Ibid.*, 36–38.

71 Ronald G. Sultana, "Social Movements and the Transformation of Teachers' Work: Case Studies from New Zealand," in *Research Papers in Education*, 6: 2 (1991), 133–52.

72 Roger Simon, *Gramsci's Political Thought: An Introduction* (London, Lawrence and Wishart, 1982), 26, 86, 101, 104, 131.

73 Peter Mayo, *Gramsci, Freire and Adult Education: Possibilities for Transformative Action* (London, Zed Books, 1999), 132–51, 155–64.

74 Michael Edwards and John Gaventa (eds.), *Global Citizen Action* (Boulder, CO, Lynne Reinner Publishers, 2001).

75 Adrian Thatcher, "Learning to Become Persons? – Three Approaches Examined," *British Journal of Educational Studies*, 35: 3 (October 1987), 248–59.

76 Brian K. Murphy, *Transforming Ourselves, Transforming the World: An Open Conspiracy for Social Change* (London, Zed Books, 1999).

77 See Francis Fukuyama, *Trust: The Social Virtues and the Creation of Prosperity* (New York, Free Press, 1996).

78 Beryl Nicholson, "Personal Histories and Social Restructuring: The Transformation of a Peasant Society," in *Sociological Review*, 44: 1 (1996), 35–52.

79 Maggie Black, *Basic Education: A Vision for the 21ˢᵗ Century, Summary Report* (Florence, Italy, UNICEF International Child Development Centre, 1999), 5.

80 See, Amir Boktor, *School and Society in the Valley of the Nile* (Cairo, Elias Modern Press, 1936), 113–122; Hussein Kamel Bahaa El Din, *Education and the Future*

(Kalyub, Egypt, al-Ahram Commercial Press, 1997); Judith Tucker, *Women in Nineteenth-Century Egypt* (Cambridge, Cambridge University Press, 1985).

81 Institute of National Planning, *Egypt Human Development Report 1998/99* (Kalyub, Egypt, al-Ahram Commercial Press, 2000), 76–79.

82 Nader Fergany, *A Preliminary Map of the Efforts Needed to Abolish Enrollment Disparity in Primary Education According to Gender* (Cairo, UNICEF, March 1995).

83 Arab Republic of Egypt, MOE, *Mubarak and Education: The National Project for Educational Reform* (Cairo, Rose al-Youssef, 1999), 11.

84 Nader Fergany, *Survey of Access to Primary Education and Acquisition of Basic Literacy Skills in Three Governorates in Egypt* (Cairo, UNICEF, 1994).

85 Mamduh Abd al-Rahman al-Riti, *Dur al-qaba'il al-'arabiya fi sa'id Misr* (Cairo, Madbouli, 1998).

86 Magdi Abd al-Rashid Bahr, *al-Qarya al-misriya fi 'asr al-salatin al-mamalik* (Cairo, al-Hay'a al-Misriya al-'Amma li-l-Kitab, 1999), 229–32, 258–63.

87 The Hawara rule spanned Abnub, Abu Maqruna, Abu Tig, Akhmim, al-'Anbariya, Ard al-Munqiziya, Asyut, Awlad Mamen, Awlad Shalul Kharfa, Awlad Tuq al-Bahary, Bahgura, Bani Jamila, Bani Warkan, Bardis, Bayada, Ballas, Edfu, Farshut, Faw, Gizirat Garagus, Garf Abu Amira, Haragya, al-Naqawa, Nikhila, Samhud, Sanabsa, Shandawil, Sharq al-Marg, al-Qabiba Qibli, Tahta, Tukh.

88 'Ali Mubarak, *al-Khitat al-tawfiqiya li-Misr al-qahira wa muduniha wa quraha*, primary manuscript source, Part 10, (Bulaq, Egypt, 'Amiriya Publications, A.H. 1305/A.D. 1885), 53.

89 *Ibid.*

90 *Ibid.*, Part 13, 51–60.

91 For a history of the South see Leila Abd al-Latif Ahmed, *al-Sa'id fi 'ahd shaykh al-'arab Hammam* (Cairo, al-Hay'a al-Misriya al-'Amma li-l-Kitab, 1987); 'Ali Barakat, *Ru'yat 'Ali Mubarak li-tarikh Misr al-ijtima'i* (Egypt, al-Ahram Strategic Center, 1982); and Ali Barakat, *Ru'yat al-Jabarti li-ba'd qadaya 'asruh* (Cairo, al-Hay'a al-Misriya al-'Amma li-l-Kitab, 1997).

92 For references on community education see, UNICEF, Community Schools: Report, Recommendations and Papers of a Seminar held in the United Republic of Tanzania, 22–29 August, 1980; John Allen, *Some Operational Issues Relating to Community Participation*, A discussion paper, UNESCO–UNICEF cooperative program, 1982; Father Gerry Pantin, *The Mobilization of Grassroots Communities: The Experience of Servol* (UNICEF, UNESCO and World Bank, 1984); Robert Biak Cin and Guy B. Scandlen, *Loving Kindness and the Five Gratitudes: Burmese Cultural Values Underlying Community Participation in Primary School Improvement* (Rangoon, UNICEF, 1986); and Ernesto Schiefelbein, *In Search of the XXI century: Is the Colombian Escuela Nueva the Right Pathfinder?* (UNESCO/UNICEF, Santiago, Chile, 1991); Sheldon Shaeffer (ed.), *Collaboration for Educational Change: The Role of Teachers, Parents and the Community in School Improvement* (Paris, IIEP, 1992); George Psacharopoulos, Carlos Rojas, and Eduardo Velez, *Achievement Evaluation of Columbia's Escuela Nueva: Is Multigrade the Answer?* (Washington D.C., World Bank, 1992); "Community-State Relationships in Africa: Case Studies on Community

Education in Africa," in AALAE Journal, 6: 2 (1992); Donatus Komba and Fulgens L. Mbunda in *The Community School and Education For All: Review of Experiences from Tanzania* (New York, UNICEF, 1993); and Cynthia Guttman, *Tous les Enfants Peuvent Apprendre, Le Programme des 900 Ecoles Pour les Deserites du Chili* (Paris, L'Education Pour Tous, UNESCO, 1993); Jean-Pierre Velis, *Blazing The Trail*, UNESCO/UNICEF Innovation series no. 4 (Paris, 1994); Malak Zaalouk, *The Children of the Nile: The Community Schools Project in Upper Egypt*, UNESCO/UNICEF Innovations series no. 9, (Paris, 1995); Cynthia Guttmen, *Voices Across the Hill: Thailand's Education Project*, UNESCO/UNICEF Innovation series, no. 7 (Paris, 1995); Andrea Rugh and Heather Bossert, *Involving Communities: Participation in the Delivery of Education Programs* (Washington D.C., Creative Associates International, 1998).

93 It is worth mentioning here that prior to and during the inauguration of the schools, parents and community members were given a full orientation on the methodology of learning in the schools and were invited to participate in and watch their children perform.

94 It is common practice in rural Egypt for ballot boxes to be placed in schools, where all citizens go to register and cast their votes.

95 An environmentally friendly technique of transforming animal dung into energy and fertilizers.

96 The "whole child" is a frequently used term in the literature of child rights, which takes a holistic approach to a child's needs. The term covers every aspect of a child's life—nutrition, hygiene, social and pyschological aspects, and so on.

97 Colombia's *Escuela Nueva* ('The New School') was a model of rural education created in 1974. It drew from and combined various features of progressive education theory and practice. In 1985 the Colombian government adopted *Escuela Nueva* as a national policy for rural primary schools. *Escuela Nueva* differs from traditional schools in several ways: it is multi-grade; uses special instructional materials; the curriculum is rural oriented; specially trained teachers are required; learning corners and small libraries are established; teachers, students, and the community all become active participants in the school; and a student government is formed. It is still considered one of the best models of its kind.

98 Shor and Freire, *Pedagogy for Liberation*, 35.

99 *Ibid.*, 33–38.

100 MOE, UNICEF and USAID, "Evaluation of Egypt's Community School Project," unpublished report, July 1995, 16.

101 *Ibid.*

102 Project Support Unit, Canadian International Development Agency (PSU/CIDA), "Community Education Project: End of Phase II Evaluation," unpublished report, June 2001, 6.

103 The National Center For Examinations and Educational Evaluation (NCEEE), *Community Schools Evaluation Project* (Cairo, NCEEE, September 2001), 116.

104 MOE, UNICEF and USAID, "Evaluation of Egypt's Community School Project," 15.

105 NCEEE, *Community Schools Evaluation*, 116.

106 Mastery learning is based on the assumption that all children can learn when provided with the appropriate learning conditions in the classroom. It does not focus
on content but on the process of mastering it, and implies a deep, rather than
superficial, understanding and learning of any subject.

107 NCEEE, *Community Schools Evaluation*, 6.

108 *Ibid.*, 123.

109 *Ibid.*, 111–15.

110 All the results were obtained from the district-level education departments in each
of the six districts of Abu Tig, Dar al-Salam, Farshut, Geheina, Manfalut, and
Saqulta. The results are usually stamped by the government and obtained annually.

111 An educational classification system developed in the 1950s by Benjamin Bloom.
It defines six levels of cognitive learning, which, in order of increasing mastery, are:
Knowledge, Comprehension, Application, Analysis, Synthesis, and Evaluation.

112 *Ibid.*, 22 and 23.

113 Barbara Ibrahim et al., *Transitions to Adulthood: A National Survey of Egyptian
Adolescents* (Cairo, Population Council, 2nd edn, January 2000).

114 NCEEE, *Community Schools Evaluation*, 24–30.

115 Nader Fergany, *Survey of Access to Primary Education and Acquisition of Basic
Literacy Skills in Three Governorates in Egypt,* a study commissioned by UNICEF
Cairo (1994), 53.

116 Population Council, *Transitions to Adulthood: A National Survey of Egyptian
Adolescents* (Cairo, Population Council, 2000), and Population Council, *The
School Environment: A Situation Analysis of Public Preparatory Schools in Egypt*
(Cairo, Population Council, 2001).

117 NCEEE, *Community Schools Evaluation*, 111–115.

118 Amina Kazem et al, *Evaluation of Community School Pupils' Learning Achievement
and Acceleration Programs in Asyut* (Cairo, NCEEE, 1998).

119 NCEEE, *Community Schools Evaluation*, 33–52 and 116–21.

120 PSU/CIDA, *End of Phase II Evaluation*, 18.

121 *Ibid.*

122 For further elaboration on this methodology see, Judith Preissle Goetz and
Margaret Diane Le Compte, *Ethnography and Qualitative Design in Educational
Research* (New York, Academic Press,1984).

123 Often a few years are added to the age of girls in some rural aeas to ease early
marriage. This also occurs when the older sister passes away and the younger
child inherits her birth certificate.

124 See Zaalouk, *Children of the Nile*; PSU/CIDA, *End of Phase II Evaluation*, 12.

125 PSU/CIDA, *End of Phase II Evaluation*, 13.

126 *Ibid.*

127 *Ibid.*

128 In-depth interviews conducted with girls from community schools in October
2001.

129 *Ibid.*

130 *Ibid.*,14.

131 Personal observation during field visit in 1993 in the village of Umm al-Kussur,
al-Akarma school.

132 PSU/CIDA, *End of Phase II Evaluation*, 19.

133 Extracts from the report and oral presentation of the two delegations from Yemen in 1997 and 1998 in Manfalut, Asyut. Members of the delegation included Mr. Abd al-Salam from the Office of the then Yemeni Minister of Education, Mr. Mohamed Majid, and Mr. Mohamed al Ghadifi, the deputy director of the Ministry of Education department in Ebb, and many others from different departments, as well as practitioners holding teaching and directing posts in schools.

134 Assessment of children's acquisition of life skills was also tackled by the NCEEE *Community Schools Evaluation Project*, in the section entitled, "Results of Students' Personality Development Checklist"; the results were very positive.

135 MOE/UNICEF, "Community Schools Project: Summary of Field Evaluation: April 1995," unpublished report.

136 PSU/CIDA, *End of Phase II Evaluation*, 13.

137 Essays written upon request of the television and radio station, Arab Radio and Television (ART) for a program called *Pen Pals in Africa*.

138 In-depth interviews conducted with girls from community schools in October 2001.

139 District report from the educational department of Manfalut, June 1994.

140 MOE/UNICEF, *Community School Project, Summary of Field Evaluation: April 1995*.

141 PSU/CIDA, *End of Phase II Evaluation*, 17.

142 This is also supported by *Ibid.*

143 PSU/CIDA, *End of Phase II Evaluation*, 13.

144 Interview conducted by Reda Alam el Din, Senior Field Supervisor, as part of research she conducted in 2002 on the impact of the schools in Manfalut.

145 Zaalouk, *Children of the Nile*, 24.

146 Fatma Qazem, *Impact Study of Women in Two Community School Sites* (Department of Rural Sociology, University of Asyut, 1993).

147 This is an area where more efforts will be made to establish inclusive education firmly and professionally in the initiative. Piloting is underway.

148 See also PSU/CIDA, *End of Phase II Evaluation*, June 2001, 12.

149 *Ibid.*, 17–18

150 Ebba Augustine, *Gender Audit: UNICEF Egypt Country Office* (Cairo, March 2000), 32–33.

151 PSU/CIDA, *End of Phase II Evaluation*, 14.

152 *Ibid.*, 12.

153 Augustine, *Gender Audit*, 33.

154 *Ibid.*

155 Shorouk is a comprehensive area-based rural development program run by the government with possible support from NGOs and donors.

156 A local agricultural bank that loans money to the poor at reduced interest.

157 PSU/CIDA, *End of Phase II Evaluation*, 18.

158 *Ibid.*, 20

159 *Ibid.*

160 Members present were Dr. Gaber abd al hamid, Dr. Kawthar Kochok, Dr. Mostafa Abd al-Samei, and Dr. Mahmoud al-Naqa.

161 PSU/CIDA, *End of Phase II Evaluation*, 22.

162 *Ibid.*, 21.

163 *Ibid.*, 22.

164 *Ibid.*, 21.

165 The National Council For Childhood and Motherhood (NCCM) is a government coordinating body established in 1989. It is chaired by the First Lady of Egypt, Suzanne Mubarak, and was established to ensure the effective application of child rights in Egypt. It is the childhood institution par excellence. It coordinates all the ministries, and although it is not an executive body, it has planning, coordinating, and monitoring powers.

166 *Al-Gumhuriya*, 9 June 2002, 2.

167 Ash Hartwell, "A Review of Egypt's Community School Project," January 1994, unpublished report.

168 MOE, UNICEF, and USAID, *Evaluation of Egypt's Community School Project*, 15.

169 PSU/CIDA, *End of Phase II Evaluation*, 25–34.

170 The unit costs were obtained through detailed research with the MOE and communities.

171 The unit costs were obtained from the MOE, GAEB, and the budget committee that served to calculate unit costs for the planning and budgeting exercise of the Girl's Education Initiative. It must be mentioned that calculations were made with the lower estimates of school buildings and equipment, originally estimated at L.E. 120,000.

172 Arthur MacEwan, *Neo-liberalism or Democracy: Economic Strategy, Markets, and Alternatives for the 21ˢᵗ century* (London, Zed Books, 1999), 13–19.

173 F. Henry Healey and Joseph DeStefano, "Education Reform Support: A Framework for Scaling up School Reform," unpublished document for USAID, June 1997, 15.

174 *Ibid.*, 21.

175 Arab Republic of Egypt, MOE, Central Administration for Educational Planning and Information, *The Third Five Year Plan, 1992/93–1996/97: Objectives and Strategies* (Cairo, 1991), 5.

176 Arab Republic of Egypt, MOE, *Mubarak and Education: The National Project for Developing Education* (Cairo, 1999), 9.

177 *Ibid.*, 7.

178 *Ibid.*, 11.

179 MOE, *Third Five-Year Plan*.

180 See Hussein Kamel Bahaa El Din, *Education and The Future* (Cairo, Dar al-Ma'arif), 1997); Arab Republic of Egypt, MOE, *Mubarak and Education, 20 years of Giving by an Enlightened President, 10 years of Education Development* (Cairo, 2001).

181 See Institute of National Planning (INP), in technical cooperation with UNDP, *Egypt Human Development Report 1998/99* (Egypt, INP, 2000).

182 World Bank, *Arab Republic of Egypt Education Sector Review: Progress and Priorities for the Future*, Report no. 24905-EGT (Washington D.C., World Bank, October 2002), 25.

183   Arab Republic of Egypt, MOE, *Mubarak and Education: Indicators of Progress in Mubarak's National Project of Education,* 1991/1992–2002/2003, 8.
184   UNESCO, *Educational Reform in Egypt 1996–2003, Achievements And Challenges in the New Century,* September 2003, 15.
185   MOE, *Indicators of Progress,* 11.
186   UNESCO, *Educational Reform in Egypt 1996–2003,* 15.
187   MOE, *Indicators of Progress,* 28.
188   See *Ibid.*; Arab Republic of Egypt, MOE and UNICEF, *The Situation of Egyptian Children and Women, A Rights-Based Analysis* (Cairo, UNICEF, 2002); MOE, *Mubarak and Education.*
189   UNESCO, with funding from the UNDP, *Review and Assessment of Reform of Basic Education in Egypt,* TSS-1 Report (New York, UNESCO and UNDP, 1996).
190   UNESCO, *Educational Reform in Egypt.*
191   Sahar El Tawila et al, *The School Environment if Egypt: A Situation Analysis of Public Preparatory Schools* (Cairo, Population Council and Social Research Center, The American University in Cairo, 2000); Cynthia B. Lloyd, *Determinants of Educational Attainment Among Adolescents in Egypt: Does School Quality Make a Difference?* (New York, Population Council, Policy Research Division, No. 150, 2001); Linda Herrera et al, *Qiyam gulus: thaqafat al-ta'lim fi Misr* (Cairo, Population Council, 2003).
192   For a discussion of educational reform see *Ibid*; Ash Hartwell, "From Projects to Sustainable Reform," presentation made for USAID in Africa, 1999; Robert W. Porter and Irvin Hicks, "Knowledge Utilization and the Process of Policy Formulation: Towards a Framework for Action," in David Chapman, Lars Mahlk, and Anna Smulders, *From Planning to Action: Government Initiatives for Improving School-Level Practice* (Paris, IIEP, UNESCO, Pergamon, 1997); Hans Reiff, "The Management of Educational Reforms—Towards a Systems Approach," IIEP reports, S35/5A; Paulston, "On the Limits of Educational Alternatives."
193   Fernando Cardozo was president of Brazil from 1995 to 2003, during which time he strengthened political institutions, expanded educational opportunities for all Brazilians, and fostered human rights and development.
194   'Positive Deviant Behavior' refers to situations in which a single school in a given community deviates in a positive way from a prevailing situation that is negative or bleak. The school may have discovered special practices or behaviors that enable it to find better solutions to prevalent community problems than other schools with access to the same resources. Positive deviance is a well known research and development methodology that is based on the assumption that solutions to community problems already exist within that community.

Index

Accreditation 74

Activity-based learning 14, 40, 41, 58, 61, 62, 63, 64, 67, 68, 69, 74, 95, 96, 105, 106, 112, 149, 153, 167

Ali Mubarak 33, 45

Ali Said (Upper Egypt) 43, 44, 45

Arab tribes 43, 44, 49

Bloom's taxonomy 111, 119

brain research 11, 12, 13, 15, 41

Canadian International Development Agency (CIDA) xii, 95, 96, 97, 102, 104, 135, 136, 154, 157, 159, 171

Carol Bellamy 2

Center for Curriculum and Instructional Materials Development (CCIMD) 37, 60, 62, 72, 96, 113, 150, 151, 164, 168, 173, 179

child/learner-centered 14, 68, 69, 96, 106, 149, 151, 167, 173, 179

Child Rights 2, 28, 32, 35, 58, 61, 72, 78, 82, 92, 105, 124, 125, 144, 179

community mobilization 45–55, 72

community participation 37, 72, 76, 96, 98, 114

conventional schools 166

cooperative learning 74

development phase 94–95

Dewey, John 3, 4

Delors, Jacques 1, 185

Education Innovation Committee 62, 94, 153, 155–156

educational reform 5, 6, 15, 24, 27, 31, 32, 153, 160, 162, 163, 164, 169

Education For All (EFA) 32

effective schools 69, 107 149, 174, 176

European Union 154, 155, 171

expansion phase 95

facilitators 40, 46, 57, 59, 63, 71, 73, 74, 76, 79, 80, 82, 83, 85, 86, 87, 88, 89, 90, 97, 105, 107, 108, 112, 113, 114, 116, 124, 125, 128–129, 137, 138, 140, 146, 147, 148

Faculties of Education (Asyut, Sohag, and Qena) 165

Female Genital Mutilation (FGM) 60, 72

Friends of Education Committee 144

girl's education 33, 104, 105, 120, 133, 135, 136, 140, 152–154, 157, 165, 169, 170, 171

Global Alliance for Transfoming Education 4

globalization 176, 179

graduates from community schools 97, 98, 104, 106, 116, 119, 125, 130–133, 149, 154, 166

Hawara tribe 44, 45, 49

Howard Gardner/Intelligences 60, 84, 85, 113

holistic educationalists 15, 16

information/reporting in community schools 65, 66, 72

Japanese International Cooperation Agency (JICA) 171

Jometein 32

kutab (Qur'anic schools) 43

leadership 26, 54, 63, 64, 67, 70, 71, 74, 76, 82, 83, 85, 86, 89, 113

learning centers/corners 74, 75

learning process 17–26, 74–88

life skills 14, 20, 21, 106, 111, 112, 125

literacy classes 136–137, 144

mastery learning 107, 191

Ministry of Education (MOE) xi, 33, 34, 35, 36, 51, 55, 56, 59, 62, 63, 64, 67, 68, 70, 71, 74, 81, 82, 91, 92, 96, 98, 99, 102, 123, 126, 136, 149, 150, 151, 153, 154, 155, 157, 159, 165, 167, 168, 169, 173
multi-ability/multi-grade teaching 30, 58, 60, 61, 81, 96, 97, 104, 112, 120, 151

National Center for Examination and Educational Evaluation (NCEEE) 37, 60, 62, 96, 97, 102, 106, 111, 112, 113, 152, 164, 168, 169, 174

National Council for Childhood and Motherhood (NCCH) 152, 153, 169
national educational standards 153, 165, 171–172
National Party 181
NGO Department at MOE 99, 151, 156, 173

Ombuds person 82, 128
one-classroom school 94, 95, 96, 97, 98, 105, 113, 136, 148, 149, 150, 151, 155, 159, 160, 166, 173
Ontario Institute for Studies in Education (OISE) 62, 63

peer learning 74
pilot phase 91–94
portfolio 22, 58, 60, 79–80, 81–82, 113, 129, 168, 169
preparatory schools 69, 166
Professional Academy for Teachers 172, 173

quality education 14–26, 27, 35, 74–88, 157, 169

school committees/education committees 39, 46, 52, 53, 57, 66, 67, 72, 90, 91–93
school management and organization 23–26

school mission statement 60, 61
site selection/school space 38
Seedbed model 147, 174
social capital 42, 43, 99
social contract 82, 89, 125
Social Dund for Development (SFD) 94, 99, 154
social groups 89
social movements 6–10, 28, 100, 101, 109, 143, 148, 160, 162
strategic planning 95, 171, 172
State of the World's Children Report (SOWC) 152
summer school 90–91
supervision/ support staff 72, 73, 74, 112, 113, 116, 129, 132, 148
sustainability 96, 157, 160
Swiss Fund 155

Tagammu' Party 181
Total Quality Management (TQM) 66, 68, 69, 96, 107, 146
training 42, 55–70, 92, 94, 95, 96, 97, 105, 137–138, 148, 149, 150, 166
transformation 25, 26, 27, 28, 29, 37, 100–102, 115–157, 161, 162–177
transnational alliances 176

UNDP 32, 171, 179
UNESCO 20, 21, 32, 171, 179, 180
UNFPA 32
UNICEF xi, 2, 20, 21, 32, 34, 35, 36, 62, 69, 71, 74, 78, 92, 93, 95, 96, 102, 125, 126, 137, 138, 147, 149, 150, 152, 154, 155, 157, 158, 159, 169
University of Asyut 93, 114
ulama 44
USAID 95, 126, 154, 170, 171

women's empowerment 138–141
World Bank 154, 155, 171
World Summit for Children 2, 3, 32
World Summit fo Social Development 3, 32